THE CHRONICLES OF BUDGEPORE

THE CHRONICLES OF BUDGEPORE

OR

SKETCHES OF LIFE IN UPPER INDIA

BY

ILTUDUS THOMAS PRICHARD

GYAN

Published by

Gyan Publishing House
5, Ansari Road
Daryaganj, New Delhi-110002
Phone: 011-47034999, 9811692060
E-mail: books@gyanbooks.com

Distribution Network
gyanbooks.com
India, USA, Canada, UK, Australia

ISBN: 978-93-6433-348-1 PB)
First Published, 1893

2nd Impression 2024

Printed at: Gyan Press, Delhi.

THE CHRONICLES OF BUDGEPORE
AUTHOR: ILTUDUS THOMAS PRICHARD

THE CHRONICLES OF BUDGEPORE

OR

SKETCHES OF LIFE IN UPPER INDIA

BY

ILTUDUS PRICHARD, Esq., F.S.S., F.R.G.S.

Of Gray's Inn, Barrister-at-law

Author of "The Administration of India from 1858 to 1869," etc., etc.

NEW EDITION

LONDON

W. H. ALLEN & CO., LIMITED

13, WATERLOO PLACE, S.W.

1893

PREFACE.

THE following Sketches, written at various intervals snatched from more serious pursuits, are intended to illustrate some characteristics of social and official life in Upper India, both in European and Native Society, and to show the quaint results which an indiscriminate and often injudicious engrafting of habits and ideas of Western civilization upon Oriental stock is calculated to produce. It may be as well to add, that there are no personal allusions throughout the book. The characters are intended to be representatives of all classes, not of individuals. And if, while seeking to amuse, I shall have succeeded in drawing attention, under the disguise of fiction, to serious abuses and defects too patent to all who have studied British India from an impartial and independent point of view, I shall not have cause to regret the time spent upon these pages.

PREFACE

CONTENTS.

CHRONICLE I.

CHRONICLE II.

CHRONICLE III.

CHRONICLE IV.

THE HISTORY OF THE BARRACKS.

CHRONICLE IX.

THE REMOUNTS.

CHRONICLE X.

CHRONICLE XI.

THE BUDGEPORE POLITICAL AGENCY.

CHRONICLE I.

A RASH PROMISE AND ITS CONSEQUENCES.

THE CHRONICLES OF BUDGEPORE.

CHRONICLE I.

A RASH PROMISE AND ITS CONSEQUENCES.

It is not the slightest use for the reader to begin by asking me where Budgepore is, for I have no intention of satisfying a vain and idle curiosity. If it is not in the map that is not my fault, for my profession is not that of a map-maker. It is enough for the reader's purpose, and for mine, that he be told that Budgepore is in India. I will further add that Budgepore is a representative place, Budgepore institutions are representative institutions, and Budgepore people representative people. As Budgepore comprises a native city and an English settlement—a station as it is called in India—it follows that the Budgeporeans consist of native and English people. If the reader thinks the natives have very hard names, that is not my fault, I did not construct Oriental languages, and Oriental appellations always have a hard sound to English ears. And if is taken as matter of offence that the English people at Budgepore have very queer patronymics, I decline to be answerable for it. If anyone is to be blamed, I suppose it is the ancestors and founders of the families whose descendants resided at Budgepore, at the time to which these Chronicles refer, and for Christian names I conclude the godfathers and godmothers are responsible. Still there is this to be said for it, that the names, although they do at first seem awkward and uncouth, will generally be understood by those of my readers who have been much in India. And to those who have not, it can make no possible difference whether a man is called Mr. Byewilwuffa or Mr. Billofsale. How it could ever have come to pass that any Englishman should have had such a designation as Mr. Kist Byewilwuffa, the Lieut.-Governor, or Mr. Dakhil Duftar, the Collector and Magistrate, or Dr. Golee, the surgeon, I cannot possibly divine. But as these gentlemen were so called, it is plainly not my business to deprive them of their family appellations or annul the work of their godfathers by calling them Mr. Smith or Mr. Jones. What would be thought of a footman, who, in announcing Sir Llwyllwgn Mautwrllg, the well-known member for Cgmwrg in North Wales, was, by way of avoiding the difficulty to call out Mr. David Williams. I shall therefore make no apology for the names of the people who figure in these pages. They would not be the same people under different names; and as they are all old friends of mine, I should be very sorry to see them called by any other.

A good many of the *dramatis personæ* that appear in these Chronicles come and go like the characters upon the stage. Others meet us all throughout the history which, like all true histories, has neither beginning nor end. There is, for instance, Mr. Wasilbakee, a Bengal civilian of high standing, who, as Commissioner of Revenue of the Budgepore division, shares with Mrs. Wasilbakee the dignity and responsibility attaching to the position of the heads of Budgepore society. Next to him in rank, comes Basil Mooltawee, the Judge, and after him, Mr. Dakhil Duftar, the Collector and Magistrate. Dr. Golee is what we call in India the civil surgeon, and there are many others who need not be enumerated here, who will, like all sensible people, come when they are wanted and not before.

It must not be supposed that, because the Budgepore people happen to have had rather peculiar names, they differed from the rest of mankind in any respect. As far as I know, human nature at Budgepore is no otherwise constituted than elsewhere, and it must not be imagined that these Chronicles are recorded for the exclusive benefit of the Anglo-Indian. On the contrary, I think it will be admitted that Budgepore red tape and whitewash much resemble the same articles in London and Paris, at any rate in the method of their application.

It remains to say a few words as to the manner in which the Chronicles came into my possession.

It so happened that in the circle of my dear and old friends who, I may safely say, have made Budgepore society what it is, there was one who had collected a number of characteristic anecdotes with which he would occasionally enliven his companions at our social gatherings. And as he enjoyed great aptitude for studying men and manners, an untiring perseverance in sifting out mysteries, and a most acute sense of the ridiculous, it occurred to me that his stories were too good to be lost, and at my especial request he consented to put them on paper, and to allow me to make what use of them I pleased. A few years before I made his acquaintance, an acquaintance that soon ripened into friendship, Sir Walter Scott's novels had been at the zenith of their fame, and my old friend had taken such a marvellous fancy to "Old Mortality" that he was always reading and always talking about it. He knew whole passages by heart, and would often repeat them with so much pathos, and such a thorough appreciation of their merits, that he acquired the nickname of Old Mortality. As such he has always been known at Budgepore, and for the last twenty years has gone by no other name.

Some considerable time, however, elapsed after the promise was first made without any show on my friend's part of an intention to fulfil it. Professional business put the matter out of my head, and it was only on my return to Budgepore, after a somewhat prolonged absence, that the idea of collecting these anecdotes through the instrumentality of Old Mortality, as we called him, recurred to me. An accumulation of correspondence, and professional details of various kinds, kept me fully employed for some weeks after my return, during which time I heard and saw nothing of the outside world. I felt the burden the more as it was Christmas, a period when, even at Budgepore, Englishmen snatch a holiday if they can, and, gathering in social circles round their wood fires, endeavour to recall in imagination the scenes of early days, and the familiar, though long-lost faces of the old friends of youth and boyhood.

One morning, when busily engaged in my office, I was suddenly accosted by the well-known salutation "A merry Christmas and a happy new year." Raising my eyes from my desk, I beheld my ancient friend. It is curious to observe the air of superiority people assume when they have just returned from Europe. The fact of having been home for ever so short a visit, or of being about to go, confers a kind of rank which I may call Budgepore rank. In possessing this, a subaltern who has just returned from furlough is a personage of much more importance in the drawing-room, the ball-room, everywhere except on parade, than his captain who has been in India for the last ten years. A man who has just returned wears the fact in his face, in his coat, in his boots: he lets everyone see that his opinions ought to carry weight. What right have old fogies and old Indians—bah!—who have not been home to rub off the rust in contact with civilisation these ten years, to put themselves on a par with him?

So that, when Old Mortality made his appearance with the unmistakable air of a man just out, I scarcely paused to ask him the question whether he had not been to England: I took it for granted, indeed, and only said as we shook hands—

"You never told me you were going."

"No," said he, seating himself by the fire, "I hadn't time—and I haven't had time either to go on with those Chronicles, and that is what I have looked in to say."

"So you have been to England?"

"Yes—a flying visit."

"Unexpected, wasn't it?"

"Decidedly."

"And what did you take home?"

"Do you mean that, or do you mean what took me home?"

"Well, yes—either way—I meant what I said."

"I will answer your first question then first. What did I take home? I took home Jimmy and Totty."

"Jimmy and Totty! and what took you home?"

"What took me home? Jimmy and Totty."

"You hadn't much time to spend on the road?"

"No, I hadn't."

"Because I was thinking that perhaps you had been spending a day or two with the Sphinx."

"Ha, ha! not bad! Well now perhaps you would like to hear a little more about it."

"It?"

"Yes—I mean my trip to England."

"And about Jimmy and Tot—what is it—Tottems?"

"Jimmy and Totty—you appear to experience some difficulty in mastering that name."

"Well, it is rather unfamiliar—probably it is less so to you."

Old Mortality looked at me for an instant out of the corners of his eyes, and answered laconically—

"Probably."

"Now, Old Mortality," said I, pointing to the heap of papers on my table that measured exactly two feet six inches in height over the whole area, "you see these papers, recollect your broken promise and don't trifle. You don't deserve to be told it, indeed you don't, but if you knew how many inquires I have had as to where you were, and when the Chronicles of Budgepore were to appear, you would grow conceited—so I won't tell you, but pray do not take up time needlessly. Let us hear all about your journey and this Johnny—"

"Jimmy, I tell you," he said angrily.

"Well, Jimmy and—the other you know."

"You don't deserve to hear a word—indeed you don't—however, as you are an old friend, I'll overlook the extraordinary remissness of your memory and tell you all about it."

"We were dining at Wasilbakee's one night. Pretty nearly all Budgepore was there. Dakhil Duftar was there and his wife, Roobakaree, too, the joint magistrate, and Mrs. Roobakaree, Mooltawee, the judge, and Mrs. Mooltawee, Dr. Golee, Captain and Mrs. Cameltrunk, Colonel Moodle and his nephew, Kamerbond, who, you know, commands the regiment—were all present. There was Doctor Nindi, the principal of the Budgepore College, Captain and Mrs. Naksha, and a whole host beside, whose names I don't just now recollect. Before dinner was announced, malignant Fate in the person of Mrs. Wasilbakee sailed up and communicated to me in a mysterious whisper her wish, equivalent to a command, that I would take Mrs. Naksha in to dinner. I bowed acquiescence, and shortly after dinner being announced, I offered Mrs. Naksha my arm and led her in to dinner, our progress thereto only being interrupted twice, by my, and then my partner's, treading on the skirt of the lady in front of us.

"Now there are certain duties allotted to every position in life, and the duty you are called on to perform when dining out is undoubtedly to talk. While your host provides the wherewithal to eat and drink, you are supposed to provide conversation for yourself and your neighbour. Under these circumstances I find that if I think of what to say I never say anything, for if you think what to say your mind inevitably passes on to thinking whether what you are going to say is worth saying, and I need hardly add that the answer is generally in the negative, so that the process ends in your saying nothing. Whereas, if you don't think what to say your flow of conversation is uninterrupted."

"All which," said I, interrupting him, "is an apology by way of preface, for your having said something very stupid."

"If you wish me to go on with my story you must not interrupt me with any superficial observations of that nature. You may keep them for your readers."

"Very well," I replied, humiliated—"no more interruptions—I am anxious to hear all about Tommy and the other."

Old Mortality replied by a contemptuous look, and proceeded.

"Mrs. Naksha and I got over the first half of the period allotted to dinner very comfortably. We discussed the usual topics. We mutually remarked that the hot weather was nearly over, and congratulated one another thereon. I observed that the season had been on the whole a very tolerable one, and my companion coincided with me. I hazarded an opinion that we should have a delightful cold season, and Mrs. Naksha endorsed that opinion. We then briefly discussed the various stations we had been located in during our Indian sojourn, and their respective merits. The last ball afforded material for a few more remarks, and we mutually wondered when the next would be.

"We then, *more Indico,* discussed the appearance and dress of every one at the table, and Mrs. Naksha told me everything she had ever heard about the private concerns of each in turn. Finally, the band was disposed of, and then came a pause.

"'I've been thinking,' said I, which was quite false, because I hadn't been thinking at all, 'of taking a run to England and seeing the Paris Exhibition on the way.'

"'Oh, how nice!' exclaimed Mrs. Naksha, 'then I shall ask you to take home Jimmy and Totty.'

"I replied of course that if I carried out my intention it would give me the utmost pleasure to oblige her; not having the least glimmer of an idea of going at all.

"She then informed me that her husband had been ordered to Peshawur. That Jimmy and Totty had arrived at that age when it was absolutely necessary they should go home, that they were extremely anxious to avoid the necessity of taking them all the way to Peshawur, and were looking out for some eligible opportunity to get Jimmy and Totty conveyed home and made over to their friends in England, that there was no one in all India to whom she would rather entrust the responsible charge than to me, and she was quite certain her husband felt the same. To all of which and a great deal more of the same kind, I replied by commonplace polite platitudes, interlarded with asseverations that my plans were by no means fixed, that the idea of going was only a passing thought, which portion of my remarks made, I found, very little impression on Mrs. Naksha's mind. In this way the rest of the dinner passed off very comfortably, and the ladies rose to leave the room.

"When we joined the ladies in the drawing-room I went and seated myself by the side of Mrs. Wasilbakee on the sofa.

"'How very kind of you!' she said, much to my astonishment, just as I sat down. She had not time to say any more when her husband came up—

"'So you are really off, Old Mortality, to the Paris Exhibition? Well done! You are quite right to go. I wish I could go too.'

"'And so very kind of him,' added his wife. 'Just think how very nice it is for poor Mrs. Naksha to be able to entrust her little ones to such good hands as Old Mortality's.'

"'And I know you will be so very kind,' added Mrs. Wasilbakee, 'as to take home for me a small packet—it is a very small one.'

"'By the way,' said her husband, 'yes, that's a good idea. I'll get you to take charge of a small parcel that I have had I don't know how long, waiting for an opportunity to send it home. It was Mouza, the Secretary to Government, gave it to me ever so long ago, and asked me to send it to England by the first opportunity that offered, and by Jove I forgot it.'

"'You go by the steamer of the 23rd, I suppose?' said Dr. Nindi, coming up at this juncture to take part in the conversation. 'There's a great friend of mine, Cripps, and his wife—charming creature Mrs. Cripps, going by that steamer. You will like Mrs. Cripps very much—clever woman, Mrs. Cripps.'

"All this time I sat as one astonished. I could realise a little the feelings of Æneas when he disturbed old Polydore's sleep. You recollect the line—

'Obstupui, steteruntque comæ, et vox faucibus hœsit,'

which we used to translate, 'I was thunderstruck, hairs stuck in my throat, and my jaws stood erect on the top of my head'—a most curious sensation that—it feebly describes my mental condition at that moment.

"'Oh yes'—I stammered, 'certainly—very nice—but to tell the truth—well—my plans are not fixed.'

"At that moment up came Naksha, grasped my hand affectionately, and said—

"'My dear Old Mortality, how can I thank you sufficiently for this great act of kindness. It has relieved us of a world of anxiety. I assure you there is no man in all India to whom I would rather entrust the sacred charge.'

"'And they are such clever, sweet children,' chimed in Mrs. Wasilbakee, 'so clever and so interesting.'

"I groaned inwardly and thought of Æneas.

"There was a pause. Immediately in front of the sofa where I was seated there was an ottoman on which Mrs. Naksha and some other ladies were sitting. In the short silence that ensued after this last remark, I heard a stifled sob; it proceeded from Mrs. Naksha, who wiped away a pair of small tears with a very small piece of lace and cambric, while her friend in an audible whisper said to her, by way of consolation—

"'But just think, my dear, such an excellent opportunity, such a good-natured, noble-hearted man, he will be so kind to them.'

"'But it is so soon,' murmured Mrs. Naksha. 'I cannot bear to think of it, he leaves by the next mail.'

"'Here's our old friend Old Mortality going to leave us,' said Wasilbakee to Colonel Moodle, who waddled up and joined the group by the sofa.

"'Yes,' said Colonel Moodle, who also seemed in league against me, 'I hear he is going to the Paris Exhibition.'

"'To England first—isn't it so?' said Mrs. Wasilbakee.

"'Oh yes,' said I, in my utter bewilderment—'certainly.'

"'Business first and pleasure afterwards,' said Rubakaree from behind. How I hated him!

"'They are such interesting children,' said Mrs. Wasilbakee. 'Jimmy's quite a precocious boy, and as for Totty——'

"The rest of the sentence was cut short by the servant handing round tea and coffee. The group in front of me separated. Mrs. Wasilbakee got up and went to lead Mrs. Rubakaree to the piano. I also arose and moved to another part of the room. Wherever I went it was the same thing over again. One asked me when I started, another wondered I had kept my intended journey so secret, a third envied me my trip, a fourth longed to accompany me, and every lady in the room one after another assured me I should find Jimmy and Totty delightful companions, and they all seemed to think it was very kind of me to take them, and that it was an excellent arrangement for all parties concerned.

"But this was not all. I soon saw another danger looming in front of me. I heard the word—I saw it on the lips of everyone—packages.

"My heart sank, I looked round, there was no escape. Every creature in that room had marked me out for its prey. So have you seen the dying camel stretched upon the sandy plain. The load is taken off his back, for he can no longer carry it, and the kafila, unable to halt, pushes on, leaving the worn-out and feeble to die upon the ground. To halt there would be to sacrifice the lives of the whole caravan for the sake of those, be they men or beasts, upon whom death has already set its seal. But scarcely has the figure of the last camel in the line of the retreating kafila passed from view behind the next sand-heap, when the flapping of wings awakens with a thrill of horror the attention of the dying creature. Instinct tells him of the fate that is in store. First one, then another, then a third, then a host of vultures and carrion birds assembled for the bloody feast, flutter in a crowd above the victim, hover in the air for an instant or two, and then swoop down upon their living prey. That was something like my position. I was as helpless and powerless to escape as that camel. So I set my teeth firmly together, and though still bewildered, yet had sufficient appreciation of my position to know there was no help for it. Once or twice the desperate idea seized me, I would mount upon a chair and make a speech. All Budgepore was there, and all Budgepore would hear me. I would say, 'Ladies and Gentlemen, I beg you to hear me. You are under a misconception altogether. I am not going to England at all, and what I said to Mrs. Naksha at dinner-time was a mere remark *pour passer le temps*, a commonplace dinner-table observation, of which she had no right to take the advantage she has done.'

"I conned over this little speech in my mind by one of those mental processes which are so rapidly executed in times of emergency. I learnt it by heart. I selected with my eye the best position—the very chair I would stand upon. It was the only hope—the only chance I had. But my heart failed me. Then came the inevitable vultures upon my yet palpitating carcass. I assure you there was not a single lady in that room, not one that did not ask me to take a package—some called it a 'parcel,' some a 'small trifle,' some 'just a tiny little thing' (I found the tiny little ones the biggest of all)—they all asked me to oblige them so far. A great many of the men, too, did the same, but them I did not hesitate to refuse.

"I reached home that night in a condition of mind more easily imagined than described. How comfortable my room looked—my writing table, my books, all to be abandoned for the discomfort, nay, the horrors, of a P. and O. steamer. I walked up and down the room for some time in a state bordering on despair. I was minded to do something desperate. Was there no release—no escape? My pistol-case was on the table. I opened it and took up my revolver and handled it for a moment fondly. It had been loaded ever since 1858. I recollected that I had been afraid to fire it off lest it should burst, and put it down again with a laugh. Then I called my servant. He came in and put his hands together as if he was going to say his prayers.

"'Pack up everything,' I said, almost in distraction.

"He asked me where I was going.

"'To England,' I said, grinning horribly in despair.

"I had had this man in my service for twenty years. On my saying this, he went away, and abstracted from all my boxes and wardrobes every single thing of every possible kind which he thought I should not miss.

"Next morning, the first thing, a note was put into my hands. It was from Naksha, and ran thus:—

"'My Dear Old Mortality,—

"'I cannot express to you how deeply I feel the obligation you are about to confer upon us. No other arrangement could possibly have suited us so well. We know your sterling qualities, and can entrust our charge to you with confidence, while we feel most grateful to you for undertaking it. I enclose a cheque on the Budgepore Bank for Rs. 1,000 to meet current expenses. Anything more you may want, please let me know. We leave for Peshawur this evening. My wife and I will bring the children in the afternoon, and make them over to you. Their things shall be sent over in the course of the day. You have placed me under a lasting obligation to you which I can never sufficiently repay.

"'Ever yours,

"'C. Naksha.'

"In the course of the morning some coolies appeared with boxes (there were four boxes and seven large bundles, just the kind of things I thought, to be comfortable, loose in one's cabin), and then clamoured to be paid.

"In the afternoon a carriage drove up. The ayah was on the box. Captain and Mrs. Naksha inside with Jimmy and Totty. Mrs. Naksha's eyes were red, and traces of recent tears were on her cheeks. Jimmy and Totty were brought up and introduced to me, and so was the ayah, who, I was informed, had undertaken for the sum of one hundred and fifty rupees, half of which had been paid in advance, to accompany the children to England. Mrs. Naksha gave me an inventory of Jimmy and Totty's things. There were three dozen shirts, three dozen pairs of socks, four pairs of shoes, six pairs of trousers, and six jackets, besides cloaks, &c., a small bag containing a brush and comb, and that instrument of torture, a small-tooth comb, a piece of soap, and sundry bits of flannel, and a sponge. Totty's wardrobe was similarly provided for, but as she was a young lady, I need not specifically detail the articles.

"I will not dwell upon the parting between parents and children. It was sufficiently painful to witness, and it was a relief when it was over.

"After this the little packages began to arrive. I devoted a room for their reception, where they were stowed away as they came, upon the ground. There were in all, by the time I started, one hundred and twenty-seven, weighing in the aggregate, ninety-six pounds eleven ounces.

"It was obvious that there was nothing left for me but to complete my preparations for the journey. I wrote and engaged berths in the next steamer, and put a bold face on the matter as became a philosopher. My philosophy, however, was sorely tried several times before I made my charge over to the affectionate aunt who was waiting at Southampton to receive it. First of all, on the morning of departure, the ayah was not to be found anywhere. Having received half the sum stipulated for the journey in advance, she not unnaturally disappeared. When I enquired for her, the other servants said her mother was sick, and thus accounted for her absence. I could not get another to accompany me, and eventually was obliged to put an outdoor servant in charge, whose especial calling it is to look after goats, and this being the nearest approximation to a nurse my bachelor household afforded, I enlisted him into the service, and started—I in one carriage, and the children and their attendant in another. We had not gone far when my carriage, which was in advance, was stopped, and on enquiry I found that Jimmy had fallen out. He fortunately fell into a heap of soft dirt or sand, and was not hurt, so we picked him up, and having enjoined on both the children the necessity of keeping quiet, and upon their attendant the duty of looking better after them, I started again. The children fortunately went to sleep after this *contretemps*, and slept for the rest of the day. We had one night to spend in an hotel, which did not pass very comfortably for me, for Jimmy and Totty having been asleep all day, not unnaturally stayed awake, and insisted on alternately playing, fighting, and crying the whole night. Next day we got to the rail, and so to Calcutta, where I engaged a brawny Scotchwoman, the wife of a soldier quartered in the fort, who consented for the sum of fifty pounds to leave her husband and accompany me to England. After this, my troubles grew less. The steamer sailed the day after I reached Calcutta. Jimmy, Totty, and I became pretty good friends before we reached Southampton, where I parted from them, and after spending three weeks in England, I set out on my way back. And here I am, come to report my arrival.

"The trouble which the landing and delivery of the packages entailed, however, is utterly beyond my power of description. The most of the time—it was not very long, certainly—that my foot rested on British soil, I was busily engaged in their distribution. A voluminous correspondence had to be conducted, and I narrowly escaped two lawsuits. There was one package directed to some confounded lawyer in some country town. Well, the wretched thing got lost, but the creature had knowledge of it, somehow. I suppose the sender had written and told him it was coming. However, that may be, I admitted having had it, and said I regretted it was lost or mis-sent. Would you believe it, he wrote back a lawyer's letter, and said I was a something or other, I forget what—I dare say you will understand, but I know it ended with a double 'ee,'* and I was bound to use due diligence in taking care of the thing. Of course, I had to go to a lawyer, too, to defend the case. His bill for costs alone came to thirty pounds. The action never came off, because a day or two before the time fixed, I received a letter in most indignant and angry terms from a man of the same name as this lawyer, to whom the parcel had been sent by mistake. The other lawsuit I got into was a nasty business, owing to my having declared the contents of a certain package to be what the sender—it was Mrs. Rubakaree, by the way, declared them to be. For some reason or other—my ill-luck, I suppose—the Custom House officers chose to pounce upon this very one out of the whole lot, and opened it, when the contents turned out to be of a very different character from what Mrs. Rubakaree had intimated, and so their suspicions being aroused they opened some twenty or thirty others, besides getting me fined heavily for a false declaration.

"This is the history of my recent adventure, and now you know what has prevented me from fulfilling my promise.

* "Bailee," probably.

There shall, however, be no more delay. I'll put my notes together and let you have the first instalment in a couple of days."

My friend was as good as his word, and in two days' time I received what you will find in the next chapter.

CHRONICLE II.

THE BUDGEPORE MUNICIPAL COMMISSION.

CHRONICLE II.

THE BUDGEPORE MUNICIPAL COMMISSION.

It pleased the Hon'ble Mr. Kist Bywilwuffa, Lieutenant-Governor, to intimate one day to Mr. Wasilbakee, the commissioner of Budgepore, in a "demi-official," his opinion that it would be very desirable that Budgepore should have its municipal commission.

The municipal commission is, as we see it, an institution essentially Indian. It is well known that the British Government is most anxious to educate the people of this country in the art of self-government. There is nothing, and we have been so repeatedly told it that we cannot refuse to believe it, that the old Bengal civilians at the head of the Government more ardently desire, than to see as much of the representative principle as possible introduced into the administration of this country. This, the reader will understand, is no new policy; they have all throughout, I mean for the last century, always held these liberal opinions, and if they have been judged to hold the contrary, it is only a proof of want of judgment among those who have ventured to criticise their acts or to review their policy. The people of India, however, as is well known, have been subjected for many centuries to all the miseries of despotic rule; and it is only of late, that is, since the British power became dominant, that they have been able really to learn what freedom is, and to enjoy its blessings. It is a work of time, however, to render races who have long been subjected to the dominion of arbitrary despots, fit to exercise the privileges of free men. And the present generation of Indian statesmen were the first to introduce the system of municipal commissions or corporations into the larger cities of Upper India, institutions which it was considered would serve in some measure to instruct the people in the art of governing themselves.

While I am writing this chronicle, a Bill is passing through the law manufactory of Calcutta, considerably modifying the existing regulations regarding municipal commissions. The reader will understand, therefore, that the Budgepore municipal commission was formed before the present, or the recent Bill (as it may, by the time these pages are placed before the public, have come into operation) became law.

It will only be necessary to remark, by way of preface, that under the old law the adoption of the system was entirely voluntary, under the new it is compulsory, that is, whenever the Government think fit to introduce it, they can do so.

Well, as I have said, the commissioner received intimation through a demi-official that it would be desirable if the residents of Budgepore would take the first lesson in the art of self-government by the introduction of a municipal commission. Accordingly Mr. Wasilbakee communicated the idea to Mr. Dakhil Duftar, the collector, and Mr. Dakhil Duftar, fully entering into the spirit of the thing, intimated by means of a public notice that there would be a meeting of the principal inhabitants of Budgepore at the cutchery the following day at 7 a.m. At the same time he sent a circular round the civil station inviting all the European residents to be present on the same occasion.

Great was the wonderment throughout the city of Budgepore as to what the "collector sahib" had summoned the inhabitants for. Various reports prevailed, which became more startling and sensational as the day wore on. Some said the Government had determined that the principal inhabitants of Budgepore should forthwith be "made Christians," the phrase "being made Christians" conveying different ideas to the minds of different men according to the various shades of feeling with which they regarded the religion of the "sahibs." Others declared that the object of the meeting was the investiture of the Budgeporeans with "khilluts" or dresses of honour for their conspicuous fidelity during the rebellion of 1857. Others averred that they knew on the best authority that there was to be a large sum exacted from them by way of a tax or a forced loan. While the Hindoos were disquieted by a rumour that an ox had been slain the day before at the cutchery, and they, the Hindoos, were to partake for the first time in their lives of a meal of genuine English roast beef, as abhorrent to them as swine's flesh would be to a Mahomedan.

Towards evening some more authentic information reached the bewildered bazaars of Budgepore. Old Gunny Lall, a very stout Hindoo mahajun, or money-lender, of great repute for his wealth, had oiled the palm of the kotwal (or native city subordinate magistrate and police officer), and he had oiled the palm of the collector's serishtadar (or record-keeper as the word literally means though its practical signification might be more correctly rendered by the word "factotum"), who for the consideration thus accorded had successfully sounded Mr. Dakhil Duftar's intentions, and through this channel there filtered out an intimation of the real object of the meeting to be assembled on the morrow. Curiosity, however, was by this means but slightly allayed, and of the twenty burghers whom the kotwal had selected as representatives of the mercantile community, but few had much sleep that night.

Duly at the appointed time the assembly met. The European community were represented by the commissioner, Dakhil Duftar, Fitzmisl, the Joint Magistrate, Dr. Golee, the Civil Surgeon, Colonel Moodle, Brigadier Haversack, and Fancy Goods, Esq., the Secretary of All Over India Trading Corporation (late Cork Screw and Co.). Thus you see all classes were fairly represented, the official classes, the military, and the trading community.

The European gentlemen seated themselves on one side of the table, the natives on the other, and Mr. Wasilbakee, as chairman, at the head. On his right, at the right-hand corner, sat Dakhil Duftar, next to him Fitzmisl, then Dr. Golee, then the two military officers. On the left, in the seat of honour, was Gunny Lall, next to him Sham Dutt, one of the modern Hindoo school, a sharp fellow who understood English perfectly, and who was placed there at the special request of Gunny Lall, in order that he might keep him acquainted with what went on, and act generally as interpreter. Next to him was Motee Lall, then Scrimmage Khan, and so on; I need not enumerate them all. Mr. Wasilbakee opened the proceedings by explaining in English first and then in Hindustani the object of the meeting. He dwelt especially on the voluntary nature of the movement, telling them that he thought the time was come when Budgepore might avail itself of the liberality of the Government, and assume charge of its own municipal institutions. He proposed that those present should enrol themselves into a committee. Their names would be sent up to the Lieutenant-Governor, and in due course of time would be published in the *Gazette*, under a notification that the Budgepore municipal commission had assumed tangible shape and form. The Surgeon and the Brigadier were to be *ex-officio* members, and also of course were the civilians. When duly recognised by Government, the commission would have authority to levy local (or *octroi*) taxes, and to expend the money so collected in local improvements.

The English gentlemen who had discussed it all before had nothing particular to say, the natives replied "jo hukm" (as ordered), and the meeting dispersed.

By that day's post the following letter went to head-quarters:—

"From No. 7351 of 18—.

"JUMMA WASILBAKEE, Esq., C.S.,

"*Commissioner of Budgepore*,

"To

"KHAS MOUZA, Esq., C.S.,

"*Secretary to Govt.*,

"*Budgepore, 1st April*, 18—.

"SIR,

"I have the honour to report for the information of His Honour the Lieutenant-Governor, that the principal native inhabitants of Budgepore have intimated their desire for the introduction of the municipal system into this city. At a meeting held this day at the collector's cutchery, a report of the proceedings of which I have the honour to append, the following gentlemen, European and native, declared their readiness to serve on the commission. The movement is entirely a voluntary one, the suggestion having of course come from me, and being readily acquiesced in.

"I have the honour to be,

"Sir,

"Your most obedient servant,

"JUMMA WASILBAKEE,

"*Commissioner.*"

In due time the notification appeared in the *Gazette*, containing the names of all those who attended the first meeting, and the day following the committee met at the same hour, 7 a.m., at the same place as before.

Proceedings having been opened by the commissioner, who took the chair, the committee took into consideration the question of taxation—what articles should be taxed.

Dakhil Duftar proposed a tax of one rupee per maund, or two shillings upon every eighty pounds of atta (flour). It was seconded by Fitzmisl, who remarked it was a sound principle of political economy to tax the necessaries of life. Fitzmisl was a competition-walla, and as such looked down upon by the older civilians. He had come out among one of the first batches of civilians, and entered the service under the new system of competitive examination. He had a decent reputation as a Latin and Greek scholar at Oxford, where he had got a second class in classics at his examination for his degree. His reputation by no means decreased when it followed him to India, and though the old school of civilians affected to look down upon him, criticised unfavourably his seat on horseback, and the cut of his shooting-coat, it was clear to me that they were a little afraid of him. He had recently taken much to the study of political economy, and was great in Adam Smith. It will be seen that the information acquired in that branch of study was not thrown away, but brought to bear upon the points that came in discussion before the Budgepore municipal committee with much advantage to that body.

The next articles that were voted to be taxed were ghee, sugar, rice, and tobacco. No objection was offered to any of these imposts, except that on tobacco, of which several of the native members expressed their disapprobation.

A little rise in the price of such commodities as grain, ghee, sugar, &c., affected them but very slightly, for they were all rich men. Had they asked the thousands of pauper families who thronged the crowded hovels in the by-ways and lanes of Budgepore, whether the scanty meal doled out daily to their wives and little children could afford diminution without injury to their physical health, they might have been answered in the negative. As a matter of course, however, no one thought of consulting them. But tobacco was a luxury any increase to the price of which touched, though in a very slight degree, the pockets of the rich mahajuns. They saw, however, that the commissioner was not inclined to abandon this tax, so they said "jo hukm."

After this there was a short pause, broken by old Gunny Lall who, acting on the prompting of Sham Dutt, who was a bit of a wag and enjoyed a joke, proposed a tax of one rupee per dozen upon "beer." At this Dr. Golee smiled, Colonel Moodle tittered, and Fancy Goods, Esq., laughed outright. Mr. Wasilbakee frowned and muttered to Dakhil Duftar something about gentlemanly propriety; and then blandly explained to Gunny Lall that "beer" was already subject to an import duty, and it would be unfair to put an additional impost upon it.

The natives during this short discussion maintained the most immovable stolidity, but a twinkle in Sham Dutt's eye showed that he had enjoyed the joke.

It was finally resolved that a tax varying in amount should be levied on the following articles: grain of all sorts, rice, sugar, tobacco, cotton, jute, indigo, salt, ghee, and milk; that fifty policemen should be enrolled who were to be stationed at the different approaches to the city (each of whom levied a tax of his own before the duty was demanded for the municipal commission), and having fixed that they would meet that day six weeks so as to allow a full month whereby to test the success of the operation, the first meeting of the municipal commission of Budgepore separated.

At the appointed time the meeting assembled again. Mr. Wasilbakee as usual in the chair. Mr. Dakhil Duftar was happy to report a favourable result to the operations of the committee. He had a sum of five thousand rupees at the disposal of the committee for local sanitary improvements.

This announcement being communicated to Gunny Lall by Sham Dutt, he rubbed his stomach with the flat of his open hand, a sure sign that he was well pleased, and said "Wah! wah!" (bravo!) and after a whisper from his mentor, asked—

"Hum logon ka hissa kitna howega? (How much will our share be?)

There was a slight titter among the natives at this. Fancy Goods, Esq., again disgraced himself by laughing outright.

Even Fitzmisl smiled. Dakhil Duftar threw himself back in his chair, and Mr. Wasilbakee looked stern.

"Yih rupiya am ke rupiye hain," said the Commissioner, rebuking the avarice of Gunny Lall. What he meant to convey was, "This money is public money."

"Am!"* quoth Gunny Lall, again rubbing his stomach, "Wah! wah! kitne bahoot am milenge." (Mangoes! bravo! what a quantity of mangoes we shall get!)

Again there was a titter. Mr. Wasilbakee did not condescend to any further explanation, but asked if any member of the committee had anything to propose.

Dr. Golee remarked, that during the past month, owing as he supposed to an unusual consumption of vegetables, there had been a great increase of diarrhœa in the city, and he suggested a duty upon vegetables.

Fancy Goods, Esq., suggested that perhaps the natives consumed more vegetables in consequence of the higher price of more wholesome articles of food.

Mr. Wasilbakee thought this was an unreasonable conclusion, for he had been careful to make enquiries through his serishtadar, who reported to him that the poorer classes were well satisfied with the tax, and that it in no way acted as a prohibitory tax upon necessary articles of food.

Dakhil Duftar confirmed that report. His serishtadar had told him the same.

Fancy Goods, Esq., looked incredulous. The Commissioner observed, that it was with the view of determining questions of this sort that the native gentlemen present were associated with them as members of the committee. He then, addressing them in Hindustani, asked the native members if they were of opinion that the tax upon the more wholesome articles of food had had any effect on the consumption of vegetables. To this the native members replied "jo hukm," or, as ordered. The Commissioner, however, not being quite satisfied with that answer, proceeded to explain to them that there was a difference of opinion among the "sahibs," some of them supposing that the tax upon grain had been followed by a larger consumption of vegetables and other unwholesome

* There are two words pronounced by Europeans in the same way One "am," meaning "public," in the sense of, for instance, deewan-i-am, a public hall of audience, and "am," a mangoe.

articles of diet, and others being under the impression that the increased consumption of vegetables was not to be attributed to that cause. He added that he himself held the latter view, whereupon the native members unanimously remarked—

"Ap kee rai buhoot daroost." (Your honour's opinion is correct.)

A tax was accordingly voted upon vegetables.

The next question proposed was "what should be done with the money," and here a great difference of opinion prevailed. One was for making a new road from the station to the city. The Brigadier thought it might be profitably expended in placing copings to the walls in cantonments. Colonel Moodle suggested that it should be expended in filling up rat-holes on the parade ground. Fitzmisl proposed gilded cupolas to the Court-house. Dakhil Duftar an open drain through the principal streets of the city. Dr. Golee thought a new dispensary should be built, and Fancy Goods, Esq., suggested that the money should be given back again. The native members being asked what they proposed to do with it, unanimously replied "jo hukm." At last Mr. Wasilbakee proposed to level and plant out with young trees a vacant space of ground at that time waste and untidy in front of Dakhil Duftar's house, and right in the heart of the station. The native members unanimously endorsed the Commissioner's suggestion, and it was accordingly carried, without there being any necessity of referring it to the European members. Old Gunny Lall, who was deaf, did not hear what had been determined on, and asked Sham Dutt how the money was to be employed.

"Collector Sahib ke waste ek bagheecha bunega" (a garden to be made for Collector) was the reply.

"Wah! wah!" replied Gunny Lall, rubbing his stomach.

Fitzmisl having been appointed honorary secretary, and Sham Dutt assistant secretary, upon a salary of 200 rupees a month, the meeting broke up.

When they met again the following month, the secretary had favourable results to report. The improvements on the waste ground in front of Dakhil Duftar's house had been proceeded with, and most of the collections from the octroi for the first month expended on them. There was of course a surplus in hand, the fruits of the second month's octroi; and without wearying my readers with a repetition of details, I may as well state that after the usual discussions, it was determined to carry out Dakhil Duftar's suggestion and make a drain through the principal street of the city. The only difference between the resolution as first put, and as carried, being that it was determined to have a covered drain some way below the surface instead of an open one.

Mr. Fileeter, the deputy collector, who was supposed to be a good (amateur) engineer, was requested to look after the construction of this useful public work.

The drain was completed about the time the rainy season set in, but there being no natural drainage, and no river to carry off the sewage, Mr. Fileeter's engineering operations resulted in the accumulation of an immense mass of filth in the shape of a morass just outside the city. About this time the cholera broke out rather severely, and Dr. Golee was glad to avail himself of the funds in the hands of the municipal commissioners to enlarge his hospital and dispensary. The most diligent efforts were made to restrain the ravages of the epidemic. Medicines were distributed *gratis*, and Dr. Golee wrote a report of thirteen sheets of foolscap, showing how the cholera would have been much worse if it had not been for the trees that had been planted opposite Dakhil Duftar's house, while Dr. Baragolee, the Inspector-General, who visited Budgepore about that time, wrote another report of twenty-six sheets of foolscap, showing how the cholera was owing to the large quantity of trees in and about the place, which developed malaria. These reports, in spite of their slightly contradictory tendency, were published in the *Government Gazette*, with a minute by His Honour the Lieutenant-Governor.

While these great and wise men were engaged in the investigation of the causes of the epidemic, my attention was directed to the same subject by a remark from a very humble individual, that is to say, my syce. As I was walking my horse leisurely along the road one evening returning to my solitary home (ah! why was it I missed that star from heaven that crossed my path and left me with seared heart a bachelor for ever!) being in a conversational mood, I, as was my wont on such occasions, addressed myself to the only available companion my syce, and endeavoured to draw forth by leading questions and remarks his opinions upon men, manners, and the times. It so happened that I pitched upon the subject of the recent visitation, and made some suggestions as to the probable cause of it, when the man said—

"When 'Taccus' came" (a tax as the personification of the evil principle, or evil demon)—"when Taccus first came the poor people left off eating grain and ate vegetables, and when Taccus came to vegetables they had not enough food to fill their stomachs, and when Taccus came to the water, the water became bad, and so all the poor people got sick and died."

This, literally translated, is what he said to me, and I pondered over his words, for there seemed to be some truth hidden underneath them.

I must here explain to my English reader that he must not from the use of the word "vegetables" get the idea of green peas and potatoes. No, the vegetables that the poor of Budgepore had to resort to when their more wholesome articles of food were taxed, were "kaddoos," or gourds, huge masses of pulpy vegetable matter like—well, I don't know what they are like. There is little or no nourishment in them. But in some parts of the country they are very cheap and grow to an enormous size. I was once told of one so large that a missionary and his family lived on it for a week. To which I replied that I had seen one so large that a missionary and his family might have lived *in* it—and so they might, for missionaries are always very small in stature, and their families, though large in number, generally small in size. The gourd I speak of was an immense one. I saw it at Dr. Honigberger's house at Srinuggur, in Cashmere.

I could not at first understand what my syce meant by "Taccus" coming to the water. But at last I discovered. I got some of the water from all the wells in the city and analysed it, and found unmistakable signs of the presence of sewage. I then made some pertinent enquiries of Fileeter as to the course of his famous drains, and the conclusion was inevitable that they had been constructed so as to allow the sewage to percolate into the city wells. This, combined with the decrease of food, and the consumption of innutritious diet, was quiet enough in my mind to account for the cholera. So I wrote a letter to the *Mofussilite*, and the editor took up the subject and wrote an article upon it. A pretty stiff one too. The result of that was the following correspondence:—

"Official. No. 10567.

"*August*, 18—,

"From

"KHAS MOUZA, Esq., C.S.,

"*Secretary to Government*,

'To

"DR. GOLEE,

"*Civil Surgeon, Budgepore.*

"SIR,—

"I have been directed by His Honour the Lieutenant-Governor, to draw your attention to an article and a letter in the *Mofussilite* newspaper of the 21st July, 18—, wherein it is stated that the recent epidemic at Budgepore is traceable to the pollution of the water by the construction of drains under the order of the municipal commission. His Honour desires that the matter may receive the fullest elucidation, and with this view I have the honour under instruction to solicit the favour of your making an analytical examination of the water from the wells in the city, and communicating the results in a report.

"I have, &c.,

(Sd.) "KHAS MOUZA,

"*Secretary to Government.*"

By the same post came the following demi-official:—

"MY DEAR DR. GOLEE,—

"You will receive an official communication from me by this day's dawk respecting the statement in the *Mofussilite* newspaper, that the wells of Budgepore have been poisoned by ill-constructed drainage. H. H. is quite convinced that there can be no foundation for this report, which has no doubt been circulated with the view of throwing discredit upon the operations of the municipal commission. H. H. will be glad to hear that his surmises are correct, and has little doubt that a scientific analysis of the water will lead to this result.

"H. H. bids me say he is much pleased with the exertions made at Budgepore to extend medical aid to the inhabitants of the city, and as the duties of the enlarged dispensary and hospital must entail considerable extra labour, he is prepared to sanction an allowance of rupees 100 a month for these duties upon application.

"Yours very truly,
"KHAS MOUZA."

Golee, who did not of course know that I was the author of the letter in the *Mofussilite*, was busy analysing the water one morning when I called at his house at chota hazree (which means a sociable cup of tea and bit of toast in the early morning), and told him all about it. I remained there and witnessed the whole operation. Dr. Golee analysed for mineral salts, and found no sewage. The result was communicated in a very able report to Government, which was shortly after produced along with the article from the *Mofussilite* in the *Gazette*, triumphantly proving the unreliable nature of so unwarrantable a publication.

The Budgepore municipal commission has now been in existence some years. It has been a remarkable success. The military and civil station no longer present the ruinous appearance they formerly had. Ornamental whitewashed walls, which require renewal every year, have been erected along all the roads. The roads themselves have been improved. The waste ground opposite Dakhil Duftar's house has been transformed into a pretty garden, where the band plays once a week. The principal roads in the civil station and the cantonment, are kept well watered; the city kotwal has built a new and rather a stylish house for himself in the Chowk or principal market-place, and Sham Dutt, the assistant secretary, has set up a carriage and pair, the most showy turnout in the whole place.

There is, it is true, another side to this picture. About 20,000 of the inhabitants of the city have emigrated to other places. The epidemic which has visited Budgepore regularly every year since the municipal commission was established, although of course the coincidence in point of time between the commencement of the one and the first visitation of the other, is only accidental, finding the poorer classes of the population with their physical strength below par from want of the necessary amount of nutritious diet, and their frequent use of vegetables as a staple article of food, has yearly swept away several thousands, chiefly women and children. The growers of country produce, cotton, et cetera, finding that they had to pay a tax if they carried their produce to the city, took it elsewhere to other spots equally favourable for transport to the coast, and the bunneas and purchasers generally, having also their own interests to consult in evading the tax, established agencies at these spots to co-operate with the producers, and thus trade has fallen off immensely. The houses in the bazaar are fast falling into disrepair, and many are ruinous, and the whole aspect of this once flourishing city is one that speaks of poverty and want. Fitzmisl, however, still proves that the municipal commissioners have been acting on the truest principles of political economy, of which science he considers himself a master. The commissioner makes diligent enquiries through his serishtadar every month as to the condition of the people, and is assured that they are delighted with the municipal commission, and quite proud of exercising so large a share in the administration. The causes of the decline of trade and general deterioration of the once prosperous city, he is assured by the same authority, is owing to the fact of three or four Europeans having become landholders in the district, and to nothing else, and Mr. Wasilbakee thoroughly endorses these views, which appear to His Honour most correct. So the one side of the picture is shown to the public in reports, blue-books, minutes, proceedings, and selections, while on the other no one cares to look.

CHRONICLE III.

THE BUDGEPORE EXHIBITION.

CHRONICLE III.

THE BUDGEPORE EXHIBITION.

CHAPTER I.

SHOWING HOW THE SKILLED ARTIZAN WAS INTRODUCED TO THE COLLECTOR.

"We are to have a Budgepore exhibition, Old Mortality, what do you think of that?" said Mrs. Dakhil Duftar to me one evening at their house after dinner.

"Yes," said I, "I am sorry to hear it."

"Sorry to hear it?" said Mr. Wasilbakee, coming up at the moment, "and why, pray—do you not think these exhibitions are great things for developing the resources of the country, giving a stimulus to trade, aiding arts and manufactures, and benefiting the artizans as well as the agricultural population?"

"No, indeed, I don't," I replied. "The principal thing they serve to develop is the rapacity of the amla and police, and the utter incompetence of their European superiors to control it. The chief thing exhibitions give a stimulus to are corruption and bribery; what they most aid in is generating ill-will, and bad feeling, and neither the artizan nor the agriculturist is one whit the better for them. The country is not prepared for them. They are in advance of the times, and worse than useless for all practical purposes."

"Ah, you are a mass of prejudice—wait till you see the exhibition! But, come, let us argue the point—how on earth can an exhibition do any of these things you say? What room is there for bribery and corruption? The collector of a district calls for the best artizan in the particular branch of industry for which his locality is famed. Say, he is a carpenter;

well, the collector sahib encourages him to produce the very best article he can possibly turn out of his workshop. He does so, gets a prize perhaps, and is a famous man for the rest of his life. He is proud of his prize medal, and hands it down as an heirloom to his children to serve as a stimulus and incentive to them to industry and perseverance."

"All very fine, my dear sir, not so fast. We have not got beyond the first stage yet. How many people, think you, will your prize carpenter have to pay before he reaches the collector sahib's presence?"

"Pay! if the fellow is such a fool as to pay money to anyone that asks him, he must do so. We can't protect people who won't help themselves."

"Suppose he is forced to pay the money?"

"I say he can't be forced—he can refuse."

"And I say he daren't refuse. If he does, woe betide him. He is a doomed man from that day forth, he will end his days in jail, happy if not tortured to death."

"Tortured to death—pooh! what nonsense you do talk. I do believe you think every official in India a wild beast that delights in torturing his fellow-creatures."

"I don't think you delight in torturing your fellow-creatures, but I think you are just as guilty as if you did, for you allow others to do so. You would, perhaps, be less to blame if you did delight in it, for then Nature would be at fault for having given you a moral organisation with blunted perceptions of right and wrong and no feeling. As it is, you deliberately blind yourself to what goes on, partly from deep-rooted prejudice and partly from indolence."

Mr. Wasilbakee and I had many such little encounters as this, and as we both understood each other, they were followed by no bad feeling or ill-will on either side. But whether he or I was right in our estimate of the probable results of the exhibition will be apparent from the following chronicle. Curiously enough, the very illustration he had used in argument served practically to demonstrate the truth of what I averred. I am not certain that it did not act as a suggestion.

It very soon became known that Mr. Byewilwuffa, the Lieut.-Governor, looked upon the Budgepore exhibition as a pet scheme. The *éclat*, it was thought, might serve to impart a little glitter and fictitious lustre to an administration otherwise weak and profitless. And all the Budgepore civilians, covenanted and unconvenanted, very soon began to see that their best chance of favour and promotion at headquarters depended on the zeal and activity they displayed in pushing forward this pet scheme. The result was, that they all more or less neglected their legitimate duties and spent their time in looking about for curiosities, or hunting up some species of country produce hitherto unheard of, or getting artizans who were recommended to them as peculiarly skilful by one of their own amla, their clerks, or moonshees, or orderlies, and setting them to work in their compounds and verandahs, making thermantidotes that wouldn't work except in models, punkahs that required a horse instead of a man to pull them, draw-wells that operated effectually with a tumbler of water on the drawing-room table, carts that combined the disadvantages of the country hackery with those of the English waggon, &c., &c. Others purchased expensive horses with a view to getting the prize at the exhibition, or bought gigantic bullocks for the same purpose. Mooltawee, the judge of Budgepore, excited great envy by displaying a buffalo with five legs which he had picked up somewhere in the district, and which everyone felt sure would carry off the prize in that department. Others took to breeding fancy pigeons, fattening ducks, geese, and turkeys. Mulligatawny, a young competition-walla, who had been a year in the country, one day saw a pony in the district with red legs and a green tail, and immediately purchased it at treble its value as a specimen of a new breed. Nor did the fever of emulation cease with the European officials. All the native subordinate officers, the tehsildars and thanadars, not to mention mookuddums, putwaries, kanoongoes, and chowkedars, who imbibed but a crude and imperfect notion of the objects of the exhibition, viz., that there was a hukm of the sirkar, or order of the Government, to collect everything that was "ajaib," or curious in the whole range of mineral, vegetable, and animal economy, left their station and their duties and went over the whole country searching for anything in the shape of a vegetable or animal monstrosity they could find. In every native collector's compound that you entered almost you would be sure to see some extraordinary freaks of nature in the shape of some mis-shapen calves, buffaloes, bullocks, or camels, waiting to be taken to the great "tamasha ghur," or exhibition. A policeman who hunted up a deformed child with no legs and without arms, was as sure of favour as if he had caught a thief. The artizans who were unlucky enough to be pitched upon as "skilled," had to abandon their work which brought them in their daily bread and spent their time in manufacturing, without remuneration, trinkets and knicknacks of all possible and impossible sorts, that could under no circumstances be of the least use to a living creature.

Meantime a spot had been selected in the vicinity of Budgepore for the exhibition building. The place was marked out and building operations commenced under the supervision of Dakhil Duftar, assisted by Fitzmisl. An inspector of police, with fifty men under him, was told off for the duty of collecting workmen, looking after their daily labour, and paying them. The way they managed it was this: There were six villages in the immediate neighbourhood of the site chosen. These villages contained a population each of from 150 to 200, men, women, and children included. The whole population of one of these villages was called out in turn one day in the week to assist in the erection of the building, the masonry work of course being performed by raj-mistrees or masons from Budgepore, the coolies being employed in carrying bricks, mortar, earth, beams of wood, &c. Dakhil Duftar would come down in the morning and see a number of coolies at work, praise the inspector for his ability in collecting so many, and would be told of course that they all came voluntarily and of their own accord. In the evening they were all seated in a line on the ground when Dakhil Duftar and Fitzmisl happened to be on the premises (when they were not, the form was dispensed with), and the allotted number of copper coin paid ostentatiously into the hand of each man, woman, or child for the day's labour, the inspector diligently recording in a note-book every rupee thus expended. Dakhil Duftar of course could not be expected to follow these coolies to their homes. Had he done so, he might have seen that as they were all marched in a line out of the grounds, as soon as they turned the corner and entered a lane lined with thick cactus hedges, they had to pass between four policemen, two on each side of the lane, who took from each individual every coin that had been paid. As was natural, of course, petitions were sent to Dakhil Duftar complaining of all this. Many of these were anonymous and received no notice; but one from Zalim Sing, a zemindar of one of the villages, complaining that his people were forcibly taken away one day in the week and received no pay, did receive attention. Zalim Sing was summoned to the cutchery, whither he went in a very uncomfortable frame of mind, having been warned all the way from his village to the cutchery by the policeman who served the summons, that he and his would rue the day he had ventured to complain to the "sahib." Arrived at the cutchery the district superintendent of the police no sooner saw Zalim Sing than he told the magistrate that he was a noted character, and that his name would be found in the list of badmashes (bad characters). The book was sent for, and sure enough there was Zalim Sing's name just as the district superintendent had said; and not only that, but the whole village had a mark against it, as being a place altogether of bad repute. So Zalim Sing was dismissed, his word not being deemed worthy of credit, and on the representation of the district superintendent, a party of ten constables and an inspector were ordered to be quartered in the village for the next six months at the expense of the inhabitants.

After this there were no more complaints of non-payment. But nevertheless the work progressed so slowly that Dakhil Duftar was seriously afraid it would not be ready in time. As it was, he and Fitzmisl had been obliged to leave all their regular work to get into arrears. The number of prisoners in the hawallat (or lock-up where prisoners whose cases have not been decided are kept confined) had increased to fifty-eight, many of whom had been in close confinement now for two months without any trial, which was strictly against the law, but who was there to see that the law was enforced? while the miscellaneous cases on the files of the collector and his subordinate had assumed formidable dimensions. So Dakhil Duftar determined to complete the work by contract, and made an agreement with a European named Bolt, who was what is vulgarly called "knocking about" the station at that time, picking up whatever work he could. Bolt went over the building with Dakhil Duftar, and examined the walls and masonry work with the eye of an experienced builder, talking very learnedly all the time, and using a great many technical terms, which much impressed Dakhil Duftar. After a day spent in examining the plans, Bolt declared his readiness to undertake the contract on certain terms. An agreement was drawn out on stamped paper and duly signed, and an advance of three thousand rupees made from the treasury. After this, Bolt mysteriously disappeared, and has never, that I know of, been heard of since. It is generally supposed that he fell into a well on his way home, or perhaps was waylaid and murdered for the sake of the three thousand rupees which he carried away from the treasury in a bag himself.

Dakhil Duftar was now sorely beset. He began to think he had better have employed the Public Works Department. Time was pressing, and what if the building should not be ready! Mooltawee felt certain there would be no exhibition at all that year, and as it was extremely doubtful if his buffalo with five legs would live for another year, he used to assemble as many of his friends as he could at his house in the morning and have the buffalo brought out for a private exhibition of his own.

At this time the Budgepore railway was in progress, the history of which I hope I shall live to chronicle hereafter, and among the engineers engaged in its construction was one Sleeper, a great friend of Dakhil Duftar's. And Sleeper came to the rescue, and having obtained permission from the railway superintending engineer to take up this work, he consented to complete the building within the prescribed time. As a railway engineer, however, he could not, of course, be expected to construct an edifice, the foundations whereof had been laid by another, and he not a professional man. So the walls had to be pulled down and the foundations laid afresh, with many alterations and improvements in the original design. Of course all this cost money, but money was forthcoming, for the Hon'ble Kist Byewilwuffa looked with favour on the scheme, and the contract was given to Sleeper for twenty thousand rupees. The material was all at hand, and Sleeper had the services *gratis* of the assistants, and overseers, and bricklayers on the railway, which unimportant work was allowed to stand over for the present, the Government consulting engineer having given it as his opinion that a few weeks' delay would not be detrimental; on the other hand it would be highly beneficial, as affording time for the earthwork to consolidate and the brickwork and masonry to harden.

A long time before matters had progressed thus far, I heard that Dakhil Duftar had given notice that all the most skilful artizans of Budgepore were to be registered, and were to be sent to the kotwallee with specimens of their handiwork before being introduced to him.

Being inclined to experimentalise a little upon the ways and means of developing genius through official channels, I summoned a trusty domestic of my own, in whose wits I had full confidence, to my counsels. I had several little knick-knacks which I had purchased in Paris a few years back. They were not of Paris manufacture, but Swiss. They consisted of very prettily carved boxes, spoons, forks, paper-knives, trays, dice-boxes, and so on. These I produced and a bag of rupees which I had taken the precaution to mark (each one separately).

"Now," said I, to my faithful domestic Selim, "you are to go and get introduced to the collector sahib as one of the skilled artizans of Budgepore, to compete for the prize at the approaching exhibition."

"But," said the astonished Selim, who evidently thought for a moment I was demented, "I am no artizan. Why should I go?"

"I know you are no artizan, Selim, but you will go all the same. Every man who wishes to be presented to the collector sahib to compete for the prizes, is to go to-morrow morning to the kotwallee and enter his name. That is all you will have to do, enter your name; do you understand? The kotwal will tell you what next to do. Take these things with you, and if you are asked what you can make, show these. I'll be bound to say no one in Budgepore will produce better. You may want a rupee or two, but don't give away more than you can help, and keep an exact account of how you spend it—give no more than you are forced to do. But recollect you are to have your name registered. There are fifty rupees in this bag, and a bank-note for fifty more. Do you understand?"

"Yes, sahib, I understand."

"Well, go."

Next morning early Selim departed. He did not return till late in the evening.

"Hallo!" I said, pretending to be very angry, "where have you been all day, sir?"

"I have been to get my name registered," said the man, rather sulkily.

"Well, that only occupied five minutes, I suppose, a walk to the kotwallee and back. What have you been doing all day?"

"If the sahib won't be angry with his slave, his slave will tell him what a net of misfortunes his slave has been enveloped in, owing to his obedience to his master's orders."

"Go on, tell me all about it."

"I went to the kotwallee at sunrise this morning, and told the chiprassee what I was come for; and he told me to wait. There were a number of others there waiting, too. We sat till ten o'clock, when I saw one of the men put a coin into the chiprassee's hand, and he was taken inside. After a time another did the same, and then a third, but when the fourth went up to follow the rest, I saw the chiprassee refuse to take the coin; it was one rupee, and he made him pay two. This went on for a long while; at last I got tired of waiting, and went up like the rest.

"'I want to go and have my name registered, sir,' said I; 'please may I go in?'

"The man held out his hand, and I slipped a rupee into it.

"'No, no, my friend,' said he, 'I've been watching you all day; you are a fine fellow with a bran new turban and such shoes! I must have five from you.'

"'Very well,' I said, and gave him the five rupees. I was then admitted into a room where I found almost all my former companions who had got in before me seated on the floor with their backs against the wall. I entered into conversation with one by whose side I happened to seat myself, and asked him how long he had been there. 'Ah,' said he, 'I saw you outside this morning; and so you have only just got in. Well, we have to wait here till our turn comes. But I see several have gone in out of their turn by paying the chiprassee at the door something.'

"'How much have you to pay this one?'

"'Oh, I don't know; I see some giving two, some three,

some five rupees, and I wish I had the money to give, and I would willingly give it to get away. I have been here all the morning, and my stomach is quite empty, and my wife is sick. I did not want to come here at all, but I was told by one of the kotwal's men that if I didn't I should be turned out of my house and have to get another, and as I am in arrears for my rent three months, this would ruin me.'

"'Well,' said I, 'I think I'll try. I have some money, and may as well spend it in this way, now I have come here, but, like you, I wish I had stayed away.'

"So I went up to the chiprassee at the door, and asked if I might go in to have my name registered.

"'Wait till your turn comes,' my friend, he replied, quite civilly.

"'But I am in a great hurry, sir, and should really esteem it a great favour if you would allow me to go in.'

"'I think you have a bag of money there,' he said, eyeing the purse.

"'Yes, and I'll willingly give you five rupees to let me go in at once.'

"'That cannot be, but I'll let you go in fifth.'

"'Take ten,' said I, pressing the money upon him, 'and let me go at once.' So he took the money and let me in.

"When I got inside, I found the kotwal seated there on one side and a man whom I afterwards found out was the collector sahib's serishtadar, on the other side. They looked at one another as I entered, and then went on with their writing. I made a very low salaam to each, and, folding my hands, addressed the kotwal.

"'May it please your majesty, this poor slave has come to register his name as a skilled artizan to compete for the prize in the exhibition.'

"The kotwal beckoned me towards him with a look of much majesty, and asked me to show him what I could make. I produced the paper-knife and other things and gave them to him.

"'Ah,' said he, 'these are very pretty, and did you make all these?'

"'Every one.'

"'And what are they worth?'

"I told him a price, five rupees, ten, and so on, just as it came into my head at the moment, for indeed I had never thought what they were worth, nor did I expect to be asked.

"'Very well,' said the kotwal, putting the things down beside him with the evident intention of keeping them, 'I'll keep these trumpery knick-knacks, they will serve as your nuzzur; go to the serishtadar sahib, and tell him you wish your name registered.'

"So I went to the serishtadar, and said very humbly, 'May it please your exalted highness, I have come, a poor carpenter, to have my name registered as a skilled artizan to compete for the prize at the exhibition.'

"'There are already too many names down on my list,' said he.

"'This will be a sad disappointment,' I replied. 'That I am skilful at such things the kotwal sahib knows, as he has done your poor slave the honour to accept a few trifling articles of my handiwork. If your majesty would be pleased to look at these things for a moment, your highness will see that I am not an impostor, and that I can really make very pretty things.'

"'Very likely, but for all that my list is so full I cannot possibly add any more,' and he went on writing.

"Fully understanding what was meant, I had resort to my bag of rupees, now pretty well diminished, and taking out ten, offered them to the great man. He pushed away my hand, and looking sternly at me, asked me if I took him for a common chiprassee, that he received bribes of ten rupees.

"'Go away, go away, you son of a dog,' he added, 'and don't interrupt me any more.'

"At this I fell on my knees, and with uplifted hands, prayed to be forgiven; and then getting out my fifty rupee note, I offered it to him very humbly, begging him to accept it as a nuzzur from his poor slave.

"This had the desired effect. He took the note, looked at the amount, held it up, and examined it before the light, and then put it down on his desk.

"'Very well,' he said, 'that will do. What is your name?'

"Now, to this moment, I had never thought what name I should go by; it had never occurred to me that I should be asked, although, of course, if I had thought about it, I must have been well aware that as I went to get my name registered, I should be certainly required to state what it was. I stammered over the question till the serishtadar got angry, and said ' Well, fool, what is your name ? '

" ' Pir Khân,' I said, at last recovering myself.

" ' Go,' said he, ' and be at the collector sahib's house to-morrow at ten o'clock, and don't look quite as much like a fool there as you do here.'

" On this I made a very low salaam, and came out. In the outer room there was many an envious eye turned upon me, as I passed out, from those who were still squatting there, like hens hatching eggs. I exchanged a few words with the man with whom I had sympathised before.

" ' I don't think I shall wait here any longer,' he said.

" ' Much better not,' I replied. ' It is better to spend your money in paying your arrears of rent, or in moving house, than giving it away here ; and ten to one, after all, if it will be of any service.' So I came away."

" And that is all the money you have brought back ? "

" Yes, sahib, that is all," he said, counting out what remained, which was thirty-five rupees.

" Keep that," I said, " you will probably want it to-morrow when you go to the collector sahib."

" Am I to go to the collector sahib ? " he asked in much surprise.

" Yes, of course you are ; didn't you go to day and get your name written down on purpose that you should go to the collector sahib ; why should I waste all that money for nothing ? "

Selim went away on this, and told all the rest of the servants that the sahib was gone mad, and the consequence was, my servant, when he brought me my dinner, eyed me askance, and trembled violently when he handed me the dishes and changed my plate.

Next day Selim went off at ten o'clock to the collector's house, and returned about one.

" Well," said I, " how have you sped—have you seen the collector sahib ? Let us hear all about it."

" When I got to the collector sahib's house this morning, I stood outside the door with seven or eight other men who were waiting there on one business or another. As no one took any notice of me I pushed my way to the front. ' Hulloo, fellow, who are you and what do you want?' said a chiprassee. 'Please, sir,' said I, 'I am a poor carpenter. I have had my name registered to compete for the prize at the exhibition, and I was ordered to come here to-day for the huzoor to see me.' 'Well, you had better wait there, and the sahib will perhaps see you when he comes out to go to cutchery; meantime, keep a little further off, and don't come crowding in close to the door.' 'If you please, sir,' I said, 'I am pressed for time, and my wife is very sick, and there is no one to give her food or medicine; if you would be so kind as to let me go in and have my business over, I shall be very much obliged.' Saying this, I slipped a rupee into the fellow's hand. 'Wait a minute,' he said, 'I'll see if I can manage it for you.'

"Saying this, he went away, and returned shortly after with another chiprassee. 'Here,' he said, 'this gentleman will take you inside; it is not every day such fellows as you get admittance to the "huzoor," but these are queer times, and we must obey orders.'

"The second chiprassee then took me rather kindly by the hand, and said, 'Come with me, my good fellow, I will see whether I can manage it for you. Come this way, the sahib is very busy this morning, and it will be difficult. But I'll do my best.'

"We had arrived by this time in a kind of outer or verandah room, where there was no furniture, but a tailor was sitting down sewing some embroidered work on the edge of a lady's petticoat. There were also a chemise and some other articles of ladies' apparel lying before him, which I suppose he had been mending. I waited there patiently by the tailor's side for at least half-an-hour, till my patience was exhausted, and I ventured to ask the tailor if he thought the chiprassee would come again.

"'I don't think it is at all likely he will come again unless he is called. You gave him nothing—don't you know the dustoor (custom)? Did you never hear the proverb, "The path through the rich man's gate is paved with silver"?'

"'Perhaps you will be so kind as to go and look for him,' said I, offering him a rupee.

"'Very well, I see you are a good fellow at the bottom, only rather stupid at first—wait here, and if anyone calls me, say you are gone to fetch me, and that I went away to drink water

"So he went inside, leaving me with the petticoat and the other things, and I could not help admiring them, they were so fine and pretty.

"By-and-by he came back again, and said, 'Unfortunately the chiprassee who brought you in was sent away on an errand, and I don't know how long he may be gone. But I have spoken to the jemadar himself for you, who promised to come as soon as he possibly could. Sit down by me, he will be here directly.'

"So I sat down. By-and-by the jemadar came. He was a very tall, dignified-looking person, dressed in blue cloth and a silver brocade belt around his waist. 'Dear me,' I said to myself, 'so grand a person as this! I shall be ashamed to offer him a rupee—I must offer him more.'

"Where is the man you spoke to me about, Kaleefa?' said the jemadar. 'The sahib is disengaged just at this moment. Now is a favourable time—if we lose this opportunity I fear he will be kept waiting all day.'

"'Oh, thank you, sir,' said I, jumping to my feet, 'I am so much obliged to you.'

"With this I followed my conductor inside, and found myself in a sort of hall, which had three or four doors opening into it. One of them was half open, and I caught a glimpse of my friend the serishtadar sitting at a table. My conductor pointed to the door as much as to say, that is the room where the 'huzoor' is—and held out his hand to me—open. I counted into it, one after another, slowly, ten rupees. He did not move till I had completed the whole ten; but I gave them to him very slowly in order that, when he had as much as was requisite, he might intimate to me he was ready to conduct me inside. Having tied up the money in a corner of his turban, he went inside the room where I had seen the serishtadar, and shortly after returned to the door and beckoned me. I stepped boldly in, and found myself in the presence of Mr. Dakhil Duftar, who was seated at a table, and the serishtadar opposite to him. The collector sahib was writing something, which the serishtadar was dictating to him in Hindustani. After a second or two, he looked up, and then looked at the serishtadar as much as to ask who I was.

"'This,' said the serishtadar, 'is a carpenter who has registered his name to compete for the prize at the exhibition.'"

"At last, then, you succeeded in reaching the collector sahib, and what did he say to you?"

"He said, 'uchchha, jao' (very well, go away), and I came away."

If Selim had entertained any doubts as to my sanity before, these doubts must have been confirmed by the roars of laughter with which I greeted this last announcement.

"So, after two days' labour and the expenditure of, let's see, how much, of exactly 75 rupees, you received this flattering encouragement, 'uchchha, jao' from the collector sahib. Well done!" and I took up the *Gazette* and read again the last paragraph of the Lieutenant-Governor's minute directing the Budgepore exhibition to be held.

"*There can be little doubt but that the exhibition will serve as a stimulus to industry, which will aid in developing genius in arts and manufactures, and by bringing the skilled artizan and the intelligent agriculturist into the notice of the authorities will afford exactly that encouragement to labour and progress which the country so much needs.*"

Next day I went to Dakhil Duftar, full of confidence in the success of my scheme. The kotwal had got the knick-knacks, the serishtadar the fifty rupee note, the number of which I had, and the rupees the chiprassees had taken were all marked. "Dakhil Duftar's eyes will be opened not a little now I should say."

I found him at home about eleven o'clock—his usual hour for going to the cutchery varied between twelve and two. I told him plainly of my scheme, its object, and success, but was a little taken aback when he remarked—

"Then it seems to me you have been nicely duped. Your man sold the things and kept the money, and has told you this cock-and-bull story. All the people about me, I assure you, are persons of integrity and character."

"Well it is easily tested," I said; "suppose, to begin with the kotwal, you ask him if he has got the knick-knacks."

"Certainly I will," said Dakhil Duftar. "He is outside. We will call him at once."

When he came in Dakhil Duftar motioned him to a chair, and as soon as he was seated, he said—

"Kotwal sahib, this gentleman has missed some little knick-knacks, a carved wooden paper-knife, trays, boxes, and one or two things of that sort. He thinks it possible someone may have taken them away with the view of passing them off as his own workmanship for the exhibition."

"The 'huzoor's' intelligence is as the sun at noonday," replied the kotwal. "Certainly it is so, your slave has these articles. They are not here, it is true, but I will send for them at once, and they will be here directly. It is as the 'huzoor' suggests. A carpenter came yesterday to have his name enrolled as a competitor for the prize at the exhibition, and presented sundry articles to me as specimens of his handiwork; they were, indeed, very well executed, and I kept them by me to show them to the 'huzoor,' as I did not know before that any man in Budgepore could produce anything like them, and I am sure the 'huzoor' will be much pleased with them."

"Now," said I, as the kotwal left the room, feeling very triumphant at my success so far, "let us try the serishtadar next, and see if he cannot find the fifty rupee note. Suppose you send for him, and say that I have lost a note of that amount, and he is to put up an advertisement offering ten rupees reward to anyone who will produce it. And don't forget to add the number, which is 047074, and that I have stopped it at the bank, and let us see what he says."

"Certainly," said Dakhil Duftar. "I don't know about the note, but it is perfectly clear the kotwal had no intention of retaining those articles. If he had, why should he have confessed to having them in his possession?"

By-and-by the serishtadar came in, and Dakhil Duftar told him exactly as I had instructed him.

"What an unlucky wretch I am," said the serishtadar, the moment Dakhil Duftar had ceased speaking, "I do believe now that is the very self-same note I received this morning for my pony. Let me see, here it is." So saying, he produced the identical note, which I recognised immediately.

"Where did you get it?" said Dakhil Duftar.

"Where should I get it from but in payment of that very pony I sold this morning to Mr. Archimedes DeCruze? The cost of the animal was fifty rupees, and Mr. DeCruze paid me in this very note. The 'huzoor' will see it is the exact sum. Only to think of its being stolen!"

"Send for Mr. Archimedes DeCruze," said Dakhil Duftar.

"I will call him. I saw him only this moment in the other room," said the serishtadar, leaving abruptly to summon him.

Mr. Archimedes DeCruze made his appearance in a few minutes, during which I looked triumphantly at Dakhil Duftar, as much as to say, "Now for the integrity and character of the people about you!"

"Did you give the serishtadar this note?" said Dakhil Duftar, showing the note to Archimedes.

"Certainly I did, sir—only this morning. I purchased a pony from him and paid him with this note."

"And where did you get it from?"

"I got it yesterday from Bankee Lall, the mahajun" (native money-lender or banker).

"Send for Bankee Lall," said Dakhil Duftar.

We had to wait a little for Bankee Lall; however, he soon came, and said, in reply to a question from Dakhil Duftar, that he had received the note from a man he did not know the day before, who asked him to change it, and he had paid four rupees, or eight per cent., for the exchange.

"Who would have thought it was a stolen note!" added Bankee Lall.

"Send for your servant, will you," said Dakhil Duftar to me.

Selim was summoned.

"What is his name?" asked Dakhil Duftar.

"*Ex uno disce omnes*," said I.

"A curious name for a native," said Dakhil Duftar, and then pointing to Selim and addressing Bankee Lall, he added "Was that the man you got the note from?"

"Certainly, it is the very same; I recognise him at once," said Bankee Lall.

"Now," said Dakhil Duftar, turning to me, "I think you'll admit you've been pretty well duped."

"There are the chiprassees, yet," said I. "Let one of them be searched, and let us see if any of the marked coin is found upon him."

"By all means. Let us go outside. I dare say we shall find one of them there somewhere with the kotwal."

So we went outside, and took Selim, now very much chapfallen and disconcerted, and who seemed to think the whole affair was a trap I had laid for him.

He soon recognised one of the chiprassees to whom he had given the money at the kotwallee the day before. Dakhil Duftar called him up at once and asked him if he had any money about him.

"Certainly I have," said the man. "I sold a ring this very morning on my way through the bazaar, and received five rupees for it. This is how I came to have so much money about me, for a poor man as your slave is does not usually carry about five rupees with him."

So saying, he produced five rupees, which Dakhil Duftar handed to me. I examined them all, and found my initials, O.M., marked on each.

"Let us come inside," said Dakhil Duftar, appearing a little impressed now with what I had said.

"Look at this rupee," he added, handing one of them to the serishtadar, "did you ever see a rupee marked like this before?"

"Oh, yes," said the serishtadar, "nearly all the rupees current in Budgepore are marked in this very same way. This is how we can always tell in our villages and elsewhere whether a man has come from Budgepore or not. If he has money marked in this way we know he has come from Budgepore, or else he must have got money here somehow. Many a 'foujdary' (criminal) case has been traced in this very way."

"Perhaps you will say the serishtadar is not an impartial witness," said Dakhil Duftar. "Let us call someone else. Call Mr. Archimedes DeCruze."

Mr. DeCruze was accordingly again summoned (I believe he had been listening all the time behind the door).

"Did you ever see rupees marked in this way, Mr. DeCruze, 'O.M.'?"

"Oh, yes, certainly," said Mr. DeCruze, examining the coin, "an immense number of Budgepore rupees are marked in this way. I once enquired of a mahajun what the letters meant, and he said they were the initial letters of a great banker who lived here formerly, Omichund Mull."

"There, you see," said Dakhil Duftar, putting the money on the table, "how you have been outwitted by that scoundrel of yours."

"Assuredly the huzoor's intelligence is as the sun at noonday," I said to myself, repeating the kotwal's words, as I drove home. And the exhibition will serve to develop genius and act as an incentive to industry.

THE BUDGEPORE EXHIBITION.

CHAPTER II.

HOW MRS. FILEETER LED THE CHOIR, AND WHAT WAS THE CONSEQUENCE THEREOF.

THE time for the exhibition drew near. The building was nearly completed. The programme of the opening ceremonies was being arranged, and amateur performers were busy practising daily for a grand instrumental and vocal concert in honour of the occasion.

A serious difficulty had arisen at this juncture which threatened at one time to be followed by fatal results as regarded the musical programme. Mrs. Wasilbakee had not returned from Simla till all the arrangements had been cut and dried She was a very good performer, and had a fine voice besides; but independently of that, if she had been proficient in neither instrumental nor vocal music, as the Commissioner's wife it would have been quite necessary that she should have taken a prominent part. I say the arrangements had all been completed before she came down, and so they had. I don't at all know how it happened, from some oversight, I suppose, and it is really impossible always to prevent mistakes in matters of this kind, but it had been so clumsily managed that Mrs. Fileeter, who had a very beautiful voice, and a nicely-educated one, too, for she had begun life as a French governess and had been herself educated in Paris, had been asked and had consented to take a leading part in the performance. I say a leading part, for if she took any part at all it must necessarily have been a leading one; as she knew a great deal more about music than any of the other amateurs, it was quite natural she should be repeatedly referred to in such matters as selection of pieces, appropriation of parts, &c.

The first day Mrs. Wasilbakee attended the practice it was at Dakhil Duftar's house. She came in a little late, after they had all begun, and had been in the room some five minutes or so before her presence was noticed, as the others were all intent on their music. She looked about and beheld familiar faces with open mouths all around her. But at the piano sat a lady she did not know. When the piece was over she shook hands with Mrs. Dakhil Duftar and a few other of the ladies who happened to be near the ottoman where she was seated.

"Can you tell me who that lady is who has been playing the accompaniment?—she has splendid execution."

"Oh, yes, that's Mrs. Fileeter."

"Mrs. who?"

"Mrs. Fileeter—the deputy collector's wife."

"How in the world did you ask her to join?"

"I didn't," said Mrs. Dakhil Duftar, "and, indeed, I don't know who did. But she plays most beautifully."

"I think I'll say good morning," said Mrs. Wasilbakee, getting up to go. "My head is so bad to-day that I'm sure I shall not be able to sing. Good-bye."

And Mrs. Wasilbakee went. But through one of those undefined processes by which public feeling becomes affected before undergoing some great change, it began to be felt in Budgepore, that Budgepore had committed a *faux pas* in asking Mrs. Fileeter to take a part in the musical programme. No doubt the change was due in a great measure to Mrs. Wasilbakee's very strong opinion on this point. Several ladies sided with her, particularly those who belonged to the Lieutenant-Governor's party, and who happened at that time to be guests of the Commissioner's wife, and many of the Budgeporeans thought it politic and proper to form an alliance in this quarter. The matter became a subject of ceaseless conversation at all the parties and little assemblies where the female sex alone was represented. In the drawing-room after dinner, before the gentlemen came in, at *chotá hazrees* in the morning, when no gentlemen happened to be present, and especially at the choir practice at the church, the *pros* and *cons* were discussed, some at first siding with the liberal party, who approved of Mrs. Fileeter, others—and the majority—agreeing with Mrs. Wasilbakee and the headquarters ladies that on no account ought she to have been asked to join. Now that the mischief had been done, it was exceedingly difficult to undo it. They could not send Mrs. Fileeter about her business, nor could the most inventive genius among the fair Budgeporeans devise any decent excuse for getting rid of her. Great as would have been the loss of her voice and advice, her taste, her accompaniment, that they were quite ready to put up with, if only the greater difficulty, that of Mrs. Fileeter's husband belonging to the 'uncovenanted service, could be by any means removed. This, of course, was impossible, and what was to be done?

Had Mrs. Fileeter conceived the least idea of the trouble her presence was giving, she would at once have relieved her friends of all their anxiety by resigning her place in the exhibition programme. I dare say that would not have been done without a pang. Human nature has its inherent weaknesses from which few of us are free, and Mrs. Fileeter would have been more than a woman if she had not experienced a little pride and gratification in contemplating the position she had been accorded in Budgepore "society." The meetings for practising were generally followed by tiffins, and, as a matter of course, Mrs. Fileeter remained to take her part in these. After tiffin, the ladies generally adjourned to croquet, and here, again, Mrs. Fileeter could not by any possibility be left out. It may readily be supposed that the ladies' croquet parties were speedily joined by the gentlemen as soon as their office work was over, and by the officers who had no office work to keep them away, as soon as they began to play. Mrs. Fileeter thus found herself within the charmed circle whose limits she would not have crossed had she tried ever so hard, had it not been for the exhibition. The question was, and my Anglo-Indian readers will see at once that it was a very difficult question, how was all this to be undone—how was Mrs. Fileeter to be got rid of? For I grieve to have to record it, that one by one Mrs. Fileeter's supporters dropped off, till at last it came to be an admitted principle, that if it were possible to get rid of Mrs. Fileeter, Mrs. Fileeter was to be got rid of. If it were not possible, then in that case it did not indeed appear exactly what would be the result, but Mrs. Wasilbakee was determined that the result should be the total abandonment of the musical programme. In dead silence or to the vulgar strains of a military band should the opening ceremonies be performed. Fairly beaten by the difficulty, none of them could overcome it. Mrs. Wasilbakee was fain to have recourse to her husband. And to him one evening she opened her griefs. His vigorous and manly intellect at once embraced the subject in all its phases.

"Pooh! my dear, is that all—why that is very easily managed."

"I declare I don't see how. I wish I had spoken to you before. You make so light of it, and I am sure it's given me many and many a sleepless night."

"You should have taken me into your confidence before, you see. You ladies always think you can do things so much better than we can, but you are obliged to come to us after all."

"But you haven't told me how you are going to do it. You will not speak to Mr. Fileeter about it?"

"Oh, no, I shall do it in a much easier way, by a demi-official."

"You don't mean to say you'll write to him! Why, he'll send the letter to the papers, and that will be worse than all."

"No, I'll write a demi-official to the Lieutenant-Governor, and have Fileeter removed at once to another district."

"There's a good creature," and Mrs. Wasilbakee rewarded her husband with a kiss, and hastened to write a short note to Mrs. Dakhil Duftar to tell her that the burden which had been hanging like an incubus on them so long was all removed as if by magic.

So Mr. Wasilbakee wrote a demi-official to Mr. Khas Mouza, and Mr. Khas Mouza communicated the contents thereof to the Lieutenant-Governor, and an order appeared in the very next *Gazette* directing the removal of Mr. Fileeter, who had been twenty years at Budgepore, to another district. Meantime an official letter was despatched to Mr. Fileeter telling him in highly flattering terms that his services were much required at Jhansie, that H.H. regretted the necessity of removing so old and well tried an officer, but that the exigencies of the public service required that the Jhansie treasury should have the advantage of Mr. Fileeter's experience.

The blow was a severe one to Mr. Fileeter. There was no increase of pay to be looked for as a compensation for the trouble and enormous expense and loss of moving; the furniture and things would have to be sold by auction, for he was ordered down at a week's notice, and it was too far to transport them—indeed he could not afford to pay for their transport. But what could he do? To remonstrate was worse than useless. He could only console himself with the reflection that the Lieutenant-Governor's flattering sentences really meant something, and that Government would never subject him to so much trouble and expense unless they intended to make it up to him hereafter in some way or other.

Of all the ladies at Budgepore, Mrs. Fitzmisl sympathised the most with Mrs. Fileeter. Mr. Fitzmisl had married before he came out, a thing which no one but a competition-walla was ever known to do. It was an innovation that came in along with the competition system. The old orthodox custom was for a civilian as a bachelor to get himself well into debt during the first few years of his service and then marry. But a competition-walla who came out married was pretty sure not to get into debt. He would have to live carefully, very carefully, to screw in fact, as the other and older branch of the service called it, to make both ends meet upon an assistant's pay. And Mrs. Fitzmisl had tasted all the bitters of poverty before her husband emerged into the full pay and position of a joint. It had, however, taught her to acquire homely habits, and habits of economy. And although she mixed, of course, in a great deal of the society of Budgepore, she did it against her will, and in opposition to her inclinations. I cannot exactly explain why this should have been a bond of union between her and Mrs. Fileeter, but so it was. Perhaps it arose from the fact that Mrs. Fitzmisl came to be looked down upon a little by the rest in consequence of her persistence in avoiding extravagance of all kinds and keeping her husband out of debt.

She shared the anxiety and distress of the other Budgeporeans in their difficulty about getting rid of Mrs. Fileeter, when once the real character of that difficulty was disclosed to her. At first she did not see, as many of the others had not seen, the gross impropriety they had been guilty of, till Mrs. Wasilbakee had shown it to them in its true light and full intensity. As soon as her eyes were opened, she acknowledged its gravity, and sought in vain, like the others, for some solution from the difficulty. Still, for all that, she did sympathise with Mrs. Fileeter, and, as I have said, was more intimate with her than any of the others.

No sooner was the transfer of Mr. Fileeter notified in the *Gazette*, and the world of Budgepore had triumphed in the success of its scheme, than its cup of joy was dashed from its lips, by the announcement made by Mrs. Fileeter herself, that she did not intend to accompany her husband, but should leave him to go on before her, get a house, and settle, &c., and she should proceed to join him after the exhibition was over. Here was a blow! But Budgepore proved equal to the occasion. Gunny Lall was spokon to, and it needed a few words of kindly advice only from the Commissioner for him to open his money-bags and invest in Mr. Fileeter's house, paying a good sum for it, on condition of immediate occupation. Mrs. Fileeter's conduct had been very much blamed. Mrs. Wasilbakee thought it was exceedingly wrong of her to let her husband go all alone to a new station, and Mrs. Dakhil Duftar agreed with Mrs. Wasilbakee, adding that it was not at all like a good wife to separate from her husband so unnecessarily. This was also the opinion of most of the other ladies, but it came with peculiar force from those two, who steadily went to Simla every year for the six months' season. However, Mrs. Fileeter would now be forced to keep her marriage vows to the very letter.

Fitzmisl, who knew nothing of all that was going on, for Mr. Wasilbakee was the only one of the gentlemen who had been taken into confidence, one day on returning from cutchery, when his wife happened to be out, found a note had just arrived from Mrs. Fileeter, and he opened and answered it. When his wife came home, about half-an-hour afterwards, he said—

"There is a note, Jane, from Mrs. Fileeter, that came when you were out. I have answered it, as I thought it was not worth while keeping it to ask you; there can be but one reply to it."

Mrs. Fitzmisl read the note, and asked with more excitement than Fitzmisl thought the matter justified—

"What did you say, dear?"

"I said of course we should be happy to see her; there is the spare room, you know, and we have no one else coming. I am very glad to be able to accommodate her."

"What *will* Mrs. Wasilbakee say?" was Mrs. Fitzmisl's rejoinder."

"Mrs. Wasilbakee! I don't see what she has to say to it."

"Ah, you don't know. You should always ask me, my dear, before you answer notes of this kind"—and Mrs. Fitzmisl ran out of the room, stopped the carriage, which was being taken to the stables, and drove at once to Mrs. Wasilbakee's.

That lady was again checked. Mrs. Fileeter had asked the Fitzmisls to put her up till the exhibition was over, and Fitzmisl had good-naturedly consented.

It is an ill wind that blows nobody good, and Fitzmisl had cause, though he didn't know it, to congratulate himself on being so good-natured. Mrs. Wasilbakee's interest with Mrs. Byewilwuffa was powerful, and, much to the amazement of Fitzmisl, he received a few days after a letter from Mr. Khas Mouza, the secretary, informing him he had been transferred to another district, and he was to proceed to join his new appointment at once. Fitzmisl, however, was a covenanted civilian, and it would not do to move him without an increase of pay, so he was promoted to the higher grade of joint magistrate, upon one thousand in lieu of seven hundred rupees a month.

Again did the Budgepore world triumph, and again was it destined to disappointment.

Mrs. Fileeter, quite unconscious of the anxiety she was causing by her movements, resolved to ask the Chillans to take her in, as the Fitzmisls were to break up their establishment at once. Chillan was Inspecting Postmaster of Budgepore, and occupied a sort of amphibious or hybrid existence, sometimes bathing himself in the full light of Budgepore "society," and sometimes laving himself in the waters situated just below that Elysium. Mrs. Chillan was ambitious. He, a sensible sort of man, was pretty well indifferent as to the circle of society he moved in, so long as he met with a welcome, and found himself in the company of people he liked and who liked him. But Mrs. Chillan was not content with this. She grieved over the want of noble aspirations in her spouse, and was resolved to force him into the higher sphere by dint of her own personal influence. The consequence was that the Chillans were always seen at all the public balls at Budgepore, but never at the private entertainments of the aristocratic world. Mr. Chillan gave in to his wife's whims on the subject good-naturedly enough, went to the balls with her, and sat them out like a man. He could, however, see, if she could not, exactly how matters stood.

Mrs. Chillan, in the equivocal position she held, hanging as it were between Elysium and the world below it, was not at all sorry to accede to Mrs. Fileeter's request to take her in. She would have a companion to accompany her to all the exhibition gaieties, a companion, too, who had made good and better footing than she had within that charmed circle she so much longed to enter. It was a lucky day for Chillan that Mrs. Fileeter bethought herself of soliciting the hospitality of his roof.

It so happened that Major Soosti, Postmaster-General, had just passed the board, and was on the point of going home on medical certificate. He was, indeed, very ill, and what made his case the more serious was, that the doctors did not seem thoroughly to understand it. However, his medical attendant described the case in the certificate as a serious, and what might prove a fatal, case of "inertia," and the Medical Board at Budgepore, who had never heard of this disease, took for granted it was a new discovery, and as none of the medical gentlemen composing the board had seen an English medical periodical, or a new medical work, for some little time, they were afraid of disclosing their ignorance if they sent the certificate back or rejected Major Soosti's application on the ground that they did not recognise the peculiar disease under which the applicant was suffering.

So Major Soosti, who had been Potmaster-General for fifteen years, passed the board and went home, just before Mrs. Fileeter went to pay her visit to the Chillans. To Chillan's great joy he was appointed to officiate for Major Soosti, and received orders to proceed immediately and take charge of the office.

Mrs. Fileeter's resources in the circle of the civil community being now exhausted, she betook herself to the military. She was intimate with the Butts. Lieutenant Butt was interpreter and quartermaster of the 78th Native Infantry then quartered at Budgepore, under the command of that distinguished officer Colonel Gotobed. The 78th N. I. was a little under-officered, as were many of the old Bengal regiments in the old days, and, indeed, I do not know that the new Bengal regiments of native infantry are much better off in these days. If the old Bengal army may be said to have been under-officered formerly, it may perhaps be said to be un-officered now. However that may be, the 78th N. I., under the command of Colonel Gotobed, had present with it the adjutant (a lieutenant, of course), the quartermaster and interpreter, and an ensign. These three officers held all the ten companies between them. The adjutant and interpreter holding four each, and the ensign two.

A short time before the period of which I am speaking, the junior lieutenant had been removed to fill the office of sub-assistant commissary-general on probation. Lieutenant Butt had applied for the appointment; he being a passed officer,* of course, as he was interpreter, but was told in reply that His Excellency was most anxious to oblige him, but that there were so many officers absent from the 78th N. I. on staff employ already, it was impossible to remove any more; notwithstanding which, within a week, the junior lieutenant, who had great interest, was removed to fill this very appointment, although he had never passed.

Mrs. Wasilbakee's interest was not confined to the civil department of the Service. She was very intimate with the Commander-in-Chief, Lady Grubb. When I call Lady Grubb Commander-in-Chief, I mean that she was *de facto*, though her husband, Sir Walter Grubb was of course, *de jure*, Commander-in-Chief. Mrs. Wasilbakee went to Simla every year, as I have already stated, and there she was a strong and powerful ally of Lady Grubb's in all the little social contests that enlivened existence in Simla saloons. The result of all this and of Mrs. Fileeter's visit to the Butts, was that Butt, much to his surprise, and greatly to his satisfaction, received a letter from the Military Secretary, Colonel Gajur, offering him the appointment of adjutant to the 28th Musalchees, an appointment he much coveted. The 28th Musalchees was a very crack regiment of irregular horse, commanded by Captain Chumcha, who got so much fame in his campaign against the Moorghies and Doongas, several of which fierce and savage

* An officer cannot hold the appointment of interpreter until he has passed an examination in the native languages.

tribes he had slain with his own hand in single combat. Mrs. Fileeter's visit at the Butts was thus cut short, for one condition of the offer of the appointment was that Butt should join immediately. This, of course, he was delighted to do, and he lost no time in selling off his furniture, and procuring a loan from the Agra Bank of two thousand rupees to pay for the uniform, which was very expensive, as it was exceedingly gorgeous, having been designed by Captain Chumcha himself, and consisting of something between the uniform of the Blues and that of the Russian Life Guards.

The triumph of the *beau monde* of Budgepore was again destined to be very short-lived, for Mrs. Gotobed having heard, of course, of Mrs. Fileeter's visit to the Butts being cut short, very kindly wrote and asked her to came and stay with them till the exhibition was over. This invitation was accepted.

And now, I dare say, you will think Mrs. Wasilbakee and the fair conspirators were checkmated. They had been checked several times before, but this looked very like a checkmate. You must, however, recollect St. Kevin—

> Ah! the good saint little knew
> What the wily sex can do.

One morning, the week after Mrs. Fileeter had moved to the Gotobeds, while they were at breakfast, a telegram was put into the Colonel's hands.

"I wonder what this can be about," said the Colonel, turning the red envelope over and over in his hand.

"Look inside and perhaps you'll find out," laconically observed Mrs. Gotobed.

"Bless me!" said the Colonel, as he read the telegram, "listen to this."

"From Quartermaster-General

"To Colonel Gotobed. Budgepore.

"The 78th N. I. is to march at once to Mirichpoor. Written orders follow by post; make immediate preparations."

"There must be something very serious the matter at Mirichpoor," said Colonel Gotobed.

"Some disturbance among the tribes, I dare say," said his wife. "I hope there'll be no fighting."

"They want an officer of experience down there, no doubt," observed the Colonel.

"Well, my dear, it is an inconvenient move for us to make just now, but it can't be helped."

Of course the news spread through Budgepore like wildfire, that the 78th N. I. had received orders by telegram to march for Mirichpoor. And in a very short time the report was supplemented by another to account for the move, viz., that some serious disturbance had broken out in that neighbourhood. There was, however, no certain intelligence, and the public were left very much in the dark till a paragraph appeared in the *Sycophant*, a paper then published at Budgepore. The *Sycophant* belonged to a joint-stock company, and the shareholders were principally officials, some of them holding tolerably high appointments in the Service. The paper prided itself on being a Government organ, and made a great deal, at least the shareholders did, of sundry scraps of most authentic information furnished to it from time to time by those of the proprietors who had access to Government records. What with circulating vast numbers of gratis copies, and supplying the shareholders with ten gratis copies each, and reducing the price of their advertisements to a figure below what any other paper would take, they managed to make a show of prosperity. Well, the *Sycophant*, fresh from the authentic sources of official information, gave its readers the following explanation of the sudden move of the 78th N. I., which had so much puzzled the public:—

"We hear that the threatening aspect of the political horizon in and about Mirichpoor has necessitated the immediate move of the 78th N. I., under command of that experienced officer Colonel Gotobed, from Budgepore.

"The regiment received its orders to march by telegram from the Quartermaster-General the day before yesterday, and there is every reason to believe that the presence, on the spot, of a regiment so efficient and so well trained, and under an officer of Colonel Gotobed's known reputation, will have the effect of speedily restoring order in the disturbed districts."

So the 78th N. I. marched exactly a week after the receipt of the telegram, but Mrs. Gotobed remained behind at Budgepore, and asked Mrs. Fileeter to stay and keep her company!

The official channels at the disposal of Mrs. Wasilbakee, and the headquarters ladies were now fairly exhausted. They had managed to get Mr. Fileeter transferred to Jhansie, Fitzmisl promoted and removed to Bareilly, Chillan had by the same means been made officiating Postmaster-General, Lieut. Butt had been appointed adjutant of the 28th Musalchees, and last, though not least, the 78th N. I. had marched to Mirichpoor. Still, Mrs. Fileeter kept her place at the exhibition choir, and used to attend the practice and sing as sweetly, and play the accompaniments as composedly, as if not a ripple had disturbed the placid surface of the waters of the Budgepore world.

We sometimes realise what unimportant and helpless creatures we are in controlling the course of events. All the influence of Mrs. Wasilbakee and the ladies of the Lieutenant-Governor's staff, which meant in reality all the influence of the Government, all the influence of Lady Grubb, which was another word for all the power and patronage of the head of the army in India, and, indeed, I may say, all the power of Government beside, were powerless to effect the removal of a weak, almost friendless woman from the station of Budgepore. And yet that very end was attained by the simplest of all possible means, nothing more than a piece of orange-peel. It happened one day that Mr. Fileeter came home from cutchery thirsty. He had been there all day since ten o'clock in the morning, and it was now six p.m. He would much have preferred not having to return tired and jaded to a solitary, dismal bungalow, and cannot one of your great gloomy bungalows, whose roof comes down to within about five feet of the ground, excluding air and light, be gloomy and cheerless when you return to it about six o'clock in the evening after a hard day's work, and find it, as you know, empty—no wife to greet you with a smile, no child to run up and catch you round the knee—well, I was saying, Mr. Fileeter returned home at six o'clock one day, and, being thirsty, ate an orange. A very simple process, yet attended with how important results! He threw the peel out in the verandah—a very untidy thing to do, but then, you see, he was a grass bachelor. In the evening, after dinner, before going to bed, he went out to take a turn in the garden, and walking across the verandah, put his foot on the orange-peel, slipped and fell, and sprained his ankle very severely.

A few days after a letter was put into Mrs. Fileeter's hand from her husband, telling her of the accident, and saying that he was confined to his bed, and likely to be so for some time, and sorry as he was to interfere with her plans and prevent her from having the pleasure of witnessing the exhibition and enjoying its attendant gaieties, he was obliged, in his helpless state, to bid her come to him. Mrs. Fileeter lost no time in obeying the summons. She prepared to start that very night.

Before she went, however, she wrote a note to Mrs. Wasilbakee, telling her what had happened, and of her intended departure, and received a very kind note in reply from that lady, saying how sorry they all were that Mrs. Fileeter was forced to leave them, and especially from such a cause, and how much they would miss her, and ended by saying she hoped she would find Mr. Fileeter better.

As Mrs. Fileeter's dak carriage rolled away with her that evening, Budgepore breathed more freely than it had done for many a long day.

THE BUDGEPORE EXHIBITION.

CHAPTER III.

SHOWING HOW COLONEL MACDARE, SINGLE-HANDED, ATTACKED THE "DEPARTMENTS."

My readers, who are behind the scenes, know well enough the secret springs that set in motion that gallant regiment the 78th N. I. *en route* to Mirichpoor. Not so the outside world, who were informed through the veracious columns of the *Sycophant* that it was the disturbed state of the district that rendered it necessary to direct the march.

This was all very well, of course, so far as the good-natured, unreflecting, put-upon, and easily-deluded public were concerned. And there is not a public in the whole of this wide, wide world which is more easily contented and thankful for smaller mercies than the Indian. Of course I mean the Anglo-Indian public. There was a native public once, but it had such a very objectionable way of maintaining its vitality, and asserting its rights that was altogether incompatible with civilised life, namely, murdering unarmed men, women, and little children, that it became necessary to put an end to its existence altogether, and it was suddenly put an end to, after a short life of one year, Ann. Dom. 1858. The Anglo-Indian public is a patient beast, extremely like a certain animal once held in much reputation in Judæa; but in modern days marked out for drudgery, ill-treatment, and contempt. If it lies quiet, it gets kicked for being lazy, indolent, and indifferent; when it makes a noise, it gets kicked for being troublesome. It has no particular food given to it, but is allowed to pick up what offal it can from heaps of vegetable refuse. It is made to do all the hard work and carry all the burdens, and although things could not go on a single day without it, nevertheless it is repeatedly told between the blows that are dealt upon its bony carcass, "that it has no business in the country, why doesn't it go out of it, but that as long as it chooses to stay, all the hard work shall fall to its share, and instead of getting half-pence in return, it shall have nothing but kicks." The fact being that the miserable half-starved creature is so weak and emaciated that it has not strength to leave the country, however much it might wish to do so.

I say it was all very well, so far as the public went, for the *Sycophant* to put in that paragraph explaining the sudden move of the 78th N. I. But you may like to know how the intelligence was received in Mirichpoor itself. And here the *Sycophant*, as they say, counted without its host, which means that he forgot that his paragraph would be read at Mirichpoor, and above all he forgot that it would be read by Colonel Macdare.

Now Colonel Macdare, who was Commissioner at Mirichpoor, was about the worst man in the whole of India upon whom it was safe to attempt to play a trick. He was a little man, but he had a large heart in a diminutive body. Though small in size, he was physically well developed, his bones might have been iron and his sinews wire, and his limbs made by nature for a model of what the human frame ought to be when best adapted for vigorous active life. A dashing fearless soldier was Colonel Macdare, one of those men of whom the Indian service may well be proud. They were more plentiful in former years than they are now.

He first came into notice in the Afghan war, where his cool intrepidity and amazing powers of endurance speedily attracted the attention of such men as Sale and Pollock. Among his other qualities he had that which I think more than anything else contains in it the seeds of greatness, the power of influencing other men. And this made him valuable as a political officer in those troubled times, when Colonel Macdare, as he was then, was known by his personal influence over wild tribes to have kept a whole district quiet, without so much as a single soldier to enforce his authority.

It is a painful reflection to make, but it is nevertheless perfectly true, that in our country, that is either in England or India, but more especially in the latter, great and noble qualities and brilliant services are not in themselves sufficient to bring a man into the position in public life he is fitted to hold. Something else is required; a man must be to a certain extent a courtier besides. He may do the most gallant deeds in the world, but unless he or his friends for him can manage a little of the "simpering in gilded saloons," his worth will not be recognised. I know there are exceptions, and I think Lord Lawrence is one of them, but these exceptions prove the rule, which certainly in the case of Colonel Macdare held good. Such services as his were fit to be rewarded with the highest appointment Government had it in their power to confer. But far inferior men, by the process known as suction, got themselves promoted, and Colonel Macdare was considered sufficiently well provided for by being made Commissioner of Mirichpoor.

There, as in every position in life he had ever held, he set himself to do his best heartily. He was an enthusiast in his work, and thought nothing beneath his notice which, if well done, would contribute to the happiness of a single human being, and which, if ill done, might entail inconvenience or loss on anyone. He was one of those men who serve the Government well. They seem to think the bargain between them and their employers involves the delivery on their part of all the powers of their body and intellect for the term of their natural life, or as long as they remain employed. There is another class of men who think the bargain involves yet more, and who in exchange for their monthly pay consider the purchaser entitled not only to their intellectual and physical powers, but something else besides.

Colonel Macdare, however, was not one of these. Government was entitled to the last drop of his life's blood, to his time, his genius, his pen, his mental faculties, but to nothing else. He never signed a despatch that was not, every word of it, scrupulously true. He never wrote one thing in an official and another in a demi-official. He never allowed the favour of his superiors or the hope of promotion to swerve him one hair's-breadth from the path of honour, justice, and truth.

There was one thing he took a real pleasure in, it was his hobby, and that was the state of his district. He would almost as soon have listened quietly to an imputation on his wife's honour, as on the condition of his district. You may imagine, then, his feelings when, opening the *Sycophant* one morning at breakfast-time (the *Sycophant* was supplied gratis to all officials of Colonel Macdare's rank), he read the paragraph already quoted, to the effect that the 78th N. I. had been ordered at once by telegram to Mirichpoor on account of the disturbed state of the district. Had a shell fallen into the room he would not have started from his chair more promptly, nay, it is probable he would not have exhibited half the emotion he did now. That anyone should breathe in secret that the Mirichpoor district was in anything but a state of absolute repose, was a thing not to be contemplated without emotion. If he had heard such a slander uttered in a small circle among his acquaintances, he would have felt it deeply; it would have given him no rest till it had been contradicted in the fullest, most decisive manner. But that the statement should appear in the columns of a newspaper, in all the imposing features of editorial type!—this was too bad. Englishmen do not tear their hair in real life. I have lived two score of years with my fellow-men, and never yet saw but one man tear his hair, and that was a native, who was apparently afflicted with the most dreadful disease that can attack the sons of Adam—he was in love. He did tear his hair: he tore his hair, his clothes, and rolled himself on the ground at the feet of the obdurate fair one in a most frantic manner. And she was excessively dirty, and very ill-dressed, and very ill-looking, and I much wondered at such an exhibition of feeling on her account. But I never saw an Englishman tear his hair except on the stage, although I have often read of it in novels. Colonel Macdare did not exactly tear his hair, but he did put his two hands to his head, and grasped the roots of his hair when he saw those lines in the *Sycophant*. Mrs. Macdare was at that time in England, and the Colonel was residing alone, and so it happened that there was no one in the room except his khitmutgar when the event occurred. Had you been there you might have seen Colonel Macdare standing in the attitude I have described, his feet a little apart, both his hands meeting on the top of his head grasping the hair, gazing with horror, indignation, wrath, and sorrow upon the columns of the *Sycophant*, which was on the breakfast-table before him, and there stood his khitmutgar just behind him, rooted to the spot and trembling with fear. All the natives were very much in awe of Colonel Macdare. He was to them as Fate, stern, inexorable, unbending; unlike Fate, in that they knew him to be just. But natives are slow to understand our motives, and cannot the least trace the connection between our actions and the intention or the will that prompts them. So when Colonel Macdare broke off suddenly in the act of cracking his egg with an egg-spoon, started from his chair, and stood erect with his two hands grasping the roots of his hair, the khitmutgar was petrified with fear, for it at once occurred to him that the Colonel had discovered something most awful and tremendous inside the egg. The khitmutgar, whose mind was intent on his master's breakfast, did not, of course, think of the newspaper as in any way connected with the Colonel's great and sudden emotion. So he kept his eyes fixed on the egg, trembling like an aspen leaf, and expecting every instant to see a huge serpent or a dragon uncoil itself, and rising from the egg-shell, develop into a full grown reptile of supernatural proportions.

While the Colonel was in this attitude, a servant entered with the morning budget of letters, and put them on the table. But, seeing his master's posture, and instinctively regarding the innocent egg as the cause of it, immediately ran away, and told all the servants, of whom there were thirty in the establishment altogether, that the "Burra Sahib" had found a "jinn" in the egg, and was bewitched, as a preliminary step to being devoured or transformed into a pig.

The report spread over the whole station in a marvellously short space of time, as reports very soon spread in India.

This exciting intelligence found the public mind in a condition only too well calculated to receive impression. Gopal Chunder, the head baboo, or clerk in the post-office, always liked to have the first news of everything, and accordingly, by a little skilful manipulation, known to the post-office employés, it was his custom every morning to open and read Colonel Macdare's newspapers before they were delivered to the orderly. This morning he had been much astonished at the paragraph in the *Sycophant* which had caused Colonel Macdare so much emotion, and, not being a very perfect English scholar, he derived from it rather a confused idea of the state of affairs at Mirichpoor. This much was clear, that a regiment was on its way, and disturbances were imminent. The *Sycophant* got its news from Government officers. He himself, when a clerk in the Adjutant-General's office a year before, had several times sent off little scraps by order of the Adjutant-General, containing the orders which were to appear in the *Gazette* the following day, and which the *Sycophant* was thus enabled to publish a day before, and no one, the baboo thought, could possibly doubt the veracity of intelligence derived from such a quarter. As soon might you look for impurities in the snow-flake, or the raindrop that falls from heaven. Bursting with the startling news, Gopal Chunder hastened off to the bazaar.

The old Eastern proverb of sowing the wind and reaping the whirlwind is well illustrated by the rapidity with which, in an Indian bazaar, a few words of alarm take root, throw out their branches, and develop their fruits. In five minutes, nay, less, it was all over the town, passing from mouth to mouth, gathering intensity as it went, that something dreadful was to happen, no one knew what—no one could tell his neighbour what calamity threatened him, but he could only warn him there was some catastrophe approaching.

The utter absence of all foundation for the rumours only increased the gravity of their nature, for everything was left to the imagination. There was a hubbub and a buzz of clattering tongues, that swelled and swelled till it filled the very air and penetrated the bungalows of the European officers.

In his chair of office sat Major Tickli, cantonment magistrate, dispensing justice.

He had just concluded the investigation in a case which had occupied two or three hours. The evening before, Muddoo Khan, a police constable, wishing to entertain a party of friends, had called at the shop of a bunneea or shopkeeper named Hulwaee, and requested him to give him two rupees' worth of sweetmeats. No coin was tendered, and the shopkeeper refused to accommodate the constable. He threatened. The confectioner defied.

Muddoo Khan went away. That night after his friends had left him, which was about ten o'clock, he called another policeman to accompany him to the house of Hulwaee, where he said he had certain information that some stolen property the police had been some time in search for, was concealed. The stolen property, which consisted of a little jewellery, or at least articles that resembled it, was found in the very place Muddoo Khan knew it would be found, for he had sent and had it put there. Hulwaee was taken away to the lock-up, and his hands being tied behind his back, a brass vessel (called a lota) full of wasps, was fastened on his stomach, and he was informed that it would remain in that position till he confessed before a magistrate.* Indian wasps are like some human beings you occasionally meet with, easily irritated, and their sting is very sharp. The first pang the prisoner felt when the poisoned shafts penetrated the skin, he bore manfully, the second weakened his resolution, the third caused him to cry out, at the fourth he begged to be released and he would confess all—anything his tormentors wanted. He was released, and the instrument of torture taken off. Begging a little cold water to relieve the burning pain, he sat down in a corner of the hut, where he was confined, till the morning. About eight o'clock his wife, who knew too well the fate that had befallen her lord, brought him some food. She was glad to escape with abuse to avoid blows, and Hulwaee, with his stomach empty inside, and swollen with the wasps' stings on the outside, was taken before Major Tickli, who, after trying the case, upon the prisoner's own confession, found him guilty, and had just sentenced him to two years' imprisonment and thirty lashes, when there was a little excitement outside, and in came a mutsuddie, or native clerk from the kotwallee, looking very important and bearing in his hand a document written in Oordoo in the usual Persian character. This turned out to be a letter or report from the kotwal to the cantonment magistrate, to the effect that there was a panic through the whole town, the bunneeas were closing their shops, burying their money and jewels, and sending their families out of the place.

Major Tickli ordered his buggy and adjourned the court. Rumour in India resembles carbonic acid gas or malaria-laden air. It first of all creeps along the ground and then ascends. There is this difference, certainly, that whereas the gas or the disease-laden atmosphere loses by degrees its noxious properties by mixing with a purer atmosphere, and so becomes

* A process occasionally resorted to by the police, and recommended by its simplicity.

diluted, rumour, on the other hand, generally gathers intensity as it ascends. So it was, that by the time the report set on foot by Gopal Chunder had reached the ears of the European officers, it had gained rather than lost in strength.

Colonel Macdare, after a while, recovered his mental equilibrium so far as to be able to go on with his breakfast; but he had hardly recommenced before the noise of wheels was heard outside, and shortly after the voice of someone asking for the Commissioner Sahib, when in walked Captain Johnson, the Deputy Commissioner.

"I know what you've come about," said the Colonel, anticipating his visitor. "You have seen the paper."

"No, I've seen no paper; at least I've seen nothing in the paper, but I have heard reports that rather astonished me."

"Astonished you, I should think they had. Read that," and the Colonel handed him the paper.

Now, Johnson, though the Colonel's subordinate officer, and in most respects very much the Colonel's inferior, was, nevertheless, better able than his chief to solve a certain kind of riddle, for you see Johnson had been several years secretary to the Secret Committee of the Indian Circumlocution Office. Whether it was that he applied the experience there gained to the matter in hand, or whether it was that his own depraved nature suggested the idea to his mind, or whether it was that he had known a similar thing done before, I cannot tell. All I know is that he immediately said to the Colonel four words—

"I see it all."

"You do!" replied the Colonel, jumping up from his seat. "It is more than I do. What on earth does it mean? Why do they send this regiment down here from Budgepore? Talk of disturbances in the district! why a child in arms might walk through it from end to end, and not hear so much as a mouse squeak."

This was a forcible simile, but the fact was the Colonel was so much excited that the incongruity of a child in arms walking about the Mirichpoor district never occurred to him.

"You see," said Johnson, "this is how it is. They wanted, for some reason or other, to send this regiment away from Budgepore. Mirichpoor was pitched upon; why, of course, I cannot say. Well, having ordered it away in a hurry, people began to talk, and it was necessary to make out there was some reason for the move. So a line is sent off to the editor of the *Sycophant*, who is kept by the Government to do their dirty work, and this is the result. They think Mirichpoor, being a long way off, and——the Commissioner being a——a military man, and holding his berth *dum se bene gesserit*, the affair will never come out."

"They think so, do they?" said Colonel Macdare, starting from his chair again and pacing angrily up and down the room. "They think so, do they? I'll tell you what, Johnson, if this is as you say, and I dare say you're right, I'll expose them; I'll track them down, the defamers of my district, I'll track them down, I'll make them confess their lie before the world. I'll worry them, I will by——"

Colonel Macdare didn't swear, and he stopped himself short ere the word passed his lips; but the vow he registered in his own mind was the result of a determined will, just as likely of fulfilment as if he had sealed it with an oath.

Here their colloquy was interrupted by the noise of wheels and the entry almost immediately afterwards of Major Tickli and then of Colonel Drew, commanding the 150th, then quartered at Mirichpoor. And to make a long story short, I may as well state, that within half-an-hour very nearly all the European officers, civil and military, stationed at Mirichpoor, were assembled in the Commissioner's room, all of course in high dudgeon as soon as they heard that there was not a word of truth in the report, although several of them went away impressed with the idea, that although the Commissioner and his own subordinate officer strongly denied the existence of any foundation for the report, this was only an official white lie, a statement put forward to allay excitement and deceive the public.

As soon as his visitors had left, Colonel Macdare began to open his morning's letters, and the first of which he broke the seal ran as follows:—

"No. 791.

"*Camp, Humble-bumble, April 21st*, 18—.

"To the Commissioner of Mirichpoor.

"Sir,—I have the honour to report that in accordance with instructions from Army headquarters the regiment under my command, strength as per margin, marched from Budgepore on the 7th instant in progress towards Mirichpoor.

"According to the route furnished me from the Quartermaster-General's office and my instructions from Army headquarters, I ought to reach the Mirichpoor district on the 6th May, and shall halt at the places mentioned in the margin on the dates specified; and I have to solicit the favour of your giving the necessary orders for supplies to be collected at each halting ground, in accordance with the indent which I have the honour to inclose.

"I have the honour to be,

"Sir,

"Your most obedt. servt.,

"ALEXANDER GOTOBED, *Lieut.-Col.*,

"*Commanding 78th N. I.*

"P.S.—I have had no instructions to proceed by forced marches, but should the disturbed state of the country render it advisable for me to do so, I beg that you will intimate the same to me, when I will leave the heavy baggage and the sick behind, and push forward in light marching order."

Colonel Macdare threw the letter No. 791, with enclosure, on the floor, and ground his heel into the paper. He then wrote to the editor of the *Sycophant* a letter, which he desired that functionary to insert in his next issue. It was as follows:—

"*To the Editor of the* '*Sycophant*.'

"SIR,—I observe in your last issue a statement put forward, as if by authority, to the effect that the 78th Regiment N. I. has been ordered peremptorily from Budgepore to Mirichpoor in consequence of the disturbed condition of that district. What may be the reason of ordering the 78th N. I. at this season so suddenly to make a long march, I know not, nor do I care; but to the explanation of that move, as set forth by you, I give the most unqualified denial. There is not, nor has there been, during the last two years, the slightest appearance of any discontent, nor the least apprehension of any disturbance in the district.

"Yours faithfully,

"PATRICK MACDARE,

"*Commissioner of Mirichpoor.*"

This letter threw the editor of the *Sycophant* into a fever, and for several days he hovered between life and death. What should he do? If he refused it, the writer would assuredly find some other channel to convey the truth to the public; and his own refusal would look bad, as a clear attempt to burke the truth. If he published it, what would Government say—what would be Mr. Byewilwuffa's feelings—what Mr. Khas Mouza's—what Colonel Donothing's, the Quartermaster-General? Nay, might not even the serenity of the halls of Olympus be disturbed, and the Governor-General himself enraged? He suffered dreadfully in the attack, became delirious and fancied that the Quartermaster-General, enraged at having something to do, was perpetually measuring him with a large wheel—first from head to foot, and then back again; while Mr. Byewilwuffa and Mr. Khas Mouza heaped piles of correspondence, in foolscap, on his head.

Colonel Macdare's letter was, however, sent in duplicate to the *Mofussilite*, where of course it appeared; and then the people began to wonder what in the world the 78th N. I. had been ordered to Mirichpoor for.

I don't suppose that anything would have transpired in consequence of the letter in the *Mofussilite*, had not Colonel Macdare, with that energy and iron will for which he was famed, followed it up by official correspondence, addressed in the first instance to Mr. Byewilwuffa, that is of course, to his secretary. In vain the usual means were resorted to—delays, obstructions, difficulties, references, objections; and in vain did Mr. Khas Mouza pile Pelion upon Ossa, red tape upon foolscap, even as in the editor's feverish dreams—all to no purpose. Colonel Macdare tossed it off, as if it were flakes of snow accumulating upon a beaver hat. He fought the paper war (and he could fight paper fights as well as real battles with cold steel and gunpowder) with as much desperation as if he was charging at the head of his old regiment. Bred in the best school of Indian military statesmanship, he could wield his pen as well as his sword. He felt his honour at stake, and he was determined to fight it out to the last, even as once in Afghanistan, when deserted by his picket in a *sunga*, he put his back against the stone wall and set his teeth, and kept at bay twenty of the enemy for at least a quarter of an hour, till succour came. But if Colonel Macdare was a dangerous foe when on the defensive, it was a much more serious matter when he assumed the offensive, as he did in this instance. Nor had he contemptible opponents. For Mr. Byewilwuffa and Mr. Khas Mouza were no mean foes, when the weapons wielded in the fight were red tape and steel pen. Colonel Macdare, in a very early stage of the conflict, saw enough to confirm the impression raised in his mind by Captain Johnson's suggestion as to the real history of the move of the 78th N. I., and the paragraph in the *Sycophant;* and he was resolved to worm out the truth through all the turnings and twistings of the Circumlocution Office, and to force from the offending department, whichever it might be, as it were at the point of the sword, a confession that the slur passed on his district was unfounded. You see he attempted a task which may fairly be regarded as Herculean in its nature, while the attempt itself was Quixotic; for he assailed a foe much larger than himself by a great many times, than the windmill against which the knight rode was taller and bigger than its assailant. Single-handed and alone, Colonel Macdare attacked the departments of the Indian Government. Well might the gods pause in their avocations in Olympus, and regard the combat with attention.

The editor of the *Sycophant*, as soon as he recovered from the fever into which he had been thrown by the excitement which Colonel Macdare's letter caused him, wrote a reply to that officer, saying that it was impossible for him to insert the contradiction; indeed, it was no longer necessary to do so, as it had appeared in other papers, but that his information was derived from official sources, and there could be no doubt as to its correctness.

Now, the editor was very ill-advised to write in this style. But the fact is, he had no more idea of Colonel Macdare's character than he had of the habits and customs of the people who live in the moon. He thought the imposing nature of the assurance, and the grand words "official sources," would at once silence his opponent, and that he should hear nothing more about it. Unhappy man! This assurance from the editor of the *Sycophant* was all that Colonel Macdare wanted. He was now thoroughly excited; his blood was warm, and his spirit aroused. He literally clapped his hands together, in token of triumphant joy, when the editor's ill-advised epistle reached him.

"Now I have them," he muttered between his set teeth; "now I have them."

I cannot tell you what trouble Colonel Macdare caused by this war with the departments. Secretaries swore when they heard his name mentioned, and clerks in the offices, even the chuprassees, grinned when they saw the well-known "Mirichpoor Commissioner's Office" stamped on the corner of the official envelope. Correspondence clerks were increased in all the English sections of the different departments; there was actually an excess in the budget that year, in the miscellaneous item of foolscap paper, owing to this tremendous war. And all because of what the old song says:—

Oh, what a tangled web we weave,
When first we practise to deceive!

and because Mrs. Wasilbakee would not go to the exhibition choir when Mrs. Fileeter played the accompaniment.

I may as well conclude the history of this little episode while I am on the subject. But you must not imagine that this war was ended at the period the events occurred which form the subject of this chronicle. Oh, no! The Budgepore exhibition passed away; even Colonel Gotobed's mortal remains mingled with their parent dust ere this war was finished. But I may as well relate the conclusion of it here, merely pausing to remark, that when the 78th N. I. came to within five marches of Mirichpoor, by which time it was the 12th of May, it was deemed better not to let the corps complete its march in the teeth of Colonel Macdare's vigorous declaration that no troops were wanted, and there being no particular place to send it to, it was ordered by telegram to march to Lahore, at which place it arrived about the 10th of June, and there it remained in camp till the September following, when it was ordered back to Budgepore.

Armed with the information supplied by the indiscreet editor of the *Sycophant*, Colonel Macdare first attacked Mr. Khas Mouza. Mr. Khas Mouza referred him to the military authorities, as the department that was concerned with the movement of troops. The letter of Colonel Macdare and the reply of Mr. Khas Mouza, after reference to Mr. Byewilwuffa, were then sent to the Military Secretary to the Commander-in-Chief, and by him returned in due course, with the reply that His Excellency had nothing to do with the movement of troops; reference should be made to the Government of India. The correspondence then went to the Military Secretary to the Government of India, and was by him returned with a reply, directing reference to the Quartermaster-General. The whole correspondence then came before the Quartermaster-General, who was quite taken by surprise at finding himself with something to do, and dictated a reply to the effect that reference had better be made to the Government of India in the Foreign Department. Accordingly, the correspondence went to the Secretary of the Foreign Department, who sent it back with a letter, saying it had nothing to do with that office; reference should be made to the Adjutant-General. Up to the Adjutant-General it then went next, who was so shocked at correspondence coming to him direct, without having gone through any of the usual channels, that he was ill and incapacitated for business for a whole week. However, at the end of that time, he dictated a very severe letter to Colonel Macdare, and returned the whole correspondence to him, devoutly wishing that Colonel Macdare was a regimental officer, so that his wig might take effect.

The correspondence, which by this time had grown to rather large dimensions, then went back to the Military Secretary to the Government of India, who returned it again. Finally, Colonel Macdare forwarded it to the Military Secretary to the Governor-General, who brought it to the notice of His Excellency. It required four stout Government House lackeys to bring the massive pile of foolscap in, and put it on the table before His Excellency.

The massive pile of foolscap, however, that required four men to carry it, did not by any means represent a tithe of the correspondence that had taken place about this case. These were only the official letters that passed between Colonel Macdare and heads of the different departments. For every one that was here, there were at least a hundred official letters written from one department to the other, and as for the demi-officials, no one could number them. You may get a little idea of this correspondence from the fact told me by Chillan, who you recollect succeeded Major Soosti as Postmaster-General, that although the burden on the State for the conveyance in mail carts, &c., of this enormous correspondence was so great, that the mail carts and runners had to be doubled, and an extra set of bags made up for every office, which cost ten annas six pie each, yet the postages for the demi-officials, which were stamped of course, covered the whole expenditure.

The correspondence, at length, having reached the Governor-General, that functionary examined it, and the result of his examination was a pencil memorandum to the Secretary to Government, Military Department, as follows:—

"78th N. I. marched from Budgepore to Mirichpoor, April, 18—; look for the order, and see why."

When the Military Secretary to Government received this pencilled memorandum, he had a search made for the old records in his office. They were found, and it then appeared that the move of the 78th N. I. had been ordered on a recommendation to that effect from Budgepore. The result was duly communicated to the Governor-General, who directed the Military Secretary to address the Budgepore Government on the subject, and ascertain the grounds of the recommendation.

But Colonel Macdare had carried the war into a region with which he was altogether unacquainted. As a military commander, he never would have committed so great a blunder as to invade a territory strange and unknown to him, or to lead his men over ground which was full of pitfalls hidden from the sight. By means of that vast system of under-currents which is ever in motion beneath the surface of life in India, everything of importance connected with the *personnel* of Government becomes known all over the country in a marvellously short space of time. That Colonel Macdare was in disgrace with the authorities, that he was regarded as an intolerable nuisance, a thorn in the side of every secretary, every head of a department, was a fact much better known to all the heads of native society in Mirichpoor than to the Colonel himself. He, indeed, was ignorant of it, for he never gave the matter a thought, and he forgot that during his official life as ruler of Mirichpoor he had necessarily made enemies of many powerful and influential men, who hated him because he had detected them in malpractices, and who feared him, while in power. That the day would ever come when the long pent-up spirit of revenge which these men harboured in their bosoms would find vent, was an idea that had never once occurred to him. Not that it would have made any difference to him if it had. He did what he had done from a sense of duty, and no consideration of personal risk would have deterred him from the course. The Asiatic who thirsts for revenge never grows weary of waiting. If an opportunity is slow in coming, "leave it to time and to me," he says to himself, and goes on watching.

After the reference to the Budgepore Government, all official record of the war with the departments becomes lost to view. Up to this time the casualties had been two secretaries driven home on medical certificate, one writer committed suicide, ten invalided, and 40 dâk horses killed from over-work.

One day people were surprised by the announcement of a sudden change in the administration of Mirichpoor. A gentleman, by name Rubbee, was appointed to the post of Deputy Commissioner, Captain Johnson having been removed to make room for him. There was a new settlement to be made shortly, and this was the reason alleged for Mr. Rubbee's appointment. It was not very long after this that sinister reports began to be whispered about, that all was not right in the Commissioner's office, and as these reports, vague at first, and undefined, began to assume shape, they would call forth the remark from those who heard them, "Who would have thought it?" "I'll never believe it." "No, no, Colonel Macdare is not the man to do that." Others would shake their heads and say it was a very serious matter, all of which tended to show that either Colonel Macdare had been doing something he ought not, or that people said he had been doing something he ought not. Colonel Macdare himself knew nothing, for no one liked, of course, to mention to him the reports that were abroad. Still, there was an uncomfortable chilly feeling about the social atmosphere of Mirichpoor society. No one seemed to be quite at home with his neighbour. The only man who was universally popular was Rubbee, and he kept almost open house, gave large shooting-parties to the officers in the district, and had a dinner-party once or twice a week, at which champagne flowed freely, and where you were sure to meet everyone in the covenanted services in turn, but never Colonel Macdare. If the Commissioner's name was mentioned, Rubbee would look mysterious, perhaps shrug his shoulders, and beg that his name mightn't be mentioned; he didn't wish *it* talked about. Now, that little word "it" was a word of marvellous significance. There they stood, those two little letters by themselves, yet what did they not imply! He did not wish "it" talked about.

What? Ah, that was the question; but then, you see, nobody ventured to ask, and so nobody got an answer.

After a short time Mrs. Rubbee joined her husband, and proved quite as general a favourite with both sexes as Rubbee had been with his own. Now Mirichpoor became more gay than ever; balls and dances followed the dinner-parties, and picnics took the place of the shooting excursions, at which all the ladies joined, but Colonel Macdare was never seen at any of them. Still, with all this show of gaiety and cheerfulness, there was a general impression that everything was not right, though what was wrong no one could have told you.

All this time Colonel Macdare kept up the war with the departments as he could. But as his official letters ceased to awaken any response, he referred the matter home, where he was known to have considerable influence with the Court of Directors.

At last it came—the crash—the electric fluid with which the social atmosphere had been so long laden developed itself, and Mr. Rubbee presented himself at the Commissioner's with an order to take over the office, for Colonel Macdare was suspended upon charges of corruption. Then followed the explosion, the lightning came first, and the thunder afterwards.

"I always knew there was something wrong in that quarter," said one.

"No man ever keeps himself aloof as the Colonel has done from his fellow kind when his hands are clean," said another.

"I hear he was very unkind to his wife," said a third, a lady speaking this time.

"Yes, they have not lived together since I have been at Mirichpoor," answered her friend.

Rubbee didn't object to Colonel Macdare being discussed now at his dinner-table, and he was discussed. And it was marvellous how acute was the knowledge of human nature possessed by all who met there, for there was not one of them, either man or woman, who had not known all along that Colonel Macdare's hands were not clean, only, of course, it was nobody's business to report it. They all knew it, everyone, and they all knew it would come out some day, and so, you see, it had.

A special commission sat, consisting of three officers, two of them being civilians and the third a military officer, to investigate the charges which Rubbee brought forward. Colonel Macdare, of course, attended, and much was he astonished at the evidence that was adduced. Six mahajuns (money-lenders and bankers) whom he had known well for years, and who, he was aware, bore him no goodwill for reasons already hinted at, produced their books, and showed items in them of large sums paid to Colonel Macdare at different times. These entries were, it is true, not in the regular row of entries, but apart, sometimes in the corner of a page, sometimes at the bottom, sometimes at the side, but as mahajuns' books are not ruled, nor are their pages numbered like an English ledger, it is obvious that an entry may be made in any part of the page at any time, and no one ever dreams, of course, of doubting an entry in a mahajun's book! They are known to regard their "books" as imbued with a certain degree of sanctity, and so, of course, it is not to be supposed for a moment they would ever tamper with them. In addition to which, Mr. Xerxes DeSouza, head clerk in Colonel Macdare's office, and now, of course, in Mr. Rubbee's (for everyone knew that Rubbee would succeed Colonel Macdare), deposed to having several times seen natives come after nightfall to Colonel Macdare's house with bags of money and go away without them.

Colonel Macdare had brought up Xerxes from childhood, he being the son of one of the bandsmen of his regiment. He had married a pretty Irish maid of Mrs. Macdare's, and the Colonel had settled the new-married couple comfortably in a little house in his own compound, and had supplied them with many comforts, nay, even luxuries, so that DeSouza was looked upon with much envy and with a good deal of respect, too, by his former associates, over whose head, by his patron's favour, he rapidly rose. The eldest son the Colonel had settled in life, but after the birth of her third child Mrs. DeSouza died, and he, alas! took to drinking to drown his sorrow, or perhaps under the influence of that mental reactionary excitement which often follows sudden emotion or any great blow, and which in little minds or minds weakly sustained by moral or religious principle, is not unapt to develop such a vice as drinking. One by one the articles of furniture, the pictures, the little comforts that had adorned his once happy home, were pawned in the bazaar, and several times the Colonel had to warn him, and at last to threaten him, that he would be dismissed if he did not mend his ways. This alarmed DeSouza, for he knew the Colonel was a man of his word, and he became, outwardly at any rate, more respectable and more attentive to his duties. Only the last hot season he had been attacked with cholera, and owed his life to the care with which the Colonel looked after him, and in the crisis of the disease personally superintended the operations that resulted in his recovery. When he was making his statement about the bags of money being brought to the house, Colonel Macdare looked him full in the face, steadily and fixedly, but DeSouza carefully kept his eyes turned the other way, and I don't suppose he would have met the glance of that quiet, calm grey eye, for the whole world. After he had been dismissed from his attendance at the court that day he went home and got very drunk. Seldom indeed, afterwards, was he seen sober. At last he fell into *delirium tremens*, and in that condition died. The state of his mind in his last moments was, as it was described to me, something dreadful. I would rather not relate it here, as such details are always painful.

Colonel Macdare must have seen how things would end, for he wrote to his wife, who was about to join him just when this affair took place, not to come, but she had started before the letter reached her; so he desired her to await him at Bombay. He was removed from his appointment immediately the report of the special commission was sent up.

India is supposed to be a great field for friendship. Doubtless the accidents and circumstances of Indian life do serve to foster the plant which, indigenous in every land, yet somehow

I cannot help fancying, grows more healthily in our own cold, phlegmatic clime. Rapid development is generally unaccompanied by soundness of constitution. You make your friends in India on board ship, at the club, or the cricket ground, or the racecourse, or as you work your guns side by side in the trenches. You lead to the altar and swear lifelong fidelity to the girl you have met four times in your life, perhaps five, and whom you may have seen once for a short time apart from the society of others. Your children scarce learn to lisp "papa" when they are taken from you; and, when you next meet them, are coarse, rough schoolboys, or young men setting out in life, or young ladies thinking of their love affairs, and when they will be married. Your bosom friend, your chum as you call him, is one morning taken ill, and the next taken to his last home; and you go to his auction, and chat pleasantly with your brother officers, and his—but yesterday—handling the different articles put up for sale, or discussing their worth with a heartless indifference; and you bid for his saddle and watch with as much *nonchalance* as if they were being sold in their maker's shop. Surely it was in India these lines were penned:—

Sleep, soldier! though many regret thee
Who stand by thy cold bier to-day;
Soon, soon shall the kindest forget thee,
And thy name from the earth pass away.
The man thou did'st love as a brother
A friend in thy place will have gained;
Thy dog shall keep watch for another,
And thy steed by a stranger be reined.

I say surely these lines were written in India. Perhaps those which follow were not:—

But though hearts that now mourn for thee sadly
Soon joyous as ever shall be;
Though thy bright orphan boy may laugh gladly
As he sits on some comrade's knee:
There is one who shall still pay the duty
Of tears for the true and the brave,
As when first in the bloom of her beauty
She wept over her soldier's grave.

You will excuse my quoting these few lines. I do not often quote poetry; and these are, to my thinking, some of the most beautiful and most touching that ever were penned.

It is, I think, partly owing to the large field over which the flowers of friendship have to bloom in this country that their colours so soon fade and petals fall off. Here to-day and away to-morrow, might be our motto. We have not time to link our souls with others in such close union as shall defy the hand of time or the rough blows of adversity. And there is all throughout our Indian life a want of depth of thought, which is striking to the new-comer, but which speedily grows upon and infects the mind. The ball-room, the billiard-room, the band, and the tittle-tattle of the drawing-room, tiffins, kettle-drums, or picnics, and large dinner parties, alternating with the drudgery of official duties, go far to make up our life.

There is, besides, among us, little of that domestic happiness —the social circle, the family ties, the reciprocal calls upon brotherly and sisterly affection; the watching and tending of declining years of parents in their old age; the strong associations of locality in places where we have lived all our lives, and our fathers before us, and which invest every feature of the scene with a halo of fond memories; the companionship of school and college days, ripening ere the interests of life have broken up the even surface of the soul, to sow it with the seeds of care;—there is little or none of all this, that, together, makes the soil where friendship blooms in healthy maturity in our own beloved land. But in place of it we have the race of life, official zeal and rivalry, constant change of scene and of companions, the glitter of a gay world, with as little permanence in its colours as the bloom on the wing of a butterfly, giddy moments of shallow happiness, loud laughter and boisterous song, or gentle tones and fleeting blushes, music, flowers, champagne, and flirting!

If you want to know the value of tropical friendship, you may see it tested at times in India. When a crow or a rabbit falls into adversity, its comrades in one case pick out its feathers, and then pick its flesh off its bones; and in the other, gnaw, and bite, and torment, till they have ridded themselves of the society of one bad mannered enough to be unfortunate. If Darwin be correct, we may all be descended from crows. If it is so, it is curious how often you find cases where the moral development and deflection from the original type has been so small.

Colonel Macdare was a sick crow. He gave no dinner parties now. Rubbee did, and Rubbee's champagne was good, and Mrs. Rubbee was pretty, engaging, clever, lady-like, and charming.

Colonel Macdare was under a cloud. It would have been troublesome to have examined into the truth of the charges, —no one had time for that; and, truth to tell, no one had the moral courage to stand up before the world and say, "I don't believe in them." So his old friends avoided him, or, if forced to meet him, spoke under constraint, and as if they felt it would be a relief to be away from his presence. The native gentry, who had formerly been so glad to cultivate his acquaintance, were careful never to let their equipages be seen standing at his door; and the ladies who in former days had danced so gaily at his parties, before Mrs. Macdare went to England, turned their heads the other way, when they passed him on the road. His house and effects were sold by public auction, and bought, most of them, by Rubbee; and one evening, accompanied by his only faithful friend, his dog, he got into his palkee and set out on a long journey to Bombay.

He never lived to reach it, and Mrs. Macdare returned to England a widow. Colonel Macdare was found one day by a traveller in a dak bungalow between Mirichpoor and Bombay in a dying state. He was speechless and scarcely sensible, and the dog that was sitting by his master's bedside looking wistfully in his face, could give no particulars. There were no servants attached to the bungalow, as is the custom in those parts, and not a soul about the place but the palkee bearers, who said the sahib had been taken ill the night before, and was almost speechless when they reached the wretched shelter where the traveller found him. He attended the dying man to the last, and did what he could to minister to his wants, but that was, alas! but little. He never spoke, but as the lamp of life flickered for an instant on the confines of two worlds, a peaceful smile stole over his handsome features, and, ere the soul left its tenement, a gleam of light shot across his dull grey eye, and there was an instant or two of consciousness, but no strength to speak. He turned his head, and looked wistfully at the well-known face of his dog; then he looked at the traveller, who was bending over him, holding his cold, lifeless hand. At that moment, a glance of recognition passed between the two men, and the traveller's heart beat wildly, and then sank again, as he saw before him the wasted, emaciated form, and pain-worn countenance of the once dashing sabreur, the staunch friend, the acute statesman, the upright, un-compromising, Christian soldier, Colonel Macdare. He pressed his hand, and the dying man feebly returned the sign. A smile lit up his countenance, and, though he was too weak to speak, the altered expression of his features told as well as if he had said it in words, that it was pleasing to him to feel the grasp of a true friend at the last moment. The next he was gone—without a struggle. The traveller with a sigh closed his eyes, and then observed for the first time that the dead man's left hand, for it was his right hand he had held, grasped a book. He took it up, and extricated it with a little difficulty, for the fingers clenched it tightly, stiffening in death. The page was thumb-worn as if the book had been a long time open at that place. The Colonel, perhaps, had been struggling to realise its contents, and had had a hard task to do so. At any rate, a pencil-mark under one of the verses showed where the reader's eye and mind had been chiefly directed. It was at the words, "Lord lay not this sin to their charge." And when he had said this he fell asleep.

The traveller could not remain in that lonely place. So, with the assistance of the palkee bearers, and his own servant, he dug a grave under a tree in the compound, as deep as he possibly could make it; and there, at sunset, he laid the body of the Colonel, and piled a huge heap of large stones over the spot, to secure, as well as to mark it. In vain he tried to induce the dog to leave it; nothing could succeed. There the creature sat, faithful unto death, till, as the moon rose on that melancholy scene, the traveller, with a heart full of sadness, set out on his long journey back again, for he had to hasten down to Bombay, to soften the terrible blow that was about to fall on the poor widow.

* * * * *

THE BUDGEPORE EXHIBITION.

CHAPTER IV.

THE PRIZE COMMITTEE.

At last the exhibition began to draw towards completion. The building constructed under Sleeper's auspices and supervision with railway material and labour, was now nearly roofed in, and intending exhibitors began to flock down in considerable numbers to the spot. There was a guard of police at the gate which led into the grounds, who exacted a fee of from four to eight annas from every native who went in; and the consequence was, that the place was not overcrowded, because no native went there unless he had some article to exhibit, or some real object to be gained by going. Isteefa, who had come to Budgepore as joint magistrate in place of Fitzmisl, was honorary secretary to the Exhibition Committee, and, of course, having no time to devote to anything else, was placed on special duty, by the Honourable Mr. Byewilwuffa's orders, leaving his legitimate duties unperformed. But as the time drew near, and the labour of despatching, receiving, and arranging the articles was really very heavy, it was found impossible for one officer, or two, or half-a-dozen, to get through the whole work. It became necessary, therefore, to strike off twenty officers altogether, covenanted and uncovenanted, for this especial duty. Some of these were judges; some judges of small cause courts, some magistrates, some assistants, some deputy magistrates and collectors—in short, it was an *omnium gatherum* of officials, who, under the orders of Mr. Byewilwuffa, were not sorry to desert the daily routine of their office work to look after the great exhibition. Some of these were struck off duty two months before the opening, some one month before. All this time, of course, cases remained undecided, prisoners were detained in close confinement in the hawallats, or lock-up, and miscellaneous matters of a thousand different kinds, such as occupy the attention of every Indian official, but utterly baffle categorising, on account of their diverse and miscellaneous character, remained unattended to pretty well all over the province.

My friend, Mr. Archimedes DeCruze, was in luck's way. Having Dakhil Duftar's interest to push him on, he very easily got appointed to a post in the exhibition, where the principal arrangement of the different articles was left in his hands.

Determined to carry out my experiment to the end, I despatched Selim with a box containing a very pretty model of a Swiss cottage, for which I had written home to France, when the idea first developed itself in my mind. This I labelled a "Bungalow," knowing that it would pass muster very well for a model of an improved style of Indian dwelling-house.

I dare say it would amuse you were I to detail all the adventures that Selim went through the day he took the model down to the exhibition. I know that he took away twenty rupees with him, and expended every one, and even then he said he had a hard fight to get his model in. But I had given him strict orders that he was not only to get his model in, but to get it put in a good place, that is in front, where it could be seen, and not buried behind a heap of rubbishy things. For this, however, that is, for allotting him a decent place for his model to stand in, he had to pay my friend, Mr. Archimedes, five rupees. I made a rough calculation, after I had seen the number of articles there, of how much Mr. DeCruze must have netted in this little business, and I came to the conclusion that it could not have been a farthing under five thousand rupees. But the exhibition was intended to develop industry, and, if that was not a development of industry, it was certainly a development of genius.

The most remarkable development of genius, however, was in the case of the Honourable Mr. Byewilwuffa himself, who could not see any reason why, when exhibitions are popular institutions in England, France, and America, where they can be elaborated and conducted by the people, they should not be equally successful in India, where there were none but the official classes to work out the idea, and that at the sacrifice of their legitimate duties.

At last the matter had progressed so far that it became

necessary to appoint judges and committees to decide upon the prizes, and this was not an easy thing to do. At least it was not difficult to find the committee, because one committee of three were capable of sitting upon half-a-dozen different classes of articles successively, but the difficulty was to find committees who had any knowledge of the subjects upon which they were to exercise their discernment.

I was on a committee with two others, Colonel Moodle and Jackson. Jackson was a young ensign who had just joined the 80th Regiment N. I., which had come to Budgepore in the place of the 78th N. I. ordered, as you recollect, to Mirichpoor. The subjects allotted to our committee to adjudge the prizes on, were as follows:—Raw Produce Department A., Sec. II., Subdivision Y., Elephants, and Fancy Pigeons, and on the morning appointed we met at the grounds.

"I hope you are up in raw produce," said Colonel Moodle as we met, and walked up to the exhibition building, "because I really am totally ignorant of the subject."

"Well, there are certainly some kinds of raw produce that I should not consider it beyond my province to pass an opinion upon, but what particular species or kinds of raw produce we may have to examine I don't know."

Most fortunately for us, we found Mr. Alsorts at the building ready to afford us his assistance. Mr. Alsorts was an intelligent member of the mercantile community of Budgepore, of the firm of Alsorts, Sizes and Co., who dealt principally in country produce. He had been very active in assisting the promoters of the exhibition, and, in fact, had made himself generally useful, having found his reward for unremitting zeal and a great sacrifice of his time by being taken a good deal of notice of by Dakhil Duftar and Isteefa, whom he used, when speaking of them to other people after this period, to call by their surnames, thereby inducing the belief in the minds of persons otherwise ignorant, that these gentlemen were personal and intimate friends of his. He was a member of the central committee, and exhibited a large number of articles, particularly in the department of raw produce, himself.

"Good morning, Mr. Alsorts," I said, "I am glad to find you here. You will help us, I dare say, to understand a little about these matters. We are the committee on country produce; Department A., isn't it, Moodle?"

"Yes," said the Colonel, referring to a ticket he had with him. "Department A., Sect. II., Subdivision Y., that's what it is, and there are pigeons and elephants besides."

"Walk this way, gentlemen, if you please," said Alsorts, just as if he was in a shop. "I shall have much pleasure in showing you the department."

So we followed him till we came to a part of the building which was filled with what looked to me like a great heap of the agglomerate you expect to find upon a spot indicated by a tall post and a board with the words, "Rubbish may be shot here."

Here, however, all the component parts of the agglomerate were arranged in an imposing manner.

I put on a very learned look, and determined to turn my attention to two things, the first was to pick Mr. Alsorts' brains, and the second to avoid making a fool of myself.

"This, gentlemen," said Alsorts, attracting our attention to a large mass of what looked like a quantity of string frayed out into its original tow; "this, gentlemen, is the department of fibres, perhaps the most interesting department in the whole exhibition. Now you see this fibre, examine it, gentlemen; you see how strong it is, how coarse-looking. Yet, gentlemen, it is capable of being worked up into the most beautiful fabric something between cambric and silk, but of a far finer texture and much more durable than either. And yet, gentlemen, this fibre is so common in India that you can get it in any quantity for a farthing a pound. One pound will make, when worked up—here I will show you—a simple arithmetical calculation"—showing us with a pencil on a piece of paper—"you see, one pound will work up into one piece of twenty yards. Now it couldn't sell by any possibility under a rupee a yard. So, you see, how profitable the discovery will be."

"That it will, indeed," said Colonel Moodle, much struck with the idea. "I almost wonder you don't work it yourself or start a company."

Jackson, who had hitherto not spoken, here remarked, "Deuced like old tow."

This was all he said, but we at once adjudged the prize in fibres to Mr. Alsorts.

He took us then to the next branch of raw produce, and

showed us a kind of earth, or what looked like common earth, but was in reality, as he explained to us, earth possessing such a large proportion of aluminum that you could manufacture a set of a dozen spoons and forks out of a spadeful of it. This valuable earth was also so common in India that you could get a cartful in any bazaar for a shilling.

"I had no idea," said Colonel Moodle, "that there was such wealth in India. Only think of making spoons and forks out of that stuff! Why, it looks for all the world like common mutti (earth). I suppose you have already realised a large fortune, Mr. Alsorts, by these profitable discoveries of yours?" Mr. Alsorts shook his head with a knowing look and a peculiar smile, such as a man adopts when he wants to convey the idea that he has not made such a bad thing out of it.

"These," he added, directing our attention to a number of ores, "are ores of iron, silver, nickel, platinum, and gold, all of which have been tested and found to be of the best quality. These ores have all been dug out of the Budgepore hills; were a company to start and work the mines, they could not make less than three hundred per cent."

"How I wish I had a little spare cash to invest in some of these things," said Colonel Moodle. "This country's a perfect El Dorado, if you only knew how to set about getting the gold out of it. Only to think of all this wealth lying under our very feet, as it were!"

"This, gentlemen," continued the indefatigable Mr. Alsorts, showing us another kind of fibre, "is a substance so common in India that any quantities of it may be obtained anywhere for the expense only of collecting. It is the fibre of neem leaves, and when manufactured in the proper way, develops into the finest cream-laid note paper you ever saw."

"Astonishing!" said Colonel Moodle. "Can you tell us, now, the apparatus that would be necessary? I have a number of neem trees in my compound; I'll certainly set about collecting the leaves."

"The apparatus is expensive," said Alsorts. "In the first place it would require a steam-engine, and that would necessitate keeping a European engineer. But if you have any idea, sir, of working the thing, you can command my services, I assure you. As soon as you have procured the steam-engine and the engineer, which is the first step, I shall easily be able to run up a building and get the machinery out. I don't suppose it would cost more than 20,000 rupees."

The next thing he showed us was what looked like a quantity of old sticks chopped up. These we found, on enquiry, were specimens of a kind of wood that elicited a most exquisite dye, something between magenta and mauve, and was so common that you only had to send out a coolie into the jungle to collect it in any quantities.

"It is a most fortunate thing we had Mr. Alsorts to show us all these things, and tell us what they were," remarked Colonel Moodle, as we came away; "otherwise we should inevitably have exposed our ignorance."

We found Jackson, who had no taste for fibres, awaiting us at the elephant ground.

There we were sadly at fault, for neither of us knew in the least what characteristic feature in an elephant constituted excellence. And there was no Mr. Alsorts there to tell us. We had left him among his fibres and his dyes.

"Let us take a turn," I said, "and see what the other committees do. I see there is a committee of native gentlemen there. Depend upon it they are occasionally as much at fault as we. We may get a hint from them."

The native committee had been all round, and had just concluded their labours, which were not small; for they consisted in adjudging the prizes on fifteen different kinds of articles, mostly domesticated birds, vegetables, &c. Their labour, however, was very much lightened by an excellent principle they had established for deciding on the respective merits of the various articles submitted to them. The committee, at the head of which was Gunny Lall, first asked if any of the specimens exhibited belonged to the commissioner sahib. If the commissioner sahib was found to have entered the list for public competition, the prize was at once awarded to him. If the commissioner had not, then perhaps the collector sahib had; and in that case, as being next in rank, he was entitled in the second place to the prize. And so it went on all down the ladder, till Mr. Fileeter's successor, the deputy-collector's fat ducks, came into prominent notice, and had the ticket, a little bit of wood, suspended by a string, tied round their necks, indicating that they had reached the highest pinnacle of excellence attainable by mortal ducks, viz., being the best of their kind.

During our walk we came upon Mooltawee, who was standing in the buffalo sheds. His specimen, on which he prided himself, had unhappily not survived. Mooltawee was standing over the prostrate carcass of the deceased buffalo, contemplating the lifeless form with affectionate regard.

"Poor thing," he said pathetically to us, as we came up, pointing to the object on the ground, "I sat up with it all night and gave it gruel and brandy, and five drops of chloroform every two hours, out of a teaspoon, but all to no purpose. It was just breathing when I got it down here."

The committee, which came up as we were speaking, however, on hearing that the dead buffalo with five legs belonged to the judge sahib, immediately awarded the prize to it.

"These monstrosities," said I, "seldom live to grow to maturity. There seems to be some stated provision that they should not, lest they should interfere with the symmetry of nature."

"Yes," said Mooltawee; "but I think in this case it was the walnuts."

"Walnuts!"

"Yes; I gave the creature some walnuts yesterday, and I think it just possible they might have disagreed with it."

"Not impossible," I thought to myself. "Who ever heard of feeding a baffalo on walnuts? This was one of the experiments in animal economy to which the exhibition had given rise."

The native committee having concluded their labours at the buffalo-shed, we returned, despondingly, to our elephants, who were all standing, wagging their trunks gently to and fro, and winking at us out of their little eyes as if they thoroughly enjoyed the dilemma we were placed in at their expense; they looked so provokingly like each other, there was no possibility of making a selection.

"Which do you think is the best?" I asked of Jackson, who, as he had been contemplating them a good long time, might, I thought, perhaps have conceived an idea of some sort as to their relative properties.

"Damn'd if I know; they are all so deuced like one another, there's no telling t'other from which."

This was not encouraging. So I turned to Colonel Moodle.

"Which do you think, Colonel, is the best?"

"It is exceedingly difficult," said the Colonel, "to say; I never saw a batch of elephants which all resembled one another so much."

"Suppose we ask the man in charge," I said. "Very often natives, who are accustomed to watch the habits of the creatures, discover virtues and faults which would wholly escape our observation."

This remark having received the assent of my colleagues, I addressed myself to a man, a sort of jemadar-looking person, who appeared to be in charge of the elephant-shed.

"Kaun hathee mazboot hai?" (Which is the strongest elephant?) I asked.

"Kya jane—sub hathee mazboot hain," was his reply. (Who knows? all elephants are strong.)

"What does he say?" asked the Colonel.

"He says they are all equally strong."

"We might choose the tallest, then," said the Colonel. "They look pretty much all of a height, but I daresay the man knows."

"Kaun hathee sub se uncha kudd ka hai?" (Which is the tallest?) I asked.

"Sub ka kudd ek hee hai" (They are all the same height) said the man, who seemed to deem us so utterly beneath his notice, as scarcely to be worth answering.

"Hem!" said the Colonel.

"Suppose we find out their age, and choose the oldest," suggested Jackson. "I have heard elephants live to be two hundred years old sometimes."

"A very good idea," said the Colonel. "But how shall we tell their age?"

"Oh, you can just go round and look at their teeth," said Jackson.

The Colonel looked at the speaker, and then at the elephant in front of him, who was still wagging his trunk to and fro, and winking his little eyes, and now flapped his ears, as much as to say, "Come, and look at my teeth if you like."

"I'll ask the jemadar," said I; "perhaps he will be able to tell us. Kaun hathee sub se bure umur ka hai? (Which elephant is the oldest?) I added, addressing him in Hindustani.

"Kya jane," said the man; "unko malum hoga to hoga." (Who knows? perhaps they know.)

"What does he say?" asked the Colonel.

"He says he doesn't know, but perhaps they know themselves."

"Well, here's one different from the rest, anyhow, without any tusks," said Jackson, pointing out one of the creatures. "I know I've read somewhere that the finest kind of elephants are those without tusks."

"I think I've read that it is the female that has no tusks," said the Colonel.

"Then we shall be all right in selecting this one, in either case," I said.

"How so?" asked the Colonel.

"According to Burns, you know. Don't you recollect he says, speaking of Nature:—

Her 'prentice hand she tried on man,
And then she made the lasses, O!"

"But Burns was speaking of young women, not female elephants," objected the Colonel.

"The principle would be the same all throughout nature," I replied. "As we find the human organisation perfected in the lovely form of women, why not seek perfection of elephantine development in the female elephant?"

"Very well, let's have it so," said the Colonel.

"To make sure, we'll ask the jemadar," I said.

"Kaun mard aur kaun madin hain?" (Which are the males, and which the females?) I asked, pointing to the elephants.

"Sub madin" (All females), said the sulky fellow.

"What does he say?" asked the Colonel.

"He says they are all females."

"Hem!" said the Colonel.

"I vote for this one," then said Jackson, pointing to another of the group.

"All right," said the Colonel, "any one you like. But why this one in particular?"

"Because it is the blackest; do you not see how black it is? It looks as if it had polished its hide with a blacking-brush this morning before breakfast."

"Very well, I agree," I said. "Let this one have the prize."

"Now the next thing is," said the Colonel, who had charge of the prize-tickets, "where shall we fasten the ticket?"

"Round his trunk," suggested Jackson.

"Or the tusk," said I.

"I suppose the creature's quite quiet," said the Colonel, advancing cautiously towards the elephant, with the ticket hanging by the string in his hand.

"Oh, perfectly," said Jackson, keeping at a respectful distance.

"They are very seldom violent," said I, retreating a pace or two.

Colonel Moodle got close up to the creature, without its apparently perceiving his approach, when suddenly it lifted its trunk perpendicularly in the air above its head, opened its huge mouth, and emitted a most frightful shriek, something between a loud squeak and a hoarse cry. Quick as lightning the Colonel turned round to run away, but his foot getting entangled in the "karbee" (stout Indian corn stalks, that form the staple of elephants' food) he fell prostrate on the ground, looking as if he expected the next instant to find himself securely lodged in the elephant's inside. Jackson was holding his sides; I could scarce restrain my laughter.

"I think it will be the best way to find the elephant's mahout (or keeper) and give him the ticket," I said, as soon as Colonel Moodle had recovered his feet and joined us, a little distance from the scene of the disaster.

So we found the mahout, who said his elephant's name was Motee, and to him we gave the ticket.

After this was over, we had only the pigeons to examine, and here we had less difficulty, for although none of us knew anything at all about pigeons, we all unanimously fixed upon one that struck us as being the prettiest, and thus concluded our labours in the capacity of prize committee.

I must say a few words in concluding this chronicle about the exhibition, and how it went off. It was opened with great *éclat*, and the programme was carefully observed. The only little mishap that occurred was at that part of the proceedings where Mr. Byewilwuffa, followed by Mr. Khas Mouza, and by the committee and the managers, secretaries, assistant-secretaries and principal visitors, two and two, were to walk up the centre aisle preceded by the band playing the

National Anthem. Unfortunately the band, which had come straight from a funeral up to the exhibition, had forgotten to take off the music that was affixed to the instruments, and the procession set out, Mr. Byewilwuffa stalking sedately along, followed by the secretary, the committee, the assistant-secretaries, the manager and assistant-manager, and principal visitors, to the tune of the "Dead March" in *Saul*. No one liked to break the order of the procession and run out and speak to the bandmaster who, was in front and at the time far away in the seventh heaven, for he had that morning made an offer and been accepted by a very pretty girl to whom he was much attached. So do sorrow and mirth, laughter and weeping, the wedding and the funeral, go hand-in-hand, as it were, in this chequered life. Mr. Khas Mouza waved his umbrella with the hope of attracting the bandmaster's attention, but the good man saw only his mistress waving her snowy handkerchief at him and not Mr. Khas Mouza's brown umbrella. The bandsmen saw nothing incongruous in it; all they attended to was that their music should be in tune and their pace likewise. So to slow time, as the chords of that magnificent piece of music, the wail of a broken heart over some beloved idol or venerated chief, swelled through the aisles and up along the vaulted roof, till its plaintive accents died away, growing fainter and fainter among Mr. Alsorts' fibres, the Honourable Kist Byewilwuffa, bearing himself majestically and little heeding the frantic gestures of his secretary, who waved his umbrella as an Indian his tomahawk at a funeral dance, perambulated the building, and, reaching his chair of state, declared the exhibition open.

"Well, Mr. Alsorts," said I, as I met that gentleman two mornings after at the exhibition building, "I hope the exhibition has been a success."

"Oh, yes, most decidedly, sir, a great success. I have cleared at the very least a lack of rupees."

"You don't say so? Well, now, how did you manage it?"

"I've sold everything, you see, and got my price, too."

"Had you much here?"

"Oh, dear me, yes; why two-thirds of the whole turn-out belongs to me."

"Does it, indeed; and have you really sold all this—rubbish, I was going to say—pointing to the mass of miscellaneous articles, furniture, chandeliers, tables, what-nots, stools, pianos, crockery, musical boxes, English toys, shawls, rugs, durries, everything, in fact, that was there in such profusion. Have you really sold all this?"

"Yes, all, and I don't mind letting you into my secret. You see, sir, I was very thick with Mr. Dakhil Duftar and Mr Isteefa all the time the preparations were going on. They found me useful. I know they don't seem quite so fond of my society now. It's no more, 'Oh, Mr. Alsorts, do just come here, like a good fellow;' or, 'Alsorts, I wish you would give me a wrinkle here;' or, 'Alsorts, you must be deucedly tired, come and take a glass of beer and a sandwich.' Ah, well, I can see as far as my neighbours; these gentlemen found me useful, and, well, I thought I might one day find them useful. So, seeing me so much with them the natives came about my place a little; well, I pretended to take no notice, but just let things run on. At last the Rajas began to come into Budgepore for the exhibition, and they came to my place too. Then their vakeels came next day to have a little conversation and to find out for their masters what this great 'shop' really meant: 'Was the Sirkar (Government) really opening a shop?' Well, I don't say that I said as much, but if the vakeels went away and told their masters that the British Government, being really very hard up for cash, had hit upon this expedient for raising the wind, and that every Raja was expected to purchase in proportion to the extent of his revenues; I say, if the vakeels told the Rajas so, how could I help it? Next day I went to all the shops in the bazaar and the city, and I bought up every single thing I could lay my hands upon in the shape of glass, crockery, clocks, anything gaudily painted and rather showy, besides all the carpets, shawls, everything in short, and sent it all here, and I've sold every d——d thing at just treble its price, and shall I not say the exhibition is a success? Long live Byewilwuffa, the jolly old buffer, say I!"

The last of the exhibition ceremonies was a grand durbar, at which Mr. Byewilwuffa presented khilluts (presents) to four of the native gentry who had been prominent in their support of his pet scheme, who were also made honorary magistrates. One of these was our old friend Gunny Lall, who, at Mr. Wasilbakee's suggestion, had opened his money bags and given 10,000 rupees towards the exhibition. Another was Salig Ram, who had been imprisoned for forgery. But his forgery had, besides getting him into prison, brought him enormous wealth, and he presented 10,000 rupees, and received the distinction and undertook the duties of honorary magistrate, in which capacity he will, I hope, always recollect to sympathize with men who are so unfortunate as to sign other people's names to bills. The third was Moona Lall, money lender, who had grown enormously rich by usury, and the fourth was Khewut Sing, who had been tried for murdering his father, and acquitted, but being a rich man, had judiciously purchased the favour of the reigning power by a grant of 15,000 rupees to the exhibition, and the loan of his elephant, the very elephant, by the way, to which we had adjudged the prize.

After it was all over, the remainder of the articles were sold by auction, Mr. Archimedes DeCruze acting as auctioneer. They fetched 15,000 rupees, and Mr. DeCruze having to receive ten per cent. as auctioneer, netted fifteen hundred by that transaction. He may have netted more, for the 15,000 rupees was never heard of again, nor, strange to say, was Mr. Archimedes DeCruze, who disappeared about that time.

Of course people wondered what had happened to him. Dakhil Duftar, who never had any but thoroughly trustworthy persons about him, thought at first he had probably fallen down a well, or been suddenly seized with cholera on his way home, and fully expected some tidings would be heard of him. But when time passed and nothing transpired, he came to the conclusion that he had been kidnapped by some of those Cabulee men who once or twice a year come down from Cabul with strings of camels laden with posteens, dried figs, apricots, &c., and return with merchandise from India, the real object of their journey, which is not to sell their own goods so much as to purchase others. Well, Dakhil Duftar was fully persuaded that some of these men had kidnapped Archimedes DeCruze and carried him off to sell him for a slave in Tartary, and so took no further steps to track him. I didn't know before that these men were ever suspected of kidnapping people in British India, no more did Dakhil Duftar, he said, but his serishtadar told him it was very frequently the case. Mr. Wasilbakee was also of the same opinion, and thought there was no doubt that Mr. Archimedes DeCruze had been kidnapped. And that opinion took the form of a settled conviction, after he had consulted his serishtadar and found that he corroborated in every particular the information furnished to Dakhil Duftar. They thought the matter so important as to justify their bringing it to the notice of the Governor-General, which they did, of course through the "usual channels," but that functionary recorded his opinion that it was one of those cases in which he "couldn't interfere." Of course no one disputed the conclusions of Dakhil Duftar and Mr. Wasilbakee. They were, no doubt, correct. Only it struck me as a strange circumstance, that only the very day before this unfortunate kidnapping took place, as it subsequently transpired, DeCruze had realised on all his Government securities to the full amount of the 15,000 rupees, the proceeds of the auction, in addition to 15,000 more which he had in Government five per cents.

There was a small deficit of 40,000 rupees altogether from the whole affair, but this was easily replaced, thanks to the *elasticity* of the resources of India, which financial people are so fond of talking about, and an additional rupee per maund on grain to be devoted exclusively to public works, being laid on by the octroi in the principal cities in the province, the surplus with something out of the *nuzzool* fund, filled up the deficit, and as Mr. Byewilwuffa wrote in his minute on the subject, "The exhibition was in every way a great success."

CHRONICLE IV.

THE HISTORY OF THE BARRACKS.

CHRONICLE IV.

THE HISTORY OF THE BARRACKS.

CHAPTER I.

THE EARLY HISTORY OF BUDGEPORE, AND HOW ANNEXATION WAS FORCED UPON US.

In the consulship of Emilius Flaccus, Quintus Metellus being Master of the Horse——What have I been writing? I meant to say, when the Hon'ble Kist Byewilwuffa was Lieutenant-Governor and Mr. Khas Mouza, Secretary, there came an order for European barracks to be built at Budgepore. You will ask what the barracks had to be built for? Well, for European soldiers to live in. And why were European soldiers to be quartered at Budgepore?

The necessity of replying to this question reminds me that I have never yet chronicled the old history of Budgepore, nor put on record the events which led to that rich and fertile province coming under the British sway. This I shall now proceed to do, very briefly. You need not be afraid, reader, of my taking up your time with a long disquisition upon the ancient history of this part of India. I shall merely trace the succession of events that led to the annexation of Budgepore. And if you have never heard or read this episode in Indian History, it must be because, like everyone else, you never studied Indian History at all.

I shall not need to go back further than the time of Mahmoud of Ghanzi in the year 1000, in whose train one of the most fierce and warlike of the Pathan tribes called the Talwarries came into Hindoostan, conquered and held the province of Budgepore.

We now pass over a considerable interval, till the time of Warren Hastings. When that great man held the reins of Government, Budgepore was a distinct province, ruled over by a Nawab, who was always called the Nawab of Budgepore.

I don't suppose he had any name, just as the Nawab of Rampore, the Maharajah of Jeypore, and other independent princes and sovereigns, it is well known, have no names, as how could they, seeing that they have neither god-fathers nor god-mothers?

Now having arrived at this stage of my chronicle, we will, if you please, leave Budgepore for the present and return to London.

One afternoon, as Mr. Leopold Scheinfeldt, a rich goldsmith of the City of London, and one of the proprietors of India Stock, was stepping into the Bear and Bull dining-rooms in Cornhill to have his midday meal, he encountered in the coffee-room of that tavern Captain Robertson, of the E. I. C. Navy, who commanded one of the East India Company's ships, half merchantman, and half man-of-war. The two gentlemen greeted one another warmly, and sitting down at the same table, entered into conversation, in the course of which Captain Robertson, remarking upon the dividends upon India Stock observed, that it was a mystery to him the East India Company did not look after their interests better than they did, for that if the Directors of the Company only did their duty to the proprietors, and protected them from being robbed by the servants of the Company in the settlements (the possessions of the Company in India were always called "the settlements" in those days), the dividends would be quite double what they were. Being asked to enter into particulars, Captain Robertson proceeded to dilate upon the state and magnificence, the luxury and grandeur of the *ménage* maintained by the governors and officers of the Company abroad. He said much upon the resources of the country, the interior of which he had visited, having been up as far as Chandernagore, and he impressed on his hearer's mind very forcibly that if stringent requisitions were sent out to the Governor of Bengal and other officers abroad, to double the revenues or the dividends, they could be doubled without any difficulty whatever.

After dinner they parted, and Mr. Leopold Scheinfeldt went back to his shop; but instead of remaining there, as was his wont at that time of the afternoon (in those days it was the custom to dine early), he desired his assistant to remain in the shop, and passed along into his own little back room, where he remained for an hour or more, with some account books before him, immersed in thought. The good man was taking stock, and reckoning what his property would be worth if the dividends on the India Stock were only doubled. The demon of covetousness had long had possession of that man's soul.

The following morning on his way to the city, for even then the more wealthy of the citizens had begun to adopt the habit of having their residences westwards, he called at the office of Mr. Lloyd Frankfort, one of the Directors of the E. I. C., and to him he told all he had heard from Captain Robertson the day before.

The following week there was a general meeting of proprietors, at which Mr. Leopold Scheinfeldt spoke his mind, and aid from private information which had reached him, he felt assured that they, the proprietors, received much smaller dividends than was right; and that if a little pressure were put upon the Governors and other officers at the settlements, much larger remittances would be made. No resolution was proposed upon this, and the meeting broke up; but Mr. Leopold Scheinfeldt was much gratified when one of the gorgeously-dressed beadles who used to vegetate in the India House came up to him in the presence of many of the other proprietors, and said that the Chairman of the Court of Directors had sent his compliments, and, if convenient to Mr. Leopold to afford him a few minutes' conversation he should be glad if he would step into his private room. Thither, accordingly, Mr. Leopold went; and there he met a small and secret conclave of those great men—the Directors. What passed it is out of my power to record. What resulted was this: that the next ship that left the docks for Calcutta took out a large bundle of despatches, addressed "To our well-beloved and trusty Governor, Warren Hastings, Esq., at Fort William, Bengal," one of which contained a missive, marked "Private and important," which caused Warren Hastings much thought. In this despatch it was intimated to that officer that unless the remittances to England were doubled in the course of the year, he would be recalled.

The contents of this despatch were not communicated to the Council; and this may be one reason why it is not to be found among the records of Government in Fort William. One reason,

I say; for another reason which may easily account for it is, that the white ants may very possibly have devoured it.

After dismissing the Council, Warren Hastings returned to his private room, and sent for his native private secretary, or meer munshi—a man, you may be sure, of very great influence, and very great talent: of very great influence, for the meer munshi of the Governor was sure to have enormous influence; of very great talent, for Warren Hastings was not likely to be served by anyone but a man of very great talent. This meer munshi kept what may be called the "Indian Doomsday Book"; that is to say—a book wherein was entered the name, history, antecedents, and surroundings of every chief and man of note in India, the amount of wealth he was possessed of, how he had acquired it, the amount of his revenues and how collected, his habits of life, his physical and intellectual attainments; in short, all that could be found out about him. It was a great book, that; great I mean not only in size, but in importance, and was kept in an iron safe under lock and key, in the strong room, where the meer munshi deposited his jewels and treasure. The Nawab of Budgepore you may be sure had a page to himself in that book.

On this occasion the record was consulted. Warren Hastings leant back in an easy chair, close to the open venetian window looking out upon the waters of the Hooghly, his forehead fanned by the evening southern breeze; while the meer munshi sat at the table near him, and read out the history and the antecedents of the Nawab of Budgepore, and all that was known about him. It was there recorded, that the Nawab was enormously rich; that he had, or was said to have, amassed ten crores* of rupees in jewels and cash; that he was a parsimonious, miserly old man, who spent most of his time in his harem, leaving the affairs of state pretty much to the management of an astute Hindoo minister, or dewan, Roy Chund; that the dewan also was reported to be very wealthy, and to be connected with nearly all the large banking houses throughout the principal cities of India.

The meer munshi finished, closed the book, and took his departure; but Warren Hastings sat in the same place without moving for a full hour, till the shades of evening had

*A crore is a million.

fallen, and the noisy crows intimated their intention of retiring to rest on the neighbouring trees.

Next day the following Minute passed the Council:—

EXTRACT FROM THE MINUTE BOOK.

The East India Company's Settlements, Bengal. Dated Fort William, 1st April, 17—.

Proceedings of Council.

The following resolution was passed this day:—

"That, with a view to increase the trade between the Settlements of the Honourable the East India Company and Great Britain, it is desirable to enter into communications with the Nawab of Budgepore, for the purpose of opening up the trade of that part of the country with the Settlement of Calcutta; and that Captain Diaper be deputed, under special instructions to be communicated to him direct from the Governor, with suitable presents, &c., for the Nawab, to arrange a commercial treaty with that prince."

What Captain Diaper's instructions were I cannot exactly say, because the copy he took with him was destroyed during the course of events that subsequently ensued; and the copy that was no doubt retained in the Foreign Office, must also have perished by those destructive little creatures, the white ants. I know he had some demi-official written instructions, at any rate, and this is the way the information reached me. Captain Diaper was sent for by Warren Hastings, and had a long private interview. What passed, of course no one can tell now. There was a young gentleman at that time in Hastings' employ as a sort of assistant private secretary and librarian. He used to conduct a good deal of the Governor's private correspondence, look after his papers and books, &c., and in short, was a sort of unattached aide-de-camp. He was drowned in the Hooghly about two years after this, but his family preserved some letters of his and a diary which he kept, and knowing that I was engaged in writing these chronicles, they kindly volunteered to let me have the use of the diary and letters. In the former I find this entry:—

"Captain Diaper having private interview with the Governor—Go in, as he is about to leave, to get some papers out of the escritoire, and hear him say: 'Well, your Excellency will excuse my speaking so plainly, but it will be necessary for my own protection should anything happen to your Excellency, which God forbid! during my absence; that I should be able, if necessary to produce your Excellency's written instructions.' Upon that, Hastings took a pencil and wrote as much as would fill a sheet of note paper on the four sides, signed it, and pushed it across the table to Captain Diaper, saying, as he did so: 'This will be quite sufficient for you, Captain Diaper.' And Captain Diaper after reading what had been written, replied: 'Quite so, your Excellency,' and took his leave."

This is all that is known about it. Captain Diaper lost his life on the mission on which he went, but neither the private letter of instructions nor the official one was found or recovered. The papers he had with him were probably distroyed, and the office copy, as I said, has no doubt been consumed by the white ants.

Captain Diaper proceeded to Budgepore, where he was courteously received by the Nawab, delivered his presents and credentials, and took up his abode in a house allotted to him, which was subsequently called the Residency. I have no means of knowing what passed between Captain Diaper and the Nawab, but after he had been there a short time, engaged, no doubt, in arranging a commercial treaty, and confining his attention exclusively to the development of trade, symptoms of disagreement showed themselves between the Nawab and his Dewan, which speedily ripened into an open quarrel. At last Roy Chund began to assemble, and enlist armed men. The Nawab's security was threatened, an *émeute* or two took place, and Captain Diaper as British Agent retired across the frontier and took up his abode in the nearest friendly state, on what might be considered British territory. He had not been there long, before he received overtures from the Nawab, soliciting the assistance of the British Government. These despatches were duly forwarded to Calcutta, and in a short time a reply was received tendering the aid of a military force, providing certain sums of money were paid down as expenses. The end of it was that a force consisting of a regiment of sepoys, two hundred Europeans, and three galloper guns, as light field guns were called in those days, were despatched to the aid of the Nawab, and five crores of the Nawab's rupees were sent in hard cash down to Calcutta, and duly shipped for

England. Soon after their arrival there, Mr. Leopold Scheinfeldt was elected into the Direction.

Meantime Roy Chund had taken the field at the head of ten thousand infantry, and five thousand horse with thirty guns. But the British Contingent, ably handled by Colonel Arbuthnot who commanded, and which consisted of the eight hundred sepoys, two hundred Europeans, and the three galloper guns, and aided by the Nawab's army of twenty thousand men, who all ran away directly the first shot was fired, easily routed them, and Roy Chund, a fugitive, was glad to seek and obtain protection in the British territory. The Nawab was then reseated on the throne which he had actually vacated, having run away from fear directly Roy Chund took the field, but three crores of rupees more were demanded and recieved by the East India Company for the expenses of the war. Roy Chund managed, through his friends the bankers, to get most of his treasure sent away, but his palace was looted, and Colonel Arbuthnot the next year retired from the service and went home, where he bought a large estate, was called the Nabob, and went into Parliament. Captain Diaper now returned to Budgepore as Political Agent, while the Nawab's crown was confirmed to him and his heirs "quamdiu se bene gesserint." Arrangements being entered into for the regular payment of a British force required to maintain tranquillity and secure the throne to its possessor.

This payment soon fell into arrears, for the disturbed state of the country had prevented the revenue being collected, and one tract of territory after another was "ceded" to the British Government in lieu of payment, till all the Nawab had left was the garden round his palace.

Meantime, the Nawab, having spent all his money, and Roy Chund having plenty at his command, the latter easily fomented disturbances, and collecting an army, marched towards the frontier. An *émeute* took place in the city. Roy Chund forced the British troops to retreat, drove out the Nawab, and seated himself upon the "musnud" or throne. The British Government then sent a force to restore order, and finding Roy Chund *de facto* sovereign, they confirmed him in the hereditary possession of the crown, which was guaranteed to him and his heirs in consideration of the payment of three crores of rupees.

All these changes did not happen without disturbance and

émeutes, in one of which Captain Diaper was killed and the Residency plundered. And it was on this occasion that the papers I spoke of just now were in all probability destroyed. At Roy Chund's death the country was involved in anarchy. The Nawab was dead also, having left a son and heir to the *de jure* sovereignty, while Roy Chund had left an adopted son, to whom he had bequeathed the "musnud," or throne.

The country was for the next few years involved in such anarchy, that the British Government, out of compassion to the people, virtually annexed it, that is, they took the revenues and maintained a Political Agent, with a considerable force under his orders at the capital.

When the two minors came of age, the British Government being obliged to choose between them, selected the heir of the Nawab as a rightful claimant of the throne, and he was installed into the office. Incessant disturbances ensued, which lasted several years. The Nawab's son and Roy Chund's adopted son died, leaving adopted sons, legitimate sons, and illegitimate sons, all of whom adopted heirs, disinherited them, and then re-adopted them, and finally they all adopted one another, till the whole question of the succession became involved in inextricable confusion. And so matters went on, till, a few years before the period when my chronicle takes up the thread of the story, the Government was forced to annex the country altogether, and Mr. Kist Byewilwuffa, then a young civilian of ten or fifteen years' standing, was deputed on special duty to "settle" it.

Mr. Kist Byewilwuffa had gained a great name in the service as a rising man, having distinguished himself very much at Haileybury, where he had gained the highest honours in law. This he had done in a fair and open field of competition, for the course of study, consisting of the second volume of Blackstone and the portion of Hallam relating to the feudal system, and the other students having gone in to the examination without reading the works mentioned, which Mr. Byewilwuffa had done, he easily distanced his competitors, secured the prize, was most honourably noticed at the public examination where Mr. St. George-and-the-Dragon, the President of the Court of Directors, spoke of him in terms of the highest eulogy, and prophesied a glorious and brilliant career for the distinguished scholar.

So Mr. Byewilwuffa on special duty, with two assistant-collectors, aided by seven hundred native "ameens," proceeded to "settle" the new province. A thorough and sound real property lawyer, as was Mr. Byewilwuffa, thanks to his study of Blackstone, Vol. II., he of course set to work to investigate the titles and the customs under which land tenures had previously existed. In doing this, the two collectors and the seven hundred native ameens were of the utmost possible assistance, because, while the collectors went out shooting, the ameens, three hundred and fifty of which were allotted to each collector, went about among the ryots and the zemindars (the labourers and the landed proprietors), and investigated the ancient titles and the nature of the land tenures. The result of these researches was duly communicated to Mr. Byewilwuffa, who at the end of two years drew up a most lucid and valuable report, which has long been looked upon as the *chef d'œuvre* of the civil service, and upon this report the "settlements" were made.

It would of course be out of place here were I to enter much into detail. I may, however, just mention one or two points, which show how completely Mr. Byewilwuffa had mastered his subject, and established the system of land tenures upon the soundest possible basis, that is to say, the old and pre-existing customs of the country, with which the Government were careful not to interfere.

Thus it was ascertained that a ryot (labourer) who had occupied land for the space of two years, and had buried any of his relations in it, acquired proprietary rights, which could not be interfered with, unless within twenty days from the date on which he deposited the remains of his relations in the soil, he had either dug a well or built a wall anywhere on the holding, in which case the title was forfeited. Thus also the occupier of a dwelling-house, if he had a child born in it, acquired a proprietary right, subject to the payment of rent, however. This proprietary right determined upon the death of the child. There was another class of sub-proprietary rights in the soil which arose in this way:—When a ryot had occupied an estate for a period sufficiently long to enable him to get two crops successively from the soil, and had afterwards dug a pukka (masonry) well, if the zemindar fell into it, provided he was taken out of the well defunct, the ryot acquired what was called a sub-proprietary right, that is to say, he could not be ousted as long as he paid the headman of the village a certain sum, and maintained a certain number of indigent Brahmins.

I must not, however, dwell any longer on these dry details of land tenures, lest I should weary my readers. Suffice it to say that the "settlement" of Budgepore secured Mr. Byewilwuffa's fame; he rose rapidly in the service, and wrote a standard work on "land settlements," besides giving Government very valuable advice in passing the great rent-law act. Of Mr. Byewilwuffa's assistants, who aided him in this great settlement, one of the collectors fell into one of the "pukka wells," which accident resulted in his gaining a freehold of six feet of ground in the Budgepore territory, the other became Commissioner. The seven hundred native ameens were appointed to various posts, lumberdars, tehsildars, thanadars, jemadars, and I don't know how many other "dars." Each ameen had been allowed seven messengers, of whom there were therefore 4,900, who were all provided for in various offices in the new territories. Each of these messengers had five brothers, who also found occupation under Government, to the number of 24,500. The province was portioned out into districts, to each of which ten uncovenanted deputy collectors were appointed, and twenty petty judges or moonsiffs. Each deputy collector had five messengers, and each moonsiff four. Jails were built everywhere, and "thanas" (small district police stations), a force of 20,000 police were raised from the other provinces and located in the new territories, and the province, to complete its happiness and prosperity, was incorporated into British dominion, and came under the "regulations."

And it is one of the most extraordinary and unaccountable phenomena I ever met with in the history of any people, that in spite of all the beneficial measures, in spite of the expense the Government went to, in spite of the admirable settlement of a man of genius like Mr. Byewilwuffa, the country languished, trade grew faint, the soil degenerated into waste land, the cities and villages became comparatively depopulated, and so besotted and sunk in ignorance were the people, that, instead of welcoming with open arms the advent of British rule, the old savage spirit of the Talwarry race still occasionally showed itself in symptoms of disaffection.

THE HISTORY OF THE BARRACKS.

CHAPTER II.

THE INSURRECTION.

The disturbed state of the province of Budgepore at length attracted the notice of Government, and they resolved to send there best man there as Commissioner. Accordingly, Mr. Kist Byewilwuffa, although the appointment was no promotion to him then, was solicited to proceed to Budgepore and endeavour to reduce the province to order. He received a most flattering letter from Government, and, of course, he accepted the office.

So Mr. Kist Byewilwuffa found himself a second time at Budgepore. On this occasion, as before, he went accompanied by his serishtadar. And he had not been there long before disturbances were quelled, and the district became as quiet and orderly as any in the whole country. For Mr. Kist Byewilwuffa, had an admirable receipt for settling disaffected provinces. He had no sooner taken up the reins of government than he caused it to be publicly known, that it was his method never, on any account, to enquire into charges against subordinate officers. Under his *régime* authority was always supported. Such a thing as a complaint against the police for torture or bribery was never to be entertained. And the result was that everything appeared on the surface eminently satisfactory, and Mr. Byewilwuffa's reputation rose in proportion.

After Mr. Byewilwuffa had been a year or two in his office as special Commissioner, the Court of Directors, for some reason or other, wrote out and called for a report upon the state of the province. I hardly know the object that prompted the enquiry, probably it was because there was a scheme on foot for reducing the army, and they wanted to know if this province was sufficiently well affected and tranquillised to enable them to adopt that measure with safety. On receiving the order to report, Mr. Byewilwuffa sent to all the collectors directing them to report each on his own district, and the collectors sending each for his native clerk, described what was wanted, and desired that the report might be ready that day week. So the reports all came in due time, when Mr. Byewilwuffa wrote a general report, reviewing the minor reports of the collectors, and the whole amounting to a Blue Book of 750 pages folio was transmitted to the Court of Directors, and eventually, laid upon the table of the House of Commons.

But I must not anticipate. The day after the report left—I need hardly say, that in it the province of Budgepore was represented as being in a most satisfactory condition, the people well affected, crime almost unknown, the revenue regularly paid, and the people cheerful and happy under British rule—the day after the report left, as Mr. Byewilwuffa was returning from his morning ride through the city, he found all the shops shut in the main street. Now he thought this was odd at that hour in the morning; at least it was not usual. By the time he had ridden (he was walking his horse) half way up the street, he was fired at from behind. The bullet whizzed past his ear, uncomfortably close. Mr. Byewilwuffa was not a coward. He knew he had been shot at. He knew he had had as narrow an escape as possible of his life, and he could not but expect that a second attempt would be made. But he did not quicken his pace. He might have put spurs to his horse and galloped off; he did no such thing. He merely turned round, and marked with his eye the position of the houses he had just passed, and rode on still at a foot pace. He had not gone ten yards before another shot was fired, and again the ball missed him, but only by a fraction of an inch as it seemed. Still he would not ride on. No other attempt was made, and Mr. Byewilwuffa reached home in safety, and bathed, and had his breakfast as usual. After breakfast he sent for his serishtadar, told him what had happened, and asked him whether the attempt was that of a private assassin or was it a symptom of wide-spread disaffection. The serishtadar replied that, "by his Honour's favour the country was never in a more tranquil state, as was it not proved to be so by the report which his Honour had only the day before sent to Government?" Mr. Byewilwuffa at once saw the force of this argument, and admitted it. He then desired the serishtadar to make enquiries, and that functionary left the house for the purpose of doing so.

Now it so happened, that there was a rich banker in the street where the shot had been fired, to whom the serishtadar was indebted one thousand rupees, and had been in debt for the last twelve months, during which time interest, at twenty-four per cent., had been duly accumulating. Of late the creditor had been rather impatient, and had once or twice rashly ventured upon dunning. It is dangerous work, sometimes, dunning people; and Heera Lall Seth of Budgepore found it so to his cost.

After an hour's absence, the serishtadar, returned to Mr. Byewilwuffa and told him that he had discovered the whole plot,—for plot there was; and in the evening he would take him to the house of a certain man in the city, in the upper room of which—so certain was his information,—a double-barrelled fowling-piece would be found which had recently been fired off. Mr. Byewilwuffa, I suppose instinctively, suggested whether it would not be better to go at once and search the house, but the serishtadar assured him that was not at all a proper thing to do, for expecting a search, the perpetrator of the deed would have concealed the weapon; by evening, no steps having been taken, he would be thrown off his guard, and the search would be likely to be much more effectual. I need not add, that Mr. Byewilwuffa entirely concurred with his serishtadar: he had entirely concurred with him for seven and twenty years, ever since he had been his munshi at Writer's Buildings, Calcutta, and kept his accounts; and was it likely he should commence to differ from him now?

Accordingly, in the evening, Mr. Byewilwuffa himself, accompanied by a native officer, two mounted police, and the serishtadar, repaired to Heera Lall's house. The shops in the bazaar were still closed. The Commissioner followed the serishtadar into an upper room. There, by the window, they found a double-barrelled fowling-piece, which, on examination, proved to have been recently used. There was no one in the house or on the premises but a watchman. And a warrant was issued at once for the apprehension of Heera Lall.

I may as well here anticipate a little, so as to complete this episode of my story. Heera Lall was tried for an attempt at murder. Fifty witnesses for the prosecution deposed to having seen the prisoner station himself at the window, gun in hand, and fire, as the Commissioner rode up the street. Fifty witnesses for the defence, deposed that, during the day in question, Heera Lall had been in his shop the whole morning, transacting his ordinary business. These witnesses were customers and constituents; and their testimony was to a certain extent borne out by the banker's day book, which contained entries, dated the day in question, relating to matters to which the witnesses had deposed. The principal feature in the case for the prosecution was the production of the fowling-piece, which had been discovered on Heer Lall's premises. During this part of the trial the prisoner's native advocate tendered evidence to show that the fowling-piece was an old fowling-piece of Mr. Byewilwuffa's, which he had once given to his serishtadar as a present; but the judge cut that part of the case short by telling the advocate not to worry the court by irrelevant nonsense; for, if the fowling-piece had been used for an unlawful purpose by the prisoner, it could make no difference whether it had been the property of the serishtadar, Mr. Byewilwuffa, or any one else. Upon which the advocate folded his hands, and murmuring, "jo hukm," or "as you order," sat down; and when Heera Lall was sentenced to be hanged, consoled his client by telling him it was his "kismat," or destiny, which did not appear to convey much comfort to the prisoner, though it was doubtless quite true.

The sentence of course went up to the Sudder, or Supreme Court, for confirmation; and there being some peculiar circumstances attending it, a full bench met to consider it. Mr. Momjama, the senior judge, delivered a long and elaborate argument, setting forth his reasons for confirming the sentence passed by the lower court; and after he had finished, Mr. Lifeffa, the second judge, said: "Well, I don't understand all that, but I say, Wind him up"; a formula for a capital sentence not unfamiliar to the criminal side of the Sudder Court.

The other judges having concurred, Heera Lall was in due time, in the language of the court "wound up."

"Bless my soul!" said Mr. Byewilwuffa, the day after the

execution, examining the following piece, "how very extraordinary; I declare this is the very identical old fowling-piece I gave Nusseer Khan (that was the serishtadar's name) in Calcutta, years and years ago. How on earth did that old rascal, Heera Lall, get hold of it, I wonder?"

The same day that Heera Lall was hanged, the report on Budgepore left the Governor-General's hands for transmission to the Court of Directors, and His Excellency in Council despatched a very flattering letter to Mr. Kist Byewilwuffa, complimenting him very highly upon the favourable report he had sent in, and adding that he had in his despatch to the Court of Directors spoken in high terms of the valuable services Mr. Byewilwuffa had rendered to the State. That complimentary letter, however, never reached Mr. Byewilwuffa, for this reason, that the runner who carried the letter-bags was murdered. For a dangerous insurrection had broken out in Budgepore. The Talwarries were such a barbarous and ignorant race that they were not content with the mild rule of the British Government. The stupid people could not see the great advantages of having jails built at their expense all over the country, and police-stations with secure lock-up houses attached. They could not realise the advantage of open courts, and a free channel of justice where a man had only to pay for what he wanted and got it directly, provided he paid enough; they were, in short, altogether too barbarous to recognise the blessings Heaven had sent them in giving them a government like that of Mr. Byewilwuffa's. So they preferred running the risk of insurrection.

In those days the Bengal army was in its prime. Its laurels were, you may say, never greener or more fresh. No regiment was ever inspected by a (Company's) General officer, but he left it on record that he considered the drill, discipline, and appearance of the ——th regiment of Native Infantry far superior to that of any English regiment he had ever met. General officers declared, at the mess tables of native regiments, that they would far rather go on service with native troops than with Europeans. And it was a proof at the same time of the sincerity and disinterestedness of these officers that when there was a campaign, they all made strong favour at Head Quarters to avoid getting posted to the command of a Black Brigade. (A Black Brigade meant a brigade exclusively of native troops.) The Governor-General wrote most flattering eulogies to the Court of Directors upon the state of the native army, and recommended diminishing the force of Europeans in the Company's employ, and getting as many of royal regiments as they could, sent home.

At the time I speak of, the 77th N. I. was quartered at Budgepore. It was considered the crack regiment in the service, and had been made "Light Infantry," for its services in Afghanistan. Colonel Moodle commanded the regiment. (That was before the amalgamation, since which he has been superseded by his nephew, Captain Kummurbund.) Young Sticklebat was adjutant. He afterwards got into the choir at Simla church, when Lady Amethyst Jones' husband was Commander-in-Chief. I mention him in this way, because it was well known that Sir Amethyst Jones left everything in the hands of his wife, who, with the assistance of the military secretary, commanded the army. From the choir Sticklebat got command of the Meddlesore contingent, one of the best appointments, in those days, going, for you were allowed to draw cavalry pay, and a contingent allowance for all the horses in the two regiments of cavalry, which were always returned as cavalry, but were in reality infantry. Colonel Moodle was a strict disciplinarian. He was unfortunately rather corpulent, but that was his misfortune, not his fault. He used to go to parade always in a palanquin, but when on the parade ground he always mounted. He had his charger drawn up alongside of the palanquin: his orderly-sergeant assisted him to get on the roof, from whence the passage to the saddle was easy. The groom carried his spurs, and when the parade was half over and the charger had carried its rider (nineteen stone) for about an hour, he put on his master's spurs, I mean he fixed the spurs in the boxes of his master's boots. I don't mean that the groom himself put on the spurs, that would be absurd.

During the hot weather there were no parades, except one for inspection and the manual and plantoon on Saturday afternoons. In the rainy season, when the ground was very wet, officers commanding companies used to go to parade with an orderly carrying two bricks. These bricks the orderly placed on the ground in front of the centre of each company, a few yards off, and the officers got out of their palanquins or off their horses, and stood upon the bricks while they put their companies through their manual and plantoon exercises, and thus kept their feet dry.* Altogether there was the best possible feeling between the officers and men of the 77th Light Infantry. The mess was a very pleasant little mess to dine at, the few ladies that were with the regiment were great favourites, and altogether a young man might find himself in a more uncomfortable billet than that of a subaltern in the 77th Native Light Infantry at Budgepore.

The disturbance at Budgepore broke out one evening early in July, 18—. A number of the citizens assembled in large crowds outside the city, which, like most of the cities of Upper India, was surrounded with gardens and garden walls and country houses that formerly belonged to the nobility and gentry of the district. Here and there were vacant spots of ground of considerable extent, and upon these vacant spots of ground the multitude assembled. Many came armed with drums, others with horns, and others with guns, matlocks, and fire-arms of various descriptions. Those who had drums beat them, those who had horns blew them, those who had fire-arms fired them off in the air, and those who had neither drums, horns, nor fire-arms, talked as loud as they could, or ran about hither and thither bawling at the top of their voices.

As soon as news of the insurrection reached the civil station, which was between the city and the military cantonment, the residents were of course much alarmed. There were about five bungalows occupied by civilians and their families, and about ten or twenty more tenanted by uncovenanted clerks, pensioners, and others. Almost all these were bungalows, that is to say, one-floor houses or large cottages, with thatched roofs of dry grass. Mr. Byewilwuffa, however, lived in what is called a large *pukka* house, that is to say, a house built of masonry, brick and mortar, and roofed with beams of wood laid horizontally and covered with mud mixed with lime, brick, &c., and a few of the rooms were roofed with large flat stones. This building, being of course much stronger and less liable to fire than the bungalows, was the rendezvous for all

* There is, I am told, still extant an old Order-book at Barrackpore, directing officers to discontinue the practice of having bricks taken down for them to stand upon while *inspecting* their companies, the same being an unmilitary practice.

the civilians and their families who left their own houses when the noise and hubbub began, as their servants told them there was a disturbance, and that they had better get out of their houses lest the thatch should be set on fire by some evil-disposed persons. Accordingly they all repaired to the Commissioner's house and assembled in the dining-room, the door of which they carefully shut and barricaded with furniture, leaving only one door open for egress or ingress.

Meantime, a half-witted idiot boy, who used to be always roaming about Budgepore, and being perfectly harmless was never ill-treated, and allowed to go and do pretty much as he liked, becoming violently excited at the noise the people were making outside the city, ran across some of the compounds (or court-yards) in the civil station, making the best of his way to the point of attraction, the place where all the noise and bustle and blowing of horns was going on. As he passed through one of the compounds he accidently came upon some loose charcoal cinders alight on the ground. They had either been thrown out of a pipe-bowl or had been let drop by some servant who had been taking some lighted charcoal for cooking purposes from one part of the premises to another. What possessed the boy it is impossible to say, but the idea seemed to seize him of doing mischief for the first time in his life. I suppose it was that he was in an extraordinary state of excitement owing to the noise and the effect it had upon his nerves. Anyhow, he took up some dry straw he found lying about, and applying the lighted charcoal to it, with his breath soon fanned it into flame, and then he deliberately set fire to the thatch of the bungalow. The brilliant blaze of light seemed to incite him to extend his experiment, and he went from house to house unnoticed and uninterrupted, and set fire to some half-dozen bungalows one after the other.

Meantime, Mr. Byewilwuffa had sent a mounted messenger to Colonel Moodle desiring him to call out his regiment at once and proceed to the focus of the insurrection and put it down. Colonel Moodle, on receipt of the requisition for military aid, wrote to the Adjutant directing him to call out the regiment immediately, and the Adjutant sent an order to the Sergeant-Major to sound the assembly and bring the men on parade. As soon as he could get his horse saddled and himself dressed, the Adjutant rode down to the parade, where, instead of finding the regiment turned out, he saw no one but the Sergeant-Major and the Havildar-Major (native Sergeant-Major) and the Pay Havildars, or Sergeants of Companies, who told him that the men objected altogether to turn out, as the weather looked threatening, and they thought it was going to rain. Whereupon the Adjutant went home, and wrote the following public letter to the Colonel:—

"Sir,—I have the honour to report that in pursuance of the instructions conveyed in your demi-official of to-day's date, I transmitted the necessary orders to the Sergeant-Major to turn out the men, and proceeded myself to parade immediately afterwards. On arriving there I found that the men objected to turn out, owing to the threatening appearance of the weather.

"I have the honour to be,

"Sir,

"Your most obedient Servant,

"JUNIUS STICKLEBAT,

"*Adjutant, 77th Native (Light) Infantry.*"

"*Budgepore, 7th July*, 18—.

On receipt of the letter, Colonel Moodle wrote to Mr. Byewilwuffa as follows:—

"SIR,—I have the honour to inform you that in accordance with the requisition contained in your demi-official of to-day's date, I issued the necessary orders at once for the regiment under my command to turn out, but I regret to find that owing to the threatening appearance of the weather, the men of the regiment under my command object to get under arms.

"I have directed a court of enquiry to sit to-morrow for the purpose of investigating the cause of this apparant dereliction of military duty, when the matter will be thoroughly sifted, and a report forwarded to Army Head Quarters through the usual channel.

"I have the honour to be,

"Sir,

"Your most obedient Servant,

"AUGUSTUS MAXIMILIAN MOODLE,

"*Commanding 77th N. Light Infantry.*

"*Budgepore, July 7th*, 18—.

"TO KIST BYEWILWUFFA, ESQ., C.S.,

"*Commissioner of Budgepore.*"

While these military operations were in progress, the state of mind of the inmates of Mr. Byewilwuffa's house may be more easily imagined than described. There were five ladies with their children there. Two of the husbands only of these ladies were present, the other three were out in the district, shooting. Those who happened to be present were the Judge and Collector, and these gentlemen were seated one in a neem tree and the other in a peepul tree in the compound of Mr. Byewilwuffa's house, double-barrelled rifle in hand, awaiting the approach of the insurgents. Each had five chuprassees who stood five under each tree. One chuprassee carried a cheroot-box, one an earthen jar containing water, one a tumbler, one a bottle of brandy, while the fifth looked on.

All this time Mr. Byewilwuffa was indefatigable in his exertions to calm the fears of the ladies, who gazed through the closed windows at the burning bungalows, and listened with beating hearts to the sound of the drums, horns, and voices of the insurgents, who, however, judging from the sounds, did not appear to be approaching nearer. Mr. Byewilwuffa attempted to allay their fears by assuring them that he had sent off early intimation of the state of affairs to Colonel Moodle, and that in a very short time the military would be on the spot, the insurrection trampled out, and order restored. What were his feelings when Colonel Moodle's letter was put into his hands! He had, however, scarcely time to realise the full effect of the communication, when his attention was attracted by piercing shrieks from the opposite side of the room, near the open door. He hastened to the spot, and found that the alarm had been occasioned by the approach of Mr. D'Rozario, the head writer in the Collector's office, armed with a brace of pistols, and accompanied by his wife and five children, who were making for the rendezvous.

All minor considerations were now resolved into the determination of the question as to whether Mr. D'Rozario, the head clerk in the Collector's office, should be admitted or not. Meanwhile the door was shut and bolted, while the question was being discussed. And it was at length resolved that, in consideration of his brace of pistols, Mr. D'Rozario should be admitted, but not his wife and children.

So the door was partially opened, and the result of the conclusion which the garrison had arrived at duly communicated to Mr. D'Rozario, who, much to the astonishment of the besieged, walked off, with his wife and five children following behind.

Meantime, however, the flames of the burning bungalows had caught the eye of Colonel Moodle, who ordered his charger and resolved upon immediate action.

THE HISTORY OF THE BARRACKS.

CHAPTER III.

THE BATTLE OF BUDGEPORE.

When Colonel Moodle reached the parade ground, he found the quarter-guard had turned out. On seeing the Colonel approach, the jemadar (native officer) formed his men in line at open order, and stood ready to present arms. After this ceremony he walked up to the Colonel, and lowering his sword in military salute said without drawing a breath,—

"Kotalgardmenekjemadardohavildarcharnaikbeessepahidonishanektumboorekchowkeedoboccusdohazarcharsowrupeeahospitalmenpainteessickmanoursubacha."

Which being interpreted signifies,—

"In the quarter-guard there are one jemadar, two havildars, four naiks, and twenty sepoys, two colours, one drum, one chair, two boxes, two thousand four hundred rupees, in the hospital thirty-five sick, and all is well."

While this announcement was being made, the sergeant-major came up, followed by a bugler who had been going about incessantly sounding the "alarm," and the "assembly," but without effect. At the command of the Colonel the bugler now sounded the "quick march," followed by "fix bayonets," and immediately some two or three hundred men appeared at the head of the lines advancing towards the parade ground. The sergeant-major and the pay sergeants then came forward and said, that "the whole regiment knew that the Colonel sahib was their father and mother, but there were in the quarter-guard a thousand rupees of half mounting (that is, belonging to the recruit's clothing fund), two hundred rupees of deserters' money, eight hundred belonging to the captains of companies, and four hundred belonging to the officers' mess and band funds; if the Colonel sahib would order the money to be distributed, there would be just three rupees to each man, the Colonel sahib was their father and mother, and he knew that the regiment was perfectly ready at that moment to follow him to England if necessary, but that if only the money was distributed the men would turn out with alacrity."

With the flames of thé burning cantonments casting a lurid light upon the heavens, the distant sounds of the insurrection in his ears, the British Indian Empire trembling in the balance, was that a time to shirk responsibility? No, he would be answerable for the money! So the order was given that the money should be distributed among his "children," and within a short hour afterwards the 77th Native (Light) Infantry were drawn up in column of companies right in front, and all ready accoutred with forty rounds of service ammunition in pouch, prepared to follow their Colonel to the cannon's mouth. So the Colonel gave the word "quick march," and to the inspiriting strains of the band, which played a march to the air of "Go where Glory waits Thee," with variations by Mr. DeSouza, the band-master, the 77th moved in column of companies across the military cantonment, and through the part of the settlement occupied by the civil residents towards the doomed city. On their way they halted for a few minutes while the Colonel detached Ensign Hughes with No. 7 Company to the Commissioner's house to protect the families of the residents.

On arriving there, Ensign Hughes was joyfully welcomed by the ladies and courteously received by the Judge and the Collector, who, from the branches of the trees where they had located themselves, directed their servants below to supply the officer with brandy-and-water and cheroots. Mr. Byewilwuffa then desired Ensign Hughes to detach a corporal's party for the protection of the Collector's cutcherry (an office were the clerks and others had taken refuge, to the number of a hundred and seventy souls, and where there were twenty lacs of treasure), and having mounted his horse and made over the civil charge to the Judge, and leaving Ensign Hughes in military command of the position, rode off to join the column under Colonel Moodle.

Ensign Hughes directed his men to pile arms, and lighting his cigar, seated himself on the compound wall.

By this time the moon had risen, and the light afforded by its rays was of great service to the troops in enabling them to wend their way among the gardens and through the lanes that formed the suburbs of the city. The insurgents, the moment they heard that the regiment was on its way, threw aside their drums, and horns and fire-arms, and ran away for several miles, when they hid themselves in the fields, leaving the city perfectly empty, and Colonel Moodle made good his approach right up to the end of the main street without the least opposition. There he halted and detached No. 5 and No. 6 Companies under Lieutenants Grimstone and Stokes, to advance in skirmishing order round the city on both flanks, availing themselves of whatever shelter might be afforded by the garden walls, the hedges and the cultivation. These officers were enjoined to proceed with caution, not to fire till they saw the enemy, and to sweep round the city one to the right and the other to the left, till they met at the opposite side, when the Colonel, who was about to charge through the main street, after carrying the position, would effect a junction with them.

As soon as these movements had been indicated, and the two skirmishing companies had started, Colonel Moodle marched the Grenadier or No. 1 Company, as it was more properly called, the corps being Light Infantry, up to the entrance of the main street. There, however, a difficulty presented itself. The company was in line, the street would only allow of men four abreast passing through it. So the Colonel halted the company a few moments to consider; the remaining six companies having been ordered to form up in close column and halt where they were till required.

With a view of effecting the necessary change of position to enable him to form four deep and so sweep the city, Colonel Moodle gave the word "No. 1, On your centre right about wheel!" The movement was effected with as much precision as if the regiment had been on parade instead of in the presence of an enemy, but when completed he found he was no nearer his object than before, the only difference being that he had now the company with their backs to the street instead of their faces. The Adjutant, seeing his commander's difficulty, suggested wheeling the company on its centre to the right. So the Colonel gave the word "No. 1, On your centre right wheel!'

This brought them up with their right flank upon the end of the street. "Right four deep!" said the Colonel triumphantly, and as the men formed in fours facing the street, he gave the word "Fire a volley and prepare to charge.—Charge!"

Now some of my readers may think that firing a volley with a whole company in "Fours," would be awkward for those in front. But this would show great ignorance. The Bengal army was quite equal to the crisis, as well as to many others, for on this as on other occasions it fired in the air.

With a deafening "Jye jye, Mahadeo!" the company charged up the street, sending the Colonel's charger with such force against the nearest house, as to cause the rider to fall against the door of a shop, which burst open and let the Colonel down gently upon a quantity of parched grain and sweetmeats put out for sale. He speedily recovered himself, however, and, remounting his charger, the floor of the shop being on a level with the saddle, kept up with the rear of his column.

The two companies who had started in skirmishing order as directed, obeyed to the letter the instructions given them, except as to not firing. The Bengal sepoy has a peculiar disposition to discharge his musket when skirmishing. In the isolated position he then holds, being separated from his comrades, he requires a little artificial aid to keep up his pluck, and it is just this aid which is imparted by the report of the musket. So, as was very natural, both the companies, as they made good their advance, kept firing, and as they fired in the air, and the volley of No. 1 Company had also been discharged in the same direction, it was not unnatural that the bullets should descend, and that a good many of them should come in contact with the heads and shoulders of some of the men in all three of the companies that were engaged, one in the centre of the city and the other two outside.

The fact of the balls striking them from above, making wounds, as the medical officer expressed it in his report, "from above downwards," naturally enough impressed the men with the idea that they were being fired upon from the upper stories and the roofs of the houses in the main street and the suburbs.

By the time No. 1 Company had completed its gallant charge, had cleared the city, and emerged in the open ground on the other side, where it halted for orders, Colonel Moodle had reached the front of the column. He found his men halted in "fours," breathless and excited. Firing was going on to the right and left of them, for by this time the two companies on their flank caught sight of the bayonets and musket barrels flashing in the moonbeams, and also became aware by other signs that they were in the neighbourhood of a body of armed men, so they advanced more cautiously but fired more rapidly. Colonel Moodle thus finding himself surrounded and his small party in imminent danger of being cut off, behaved with great presence of mind. He adopted the same manœuvre that Brigadier Colin Campbell, afterwards Lord Clyde, did at Chillianwalla, when he swept the Sikh position after the check our arms received upon that famous field. He first of all formed line from "fours," and then ordered the rear rank to "right about." He then gave the word "Front and rear ranks fire a volley, and file firing from right to left!" The firing was kept up until all the ammunition was expended, and then it ceased. Meantime the two skirmishing companies having expended their ammunition, also ceased firing.

Colonel Moodle finding now that all opposition had ended, thought it would be useless to attempt to follow up the enemy, because he had not the least idea in which direction they had retreated; he determined therefore upon returning to his lines, the object with which he had been called out having been satisfactorily accomplished. So he marched his men back again, taking the wounded with him, of whom there were a great many. Several severe contusions had occurred from the bullets striking the men in their descent, and, besides that, charging in the formation known as "fours deep" is not one of the movements down in "Torrens," the drill book at the time in vogue, and the 77th Native (Light) Infantry had never practised it. The consequence was that except the four men in the rear rank who were unhurt, there was not a single sepoy in the whole company who was not more or less injured by bayonet thrusts. Some of the wounds were very serious indeed, and a few actually proved fatal. But I need not enter more into detail upon this part of the subject.

Upon rejoining the main column, Colonel Moodle sounded the "assembly" and called in the two skirmishing companies, and prepared to march the regiment back to its lines. Another casualty had meantime occurred.

The Christian drummers, expecting a night of it, had brought out with them a good deal of liquor, and Mr. DeSouza, the band-master, having partaken too freely of it, unfortunately seated himself with considerable violence on the big drum, the parchment gave way, and Mr. DeSouza was precipitated into the drum, into which he fell in a very awkward position, for being a very stout man he was wedged in, his head and feet sticking out in a most helpless state. It was with much difficulty he was extricated, when, having sufficient sense to perceive the possible consequence of his intemperance, he made out that he had been struck on the head by a spent ball.

As soon as all arrangements for conveying the wounded were completed, the regiment marched back to their lines, the band playing, "See the Conquering Hero comes," with variations.

Mr. Byewilwuffa, who exposed himself almost recklessly the whole time to fire, riding about here and there with the view of procuring information, left the column as they passed through the civil lines and repaired to his house, where he found the inmates had made themselves comfortable for the night, and had gone to sleep. Ensign Hughes remained at his post, sitting on the compound wall, still smoking cigars. The Judge and Collector had both fallen asleep; the one in the neem, the other in the peepul tree; and the five chuprassees had followed their example, lying at full length upon the ground at the foot of the trees. The Judge's attendants were, however, rudely awakened by that gentleman in his sleep shifting his position, and so falling down, when he alighted upon the five chuprassees, who made a great deal out of the story afterwards, and spread the report that the "hazoor" had been struck by a spent ball, and might have hurt himself severely in his fall, had not his faithful slaves caught him in their arms.

The following is a copy of the despatch forwarded by Colonel Moodle, and contains the official, and therefore the correct account of the affair; although it will be seen that it differs in no material point from the account I have given, but enters of course less into detail.

I must explain, that the Budgepore command was at this time a sort of semi-independent command; that is to say,

Colonel Moodle, who commanded the station without having the rank of a brigadier, corresponded direct with the Major-General commanding the division.

"*Budgepore, July* 10*th*, 18—
No. 73674.

"From
"LIEUTENANT-COLONEL A. M. MOODLE,
"*Commanding 77th Native (Light) Infantry.*

"To
"CAPTAIN GRAMPION NORVAL,
"*Assistant Adjutant-General,*
"*Nursingpore Division.*

"SIR,

"1. I have the honour to report, for the information of Major-General Cradle, commanding the Nursingpore Division, that a dangerous insurrection having broken out in Budgepore on the 7th instant, Mr. Byewilwuffa, C.S., Commissioner and Governor-General's Agent, sent a requisition to me to proceed to the spot, with the 77th Native (Light) Infantry, under my command, and aid the civil authorities.

"2. Accordingly, I marched from the parade ground about 8 P.M. on the 7th instant, with 800 bayonets, 40 rounds per man in pouch, and 200 in reserve.

"3. The reserve ammunition did not follow the column, as directed, in consequence of the absence of the Commissariat Gomashtah in charge of the Government camels, who had gone to a wedding.

"4. I halted the column in the civil station for the purpose of detaching Ensign Hughes with No. 8 Company, 77th Native (Light) Infantry, to protect the civil residents, the Government records and treasure.

"5. I have the honour to record here my high sense of the very efficient manner in which Ensign Hughes conducted these operations. Owing to the judicious measures adopted by that officer the lives of the civil residents were protected, the Government records preserved, and two lacs of treasure saved to the State.

"6. After detaching Ensign Hughes upon this duty, I proceeded with the remainder of the 77th Native (Light) Infantry, now reduced to 720 bayonets, to the focus of the insurrection, the city of Budgepore.

"7. Upon the approach of the column, the enemy, who had previously taken up their position in the open plain near the city, whence they deputed bodies of men to fire and plunder the bungalows of the civil station, retreated, to take up a stronger and much more formidable position within the city itself.

"8. I would mention here, that throughout the whole of the operations that followed, I was accompanied by Mr. Kist Byewilwuffa, C.S., who, in spite of a heavy fire, was unceasing in his efforts to procure information.

"9. Having reason to believe that the enemy were now determined to oppose us with street-fighting,—the most difficult military operation to conduct effectually with native troops, owing to their high spirit and generally uncontrollable ardour in the field and when under fire,—I detached two companies, Nos. 5 and 6, under Lieutenants Grimstone and Stokes, to proceed on either flank of the city in skirmishing order, taking advantage of such shelter as might be afforded by the suburbs and the cultivation, with instructions to make good their advance and clear the ground of such bodies of the enemy as might be lurking behind the walls and in buildings, and cultivation round the city.

"10. Having seen this movement in progress, I formed up No. 1 Company under my own command; and after firing a well-directed volley at the roofs and upper storeys of the houses of the main street, charged through the street and swept it completely from end to end.

"11. After clearing the city, I halted on the opposite side in tolerably open ground, where for some time I was exposed to a pretty constant fire from both flanks. In imminent danger of being cut off if I allowed the enemy to gather strength from confidence and approach too close, I faced my rear rank to the rear, which thus became their front, and maintained a stead fire from right to left.

"12. This effectually quelled the enemy. He retreated with such rapidity as to prevent me from following him up, from my inability to discover the direction in which he had retreated.

"13. In spite of the rapidity of his retreat, the rebels carried away with them the whole of their killed and wounded, which, to judge from the nature of the fire that we kept up, must have been very numerous.

"14. Upon finding that the operations detailed above had completely succeeded in their object, I, with the concurrence of Mr. Kist Byewilwuffa, moved off the ground, which a single company of the 77th Native (Light) Infantry had so gallantly won and bravely held against overwhelming odds, and rejoined the main column, which, I forgot to remark, I had left drawn up in quarter-distance column, under command of Captain Chashma, about two hundred yards from the entrance to the city.

"15. I was here in due time rejoined by Lieutenants Grimstone and Stokes, with the men under their command. A report from these officers, detailing the operations conducted so efficiently and successfully by them, accompanies this letter.

"16. It is not to be expected that military operations requiring the dislodgment of an enemy well provided with arms and ammunition, from a post so strong as the walls and houses of a native city, could be conducted without some casualties. And I regret to add that my loss was severe. In No. 1 Company I had seventy-six men wounded; twenty-six severely, three or four I fear mortally, and the rest slightly. The precision of the fire, and the effective nature of the charge, is shown by the fact, that the only four men in this detachment who escaped altogether were the four men in the rear.

"17. Many of the wounds are severe bayonet thrusts, the others mostly contusions from spent balls.

"18. The enemy had no artillery.

"19. In Nos. 5 and 6 Companies, that were engaged in operations on the two flanks of the city, there were no casualties beyond a few severe contusions from spent balls.

"20. It is now my pleasing duty to bring to the notice of the Major-General those individual members of the force whose behaviour on the occasion was such as to call forth my warmest encomiums, and to suggest the hope that the Major-General will be good enough to bring their names to the favourable notice of His Excellency the Commander-in-Chief and the Government of India.

"21. My second in command, Captain Chashma, ably held the position entrusted to him with the main column. He was well supported by Lieutenant Higginbottom, and Ensign Scattersmalls, of whose conduct he speaks most favourably.

"22. The eminent services performed so efficiently by Ensign Hughes, whose gallantry and coolness is only equalled by the modesty with which he disclaims all merit for his services, I have already touched upon.

"23. Lieutenants Grimstone and Stokes deserve my warmest commendation, for the distinguished manner in which they carried out the difficult and arduous duties entrusted to them. The Major-General, being an officer of much experience, knows too well for me to enlarge upon it, the difficulty of dislodging an enemy strongly posted in the suburbs of a native city.

"24. Ensign Peajacket, who led No. 1 Company, under my immediate orders, behaved most gallantly. The manner in which, sword in hand, he headed the detachment through the street of Budgepore, exposed to a heavy galling fire, cannot be too highly spoken of.

"25. Subadars Pandy Tewary, Tewary Pandy, Chowbey Pandy, Pandy Chowbey, Tewary Pandy Chowbey, Chowbey Pandy Tewary, Ajoodia Tewary, Hunnooman Chuckemup Doorbijie Runamak, and Seetal Lickemup, behaved in a soldier-like and most exemplary manner. Cool under fire, they evinced that presence of mind which in a body of native officers is the sure prelude to success.

"26. Jemadars (here follow the names of ten jemadars, which I need not transcribe), were equally as worthy of commendation as their immediate superiors.

"27. It would be impossible for me by any words I could use, to do adequate justice to the gallant and steady conduct of havildars—(native sergeants) (here follow the names of forty havildars).

"28. Equally praiseworthy was the behaviour of the following non-commissioned officers (here follow the names of all the naikes or native corporals in the regiment).

"29. Quartermaster-Sergeant Grimes made the most efficient arrangements for the reception of the ammunition camels, which, however, did not arrive.

"30. To Sergeant-Major Russell I am deeply indebted, for the efficient manner in which, at the head of the convalescents, he remained in his bungalow, and held out the position at the same time that he protected the lines, the quarter-guard, the rear-guard, the bells of arms, and the hospital.

"31. For these services I trust I may be excused, if I venture to suggest that Sergeant-Major Russell might not be unaptly rewarded with a commission.

"32. Of the medical arrangements, it is impossible for me to speak too highly. Assistant-Surgeon Pickemup was at his post the whole time, having taken up an excellent position under cover of a wall, where he was ready to attend to the wounded and relieve their sufferings. As it was a sultry night, the Assistant-Surgeon had had the forethought to come provided with a stock of iced water, which, with the spirits he also had in readiness, was of the utmost service in relieving the thirst of the wounded men.

"33. The dooly bearers behaved in a manner that is quite beyond all praise. As there are only two and-a-half allowed by regulation to each dooly, and only one dooly (as we had not time, so sudden was the emergency that called us into the field, to get our service complement), considerable difficulty was experienced in making the necessary arrangements, which, nevertheless, the Assistant-Surgeon did succeed in making most effectually, for the accommodation of all the wounded.

"34. It may not, perhaps, be out of place, and I trust I shall not be considered overstepping the limits of my duty, if I bring to the notice of the Major-General, for subsequent reference to Government, should the Major-General consider my suggestions worthy of such reference, that the allowance by regulation of two and-a-half men to each dooly is occasionally productive of some inconvenience, especially when a regiment is called upon suddenly, as on the present occasion, to take the field.

"35. I have the honour to annex official returns of killed and wounded, and to be,

"Sir,

"Your most obedient servant,

"AUGUSTUS MAXIMILIAN MOODLE,

"*Commanding 77th Native (Light) Infantry.*

"Return of killed and wounded in the 77th Native (Light) Infantry, in the military operations at Budgepore:—

	Killed	0
Wounded	Mortally	4
	Severely	26
	Slightly	56

"*Miscellaneous*:—Band-master DeSouza knocked into the middle of the big drum."

"Enclosure.

"From No. 1

"LIEUTENANT GRIMSTONE,
"*Commanding No. 5 Company,*
"*77th Native (Light) Infantry.*

"To

"LIEUTENANT STICKLEBAT,
"*Adjutant 77th N. L. I.,*
"*Budgepore, July* 10, 18—

"SIR,

"I have the honour to report that in pursuance of verbal instructions from Lieutenant-Colonel Moodle, commanding the regiment, on the night of the 7th July, No. 5 Company under my command advanced in skirmishing order to the right of the city of Budgepore, with orders to sweep the right flank of the city and clear the suburbs.

"The difficult nature of the ground, consisting of brick walls, gardens, garden houses and occasional cultivation, rendered it necessary to proceed with the utmost caution. The enemy had a very strong position, and so effectually were they concealed under cover of the walls and the cultivation, that during the whole of the operations they effectually succeeded in screening themselves from view. The admirable behaviour, however, of the men of No. 5 Company under my command enables me to report a most successful accomplishment of the object intended to be effected by our advance. Making good our ground inch by inch we proceeded without a single check from the spot where we left the main column right round the right flank of the city in skirmishing order, firing as we advanced, till we reached the extremity of the city walls. Here, for some time, a very sharp fire was maintained.

"The enemy retreated so rapidly as to render hopeless any attempt to overtake them. They also succeeded in carrying away with them the whole of their killed and wounded, which, judging from the rapidity and precision of the fire kept up, must have been very great.

"I have the honour to bring to the notice of the officer commanding, the names of the following non-commissioned officers and men of No. 5 Company, who especially distinguished themselves upon this occasion. (Here follow the names of the havildars, naiks, and all the men of No. 5 Company.)

"I have the honour to annex an official return of the casualties in the company under my command.

"And to be,
"Sir,
"Your most obedient servant,
"SURPHUR GRIMSTONE, *Lieut.*,
"*Commanding No.* 5 *Company*, 77*th N. L. I.*"

Return of killed and wounded in No. 5 Company at the battle of Budgepore on the night of the 7th July, 18—

	Killed	0
Wounded	Mortally	0
	Severely	0
	Slightly	0
	Total	10

Lieutenant Stokes' despatch was the same as Lieutenant Grimstone's, *mutatis mutandis*, except that his return of casualties was a good deal more serious than that of No. 5 Company.

The result of this affair as concerns the officers and the regiment engaged were as follows:—

Lieutenant-Colonel Moodle was made a C.B., Captain Chashma obtained his brevet majority. All the native officers received the order of the Star of India—I mean the Order of British India, and the 77th Native (Light) Infantry were allowed to carry the name "Budgepore" upon their colours, and were to be known henceforward by the distinctive appellation of the "Governor-General's Own." While Sergeant-Major Russell was rewarded with an ensign's commission.

Now it so happened that the report of Mr. Byewilwuffa representing everything at Budgepore as *couleur de rose* was accidentally delayed in transit. It consequently reached the Court of Directors at the same time as the subsequent report detailing the military operations. You might, perhaps, run away with the notion that the Court of Directors would not be very well pleased at receiving on one and the same day two reports varying so materially as did the two official documents from Mr. Byewilwuffa. But the fact is the discrepancy proved the stepping-stone to Mr. Byewilwuffa's attainment of the Lieutenant-Governorship. For, argued the Directors, this officer has shown a marvellous degree of penetration, and a prudence which cannot be too highly commended, in that he has forwarded the official reports in so convenient a form, a form which enabled the Honourable Court to suppress altogether one set of despatches and to lay the other before the proprietors, the public, and the House of Commons. Whether the second report containing the account of the military operations, should be published or not, depended upon whether the morning papers next day contained any allusion to them. The *Times*, however, was silent. The fact is that an account of the battle of Budgepore had been sent to it and to the *Daily News*, but nothing having been previously known of the existence of any causes likely to eventuate in military operations, the *Times* thought it a hoax, and before publishing anything determined to make enquiries at the India House. The reply to these enquiries was that no account of any military operations had been received with the last Indian Mail. So the *Times* was silent, and the *Daily News*, which waited to see what the *Times* said, was silent too.

Mr. Byewilwuffa had thus, as it appeared, helped the Court out of a dilemma, and saved it from the disagreeable duty of announcing unpleasant news. Which conduct recommended itself so strongly to them that in their next despatch to India they directed that Mr. Byewilwuffa should be nominated to the Lieutenant-Governorship of the province on the first vacancy.

This was one result. The other result was the order to quarter for the future a European regiment at Budgepore, and so barracks were ordered and estimates called for.

THE HISTORY OF THE BARRACKS.

CHAPTER IV.

THE COMMITTEE PROCEED TO SELECT A SITE FOR BARRACKS.

I HAVE related in a previous chapter the circumstances that led to the location of a European regiment at Budgepore; that is to say, to the order for barracks to be erected. And as the first step, how estimates and plans were called for.

The reader, perhaps, may ask how it was that the preliminary step was taken so long before the design was carried out; for at least two years elapsed from the date of the occurrence related in the last chapter, to the period when the committee assembled to select a site for the barracks.

The fact is, the estimate had to go before the Military Board, and the Board being at that time occupied in a very important investigation, the estimates were laid aside till the more pressing business was completed.

It was the practice in those days, as I dare say many of my readers will recollect, for every regiment in the Company's army to send in twice a year, on the 1st May and 1st November, what was called a half-yearly return. This was a return of all the arms, accoutrements, ammunition, camp equipage, &c., attached to the regiment. There were eight columns in this return: three showing the articles with the regiment up to date of last half-yearly return, "serviceable," "repairable," and "unserviceable." Then there were two columns, "received and expended" during the past half year; and three more columns, showing what were then in store, "serviceable," "unserviceable," and "repairable." These returns were very carefully examined by the Assistant-Secretary to the Military

Board, who drew his pay and staff salary of about seven hundred a month besides. They were then examined by seven baboos, who in regular gradation as 1st assistant, 2nd assistant, and so on, aided the assistant-secretary in his duties. If any discrepancy in the figures was observed, it was pointed out to the assistant secretary, who brought it to the notice of the deputy-secretary, who reported it to the secretary, who laid it before the Board.

Now it chanced that the half-yearly return sent in from the 77th Regiment Native Light Infantry, the very same corps that so distinguished itself at the battle of Budgepore, as has been reported above in these Chronicles, two years before, had a discrepancy. Under the head, "Scabbard Bayonet Musket," present at the termination of the half-year preceding, there were 1,356. None were down as received or expended during the year; and in the column of articles in store at the date of the return there appeared 1,355. There was, therefore, one missing!

The matter was reported to the officer commanding the 77th N. L. I., who referred it to the Interpreter and Quartermaster, Lieutenant Jenkins; who replied that, in taking over charge from his predecessor, he had signed a receipt, certainly, for 1,356 bayonet scabbards, but in taking stock he had found there were actually only 1,355; so he had entered the exact number. As he was to blame for the slight inaccuracy, he was quite ready to re-imburse the Government the value of the article lost. A new bayonet scabbard was priced eight annas, or one shilling; as this was an old and unserviceable one, its probable value was about three annas, or fourpence-halfpenny.

This method of settling the matter, however, did not at all satisfy the Military Board; and after an enormous deal of official correspondence the whole case was sent up to the Commander-in-Chief. Sir Amethyst Jones at that time held the appointment. Sir Amethyst Jones consulted Lady Jones, Lady Jones consulted the Adjutant-General, and the Adjutant-General consulted the Judge Advocate General; and again the case was returned to the Military Board.

In the meantime one of the seven baboos in the secretary's office had discovered, in looking over some musty old records, that the number of bayonet scabbards, 1,356, was the number which was inserted in the half-yearly return of the regiment on the 1st November, 1806, and that on the 1st May, 1806, the number was 1,355. The discovery was duly laid before the Board, who directed the whole of the returns to be examined between that date and the present year. This involved a great deal of trouble, because many of the records were mislaid, and many missing; and the records in the offices of the Assistant and Deputy Quarter-master General all over the country had to be searched and ransacked. It was owing to this that the estimates and plans of the Budgepore barracks became forgotten; indeed, they were overlooked altogether.

I will now, in a few words, relate how it came to pass that the estimates and plans were recovered from the oblivion into which they had fallen.

You will recollect that I stated at the commencement of this Chronicle, that it was in the time of Mr. Kist Byewilwuffa that the barracks were built; that is, when this eminent official was Lieutenant-Governor. You will also recollect that it was when he was Commissioner of Budgepore, some years before, that the insurrection took place, which was followed by the battle of Budgepore, and that again was followed by the determination of Government, upon Mr. Byewilwuffa's report, to quarter a European corps at the station.

The overland mail one day brought the Hon. Kist Byewilwuffa a letter, which caused him at least five minutes' thought. It was from an old friend of his family, Lady Cecilia Toddleton, and ran thus:—

"MY DEAR MR. BYEWILWUFFA,

"My nephew, James Stuart, has been now five years in India. He is in the Engineers. In what part of India he may be, I have not the least idea, but I am told he went to Bengal some five years ago; and as he has not been back since, I presume he is there now. Ellen tells me he has not got on at all, having no one out there to give him a helping hand. If you can do anything for him, please do.

"I do not know enough about military affairs in India to suggest any particular line in which his interests may best be served. But if you could make the poor boy a general or a colonel, or something of that sort, I dare say it would be as much as he could look for.

"Clara and Adelaide were over here in the spring; they

have promised to come and see me at Christmas, and I hope Joe will spend part of his Christmas holidays at the hall.

"Believe me, yours sincerely,

"CECILIA."

Clara and Adelaide were Mrs. Byewilwuffa's two elder daughters. Lady Toddleton had a very pretty house and estate in Sussex, and a comfortable income of about ten thousand a year. Mr. Byewilwuffa, therefore, was very glad to keep on good and friendly terms with the kind old lady, who in their younger days, so it was said, had been a sort of flame of his. It was no small advantage to his girls to have the *entrée* of Lady Toddleton's house, were they not only enjoyed their visits very much, but met all the best county families.

I must here, at the risk of digressing unwarrantably, pause for an instant, to relate how it came to pass that Mr. Byewilwuffa had a son with such a plebeian name as Joe. I might as well relate the little incident here, otherwise I may forget it altogether. For, not only was Mr. Byewilwuffa's son named Joe, but Joe was his eldest son, and this is how he came to be called by that name.

Being on very intimate terms with Mr. Byewilwuffa, I was asked to stand proxy godfather when the infant Joe, the son and heir of the House of Byewilwuffa, was christened. The name was duly given to me beforehand, and it was to be Hastings Clive Prinsep. What could have made me forget myself I cannot tell. But my head was running on all sorts of nonsense during the time the service was being read, which was exceedingly wrong, I know; but sometimes you have not that power over your thoughts which you ought to exercise. And to tell the real, honest truth, I was in my mind quizzing my good friend Byewilwuffa a little, and thinking that such a complete, thorough-bred official as he was, ought to give his children appropriate Christian names. So, when the chaplain turned his head towards me, and said abruptly, "Name this child," I inadvertently replied, "Jo hukm"; a formula, meaning "As you order," in the mouth of every native whenever he receives anything in the shape of instructions from his European superior. Upon my saying this, Short, that was the chaplain's name, went on with the service "Jo hukm,"

&c., and Mr. Byewilwuffa's son and heir became "Jo Hukm Byewilwuffa."

Now you will, I knuch say at once that such a thing was totally impossible, because Mr. Byewilwuffa would have himself perceived the mistake in time to stop the chaplain. But, if you had ever heard Short read the service, you would not say so. Short was his name and short his nature. He was as thorough-bred an Indian chaplain as Mr. Byewilwuffa was in his way an official. I do not mean so much in respect of his social qualities, as his professional habits and capabilities. Socially speaking, he was a valuable member of society. He had a good seat on horseback; looked after the Budgepore pack, about which I may have something to say one of these days, was a capital hand at billiards and whist. If you might judge of the importance he attached to his clerical duties by the amount of time he spent over them, you might say he hardly gave them their due weight. He made a bet once in my hearing, that he would get through the morning service, sermon and all, in seventeen minutes and a-half, and the bet having been taken, he set the clerk to time him. I need hardly say he won. You required to "look alive," as they say, on going to church, when Short performed the service. He was a little man, and very rapid in his motions. He had a method of locomotion more like hopping than anything else. He hopped up the aisle into the reading-desk, gabbled away the preliminary exhortation, down on his knees, up again, jumped through the psalms, shot through the lessons, down on his knees again, away through the prayers with most irreverent haste, up again, out of the reading-desk, up into the pulpit, down again and back to the vestry, so that you really felt as if you could not draw a breath from the time you entered the church till you left it. So the fact was, that Short having got the name from me, rattled through the remainder of the service, and was at the end of it before Mr. Byewilwuffa, whose presence of mind totally deserted him, had time to realise the mistake, or the necessity of correcting it. Then, when all was over, with a reproachful look at me, he followed Short into the vestry. Not an instant scarcely, as it seemed to us, had elapsed, since Short had completed the service and retired, and we had rejoined him in the vestry; yet, in that short space of time, he had half-divested himself of his surplice, and was lighting a cheroot, the clerk holding a lighted coal in a small tongs, the church-bearer standing behind with Mr. Short's cheroot box. Mr. Byewilwuffa remonstrated, but in vain. He insisted that the intended Christian name of his son should be inserted in the register, but Mr. Short wouldn't hear of it. And the aggrieved father was forced to content himself with the reflection that the initials J. H. would look like Joseph Henry; and for the rest, if his son went through life by the name of "Joe," it would always be supposed that it was the usual abbreviation for Joseph.

But to return. The Lieutenant-Governor had Lady Cecilia's letter in his hand, and was still cogitating upon the contents, when Mr. Khas Mouza, the Secretary, came in with some papers for signature. After they were signed, Mr. Byewilwuffa asked his Secretary if there was any vacancy in the Public Works Department in any situation which might be appropriately filled by an Engineer officer of about five years' standing. Mr. Khas Mouza couldn't recollect, but intimated that if his Honour wanted to oblige any of his friends, it would not be difficult to recommend the institution of some public work. It was very desirable, he thought, that another canal should be undertaken, from the Ram Jumna into the Budgepore district. I say "another," because one had already been executed; but as in its construction it seemed to have been designed for taking water up hill, it had not succeeded so well as might have been expected. Mr. Byewilwuffa thought the Supreme Government would hardly sanction another canal, at any rate till the bed of the old one had got filled up somehow. Mr. Khas Mouza then suggested a branch from the Grand Trunk Road. Mr. Byewilwuffa enquired where the branch was to run to, but Mr. Khas Mouza thought that was a secondary consideration altogether, and that it might be led round the neighbouring villages over an area of a few thousand square miles, so as to develop the resources of the district. Mr. Byewilwuffa, however, said he was not prepared to recommend that, as no progress having as yet been made with the Grand Trunk Road at all in the province, it might look premature to commence upon the branches. Mr. Khas Mouza then suggested the erection of a masonry pier and landing-place at Gurmuckteser, with wharves and steps for men to go down to the water, and a covered way for women; for, as the Secretary suggested, it was very desirable to prevent indiscriminate bathing by both sexes at one spot. After some discussion, Mr. Byewilwuffa rejected this proposition, on account of the large outlay that would be required. Mr. Khas Mouza then suggested a new church at Budgepore. To this also the Lieutenant-Governor had some objection, "but," said he, "this allusion to Budgepore reminds me that some years ago barracks for a European regiment at Budgepore were sanctioned and estimates called for; what became of those estimates, Mouza, and why where the works never commenced?"

Mr. Khas Mouza said he didn't know, but would see if there was any record in the office that would give the required information.

The result of this conversation was, that after about three months' correspondence the estimates were disentombed from some crowded shelf where the records of the Military Board were kept, and in due time the necessary orders were issued for the construction of the barracks, Lieutenant James Stuart being appointed by Government to supervise the works.

Stuart's senior officers gnashed their teeth at so good an appointment being thrown away upon so young a man, but they did not wonder at it, for his connection with Lady Cecilia Toddleton was well known in the regiment.

The next step was the selection of a site for the barracks. And for this a committee was appointed—the members of which were the Superintending Surgeon of the Budgepore division, Dr. Tincture, the Brigadier, whose name was Haversack, and the senior Engineer officer on the spot, Major Wrangler of the Engineers, the Commissioner of Budgepore being requested to attend. The committee was exceedingly well selected for the purpose. None of the members, except Major Wrangler, had ever had anything more to do with European troops than just seeing them on parade or in barracks. Brigadier Haversack had been thirty-eight years with a native regiment, and only recently promoted, and there were no European troops at all under his command. Dr. Tincture was a little aged. He had been an able man in his time, and had written two or three works to prove that malaria was generated by vegetation. This was his favourite theory, and one that he carried out in practice as far as he could. He had all the trees, shrubs, flowers and plants of every kind rooted up from his garden, and the grass and weeds that made their appearance occasionally on the surface, regularly scraped away directly they showed their faces above ground. During the rainy season I have seen as many as thirty men at a time in his compound, all engaged in waging war with nature and repressing its rather energetic efforts to clothe the ground with verdure.

If he had been allowed he would, of course, have carried out this principle in the cantonment also, but this was put a stop to by the Brigadier, who had a contrary opinion, and thought the growth of trees and vegetation most beneficial. Of late years Dr. Tincture had become rather crotchety. He was getting old, and ought to have been invalided or pensioned. One of his quaint conceptions that every now and then seized upon his mind was, that he was a heap of grain. And when under the influence of this peculiar delusion, it was sometimes painful, at the same time ludicrous, to witness the state of alarm into which he was thrown if a horse, or a cow, sheep or goat approached him.

Major Wrangler had a most hearty contempt, as you may suppose, for his coadjutors. He was a thoroughly scientific man, devoted to his profession, in the prime of youth and vigour, and looked with some disdain, as I am sorry to say that young men sometimes are prone to do, upon the infirmities of old age and those labouring under them. Conjoined with this disdain for age was a somewhat similar feeling for everyone who did not belong to the Engineers. The feeling was, you will allow, very foolish in both cases, because in the first it is folly for us to despise that which most likely will one day be ours, and which, if it is not, we shall wish most heartily it might be. We must either grow old, or die before we grow old. And in the latter case we should certainly prefer the other alternative. To despise old age, therefore, is foolish, if no harsher term can be applied to it. I speak feelingly on this point, being an old man myself, and having occasion sometimes to think that if the present generation of young men were a little more mindful of the principle "seniores priores," than they are, it might be better. But let that pass. I will not moralise, my business is to tell stories.

As to the other of Major Wrangler's notions, his contempt for men who did not belong to the Engineers, this was equally silly, for what would become of the world if everybody was an Engineer? Why, it would be scooped inside out, and there would be no place left to live in.

The first morning the committee met they resolved, *nemine contradicente*, that the best plan would be for each member to make an expedition by himself, riding or driving or walking, just as he might fancy, and take a look at the ground. They might then meet and compare notes, and any particular spot that appeared eligible to any two of them, might then be visited by the committee collectively. So they all set out, Major Wrangler going across country on horseback, Brigadier Haversack in a buggy, and Dr. Tincture in a palanquin.

Two of the members of the committee were, however, destined to meet without appointment. For as Major Wrangler was returning home after scouring the country in all directions for about fifteen miles, he espied what at a distance looked like a buggy hood standing upon the ground. On reaching the spot he found it was, indeed, a buggy that had sunk in soft earth up to the axles and a little over, the horse, of course, being proportionately enveloped also, that is to say, being stuck fast up to his hips.

As Major Wrangler rode up, the groom, who was standing up inside the buggy, leaning against the splashboard, made signs to him to beware of something and to advance cautiously. So he called out, "What's the matter?"

"Who's that?" said Brigadier Haversack, thrusting his head out through the opening in the hood behind. "Oh, is that you, Wrangler? Ride back to cantonments, that's a good fellow, as hard as you can, and get some assistance. Desire Cameltrunk to send out an elephant and ropes with the least possible delay. I have got stuck fast here. And I'm afraid the buggy is momentarily sinking further."

"But how on earth did you get there, Brigadier? There is no road here."

"Road! of course there's no road. If we confine ourselves to beaten tracks, how shall we ever do our duty properly? I came here in accordance with our resolution to look for a site for the barracks. I thought this plot of ground would do admirably, and was driving across it, when all of a sudden

I got into this slough of despond; and here I am, you see. Make haste, there's a good fellow; send the elephant."

"And was this the place you selected for a site for a barracks?"

But Major Wrangler did not wait for a reply, he had recognised the spot and understood the state of affairs, and felt really anxious to get assistance as speedily as possible.

The Brigadier's position was a great deal more awkward than he himself believed.

The plot of ground he had approved was a spot which had been selected a year or two before by a committee of civilians for a grand "sanitary" experiment. Mr. Byewilwuffa had directed three of the commissioners of districts to meet together and consult as to the best method of disposing of the filth and refuse of jails and large cities; and they had unanimously resolved to try the plan of digging an enormous pit in the ground, some miles outside the city of Budgepore, as an experiment, and there depositing the matter which it was deemed desirable to get rid of. The pit, after being filled, had been covered over with a layer of earth; and it was thus, in this eligible site for barracks, that the Brigadier had met with this mishap.

The circumference of the pit was about sixty yards, and its depth twenty feet. The treacherous soil had borne the superincumbent weight of the buggy for a yard or two, and then had given way all round. The horse floundered dreadfully; the Brigadier whipped him on, and he managed to extricate himself and the buggy by struggling on to a portion of the soil which happened to be a little firmer than the rest. And there they were upon an island, as it were, in the centre of a bog or slough, which, however, gave uncomfortable premonitory symptoms of breaking up; and already the horse's legs and half the wheels had become imbedded.

Major Wrangler thought he perceived symptoms of the earth altogether giving way; in which case nothing could have saved the Brigadier, the syce and the horse, from destruction.

Such a fate was too horrible to contemplate; so, although his contempt for the Brigadier was so great that he really thought it would be no loss to the world if he were totally submerged, yet better feelings overcame him; and, setting spurs to his horse, he never drew rein till he reached Captain Cameltrunk's door.

Captain Cameltrunk was, you recollect, the Executive Commissariat officer of Budgepore; and when Major Wrangler arrived he was in the bath—a large swimming bath in the compound in which Captain Cameltrunk and his friends disported themselves in the morning and evening during the warm weather. It was a good-sized bath, being fifty feet long and twenty-five wide, and seven feet deep. It was kept filled from a well close by, the water being drawn up by Government, otherwise called commissariat, bullocks, which, by regular exercise thus afforded them, were kept in good health. When Major Wrangler mounted the steps and entered the bath room, he had some difficulty in distinguishing his friend Cameltrunk from among forty other individuals, all in the same costume exactly, that is to say—well, all in their bathing costume, which was very simple and unpretending, and remarkably uniform. Of the forty individuals in the water, at least twenty were poised upon mussucks, or inflated sheep-skins, in which water is carried in the East, and which, when filled with air and put in on all fours upon the water, float upon the surface, so that bathers can sit astride upon them and paddle themselves abcut as if they were riding on horseback.

This is a very favourite amusement with Anglo-Indians; and various are the sports, feats of skill in horsemanship, if I may use the word, to which the use of this innocent method of recreation gives rise. Wrangler, after a while, discovered Cameltrunk; but it was no wonder he had a little difficulty in finding him out amid such a crowd, for he was floating on his back, with a lighted cigar in his mouth, his legs extended at right angles, straight up in the air, and balancing on the upturned soles of his feet a "mussuck," or inflated sheep-skin, with a little native boy seated on the top. This peculiar attitude he had assumed by reason of a wager laid by a brother officer, that he would maintain that position a certain time. At Wrangler's call, however, and on hearing that some business of importance required his immediate attention, he surrendered the mussuck and the little boy to his neighbour, who took them upon his back, and swam to the side of the bath.

"What is it, old fellow?"

"The Brigadier is in a deuce of a mess; I don't know how the devil to get him out of it. I want you to let me have an elephant and some ropes, directly."

He then proceeded to describe the position in which he had left the Brigadier. Cameltrunk, meantime, had scrambled up the side of the bath, and was drying himself with a towel, making that peculiar noise, half hissing, half whistling, that all ostlers do when they are cleaning horses, and some other men when they are cleaning themselves. Cameltrunk was rapid in his movements, and by the time Wrangler had finished his story was already half dressed.

"I'd send the elephant with pleasure," said he; "but I don't see how it's to be done. Who's to sign the indent?"

"Sign the indent; why you don't mean to say, that when the Brigadier is in danger of losing his life by a fate too horrible to think of, you stickle about an indent!"

"I can't help it, Wrangler. I'm very sorry for the Brigadier, but I couldn't let the elephant go without having the indent signed, and it must be signed by the officer commanding the station."

"Can't the second in command sign it? Colonel Sungeen, won't his signature do?"

"Why, man, you know as well as I do that it won't do," said Cameltrunk, irritated by his friend's ignorance of standing orders—"of course it won't do; Brigadier Haversack commands the station."

"He won't command it much longer. Well, look here, you order the elephant down sharp and a coil of ropes. I'll get the indent drawn out meanwhile, and we'll make the Brigadier sign it before he's pulled out. Will that do?"

"Well, I suppose, under the circumstances, I should be justified in reading the regulations so as to admit of that arrangement; but we cannot supply our ropes, you must get them from the barrack-master's yard."

"Oh, all right, that will be very easily done," said Wrangler, intimating that in the Engineer's department there were no fetters put upon the discharge of obvious duties by a punctilious adherence to silly regulations.

So leaving Cameltrunk, who by this time was dressed, and

was already surrounded by a crowd of nude inquirants asking while they dried themselves what the deuce was up, Wrangler hastened off to the Brigade-Major's office to tell the baboo to make out an emergent indent in duplicate for an elephant "on command"—thus it was expressed by the rules of the service—and then rode down to the barrack-master's yard, which was in his own department, but not presided over immediately by him, but by an officer junior to him.

Here he found Sergeant Stack, the Barrack-Master-Sergeant, a good, trustworthy non-commissioned officer, who had been in the department for eleven years and had sole charge of everything. His pay was 120 rupees or £12 a month, and he was so thrifty that he had *saved* enough to build himself one of the best houses in the place, where he lived in state and style quite equal to that of the Brigadier himself.

Here he got a coil of good strong rope which had been sent from England for the church bells. This was sent up to his house. As soon as the necessary arrangements were complete, he got into his buggy, and taking with him the ropes and a couple of very long bamboos, drove to Cameltrunk's house to pick up that officer, who also got into the buggy with the indent, a portable inkstand and pen, and the two drove off together; the elephant had preceded them, having been sent off at once with orders to the mahout or driver to make all possible speed to the place where the Brigadier was imbedded.

When they got there, what was Wrangler's horror to see no trace any longer of the Brigadier's buggy and horse, or of the syce, or the Brigadier himself.

"Good heavens!" he exclaimed, "how shocking; we are too late!"

"Who on earth will sign the indent!" was Cameltrunk's remark.

But Wrangler did not hear it. He had leapt out of the buggy, and beckoning to a labourer, whom he recollected having seen near the spot before, to come up, he advanced to the edge of the morass or pit and began sounding with one of the long bamboo poles. His object, of course, was to find out where the buggy had sunk, so as to get out the vehicle and recover the bodies of the unfortunate Brigadier and his servant. But without avail. He toiled and toiled till the perspiration (for the sun was fiercely hot) streamed down his face, but no trace of the lost ones could be discovered.

It may be as well to state here in a few words what had befallen the Brigadier.

About three minutes after Major Wrangler had ridden away, a zemindar of the neighbourhood, who was called Raja Tukht Sing, came by, with one or two followers, on an elephant. Seeing the buggy imbedded in the morass, he immediately called to the labourer who was in a field close by, and told him to go to the next village and get a rope. The rope was brought, and after about half-an-hour's labour the buggy and its occupants were extricated, and the horse none the worse for the mishap, except being a good deal bespattered and bedaubed with mud, &c. The Brigadier tendered his hearty thanks for the timely aid thus afforded him, and drove home.

Major Wrangler, at last, being worn out and in despair, sat himself down, and, turning to the labourer (Cameltrunk having remained in the buggy all the while an inactive spectator of the scene), asked him to point out the exact spot to which their researches should be directed. The man indicated the place which was precisely where Major Wrangler supposed it to be. He then put the question—

"When did the buggy sink?"

"It did not sink," replied the man; "it is gone away."

"Gone!" said Wrangler, leaping to his feet. "Gone! and why didn't you tell me before?"

Whereupon he took to cuffing the labourer most unmercifully about his head and ears. After giving vent to his feelings in this manner, he rejoined Cameltrunk and told him it was all right, the Brigadier had gone home.

Cameltrunk looked hard at his friend—hard and anxiously. He was afraid he was suffering from aberration of intellect. He had come to him in a most excited state that morning, and told him a most improbable story, which was utterly uncorroborated by circumstances: he had asked him to "issue" an elephant without an indent, and had ended by beating a labourer who had been patiently rendering him all the assistance in his power.

"Hadn't you better let me drive home?" said Cameltrunk, taking the reins as Wrangler got into the buggy. Wrangler seated himself in silence, and allowed his companion to drive him back to cantonments.

Meantime, for it was now mid-day, the labourer also went home. His dwelling was a hut, built of mud, and about twelve feet square, plastered inside with mud mixed with cow-dung, and containing for furniture an old clumsy cot and an earthen pot for water. His wife was squatting on the ground near a few embers preparing the homely dinner, which consisted of a few cakes made of meal; these she was patting in her hands over the fire. Two small children, perfectly naked, and covered with flies, lay on their stomachs on the floor beside her. That was the labourer's domestic circle, and the description of his home will pass for a description of the home of many tens of millions of the peasantry of India, who, as is well known, are so exceedingly well off under British rule. The head of the family and master of the house, sat down on the ground in the doorway, and his wife put a pipe into his hands in silence. He took a whiff or two, and then his conversational powers being developed, he told his wife all that had happened that morning, and ended by asking her "And, now, why did the sahib beat me?"

He had been revolving that question in his mind ever since.

"The sahibs always beat everyone," said the wife, still patting the cakes—first on one hand, then on the other.

"You speak like an ignorant woman," said the man. "It is not so. I say, why did the sahib beat me?"

"If I am an ignorant woman, why do you ask me," said the wife, offended.

The labourer, who was a philosopher in his way, saw the force of that remark, and was silent. At last he said, muttering to himself, "One sahib gets into the slough, Raja Tukht Sing comes by and sends me to get ropes. I get ropes, and the sahib is taken out. Then the other sahib comes and looks for the first sahib, and when he does not find him he beats me; he is angry because I helped to get the first sahib out."

That was the only conclusion the labourer could arrive at. He was a philosopher, you see; and being aware that effects must have a cause, he endeavoured, in his simple and untutored mind, to trace the connection.

Meantime Cameltrunk and Wrangler drove back in silence, being lost in thought. Cameltrunk, however, was the first to break the silence; and, as he got down, he said:

"Deuced unlucky; who *is* to sign the indent?"

You see he was a philosopher as well as the labourer: which was the greater philosopher of the two, I leave you to judge.

So Wrangler drove on to the Brigadier's, where he found him at breakfast, and had the pleasure of congratulating him on his escape.

THE HISTORY OF THE BARRACKS.

CHAPTER V.

INTRODUCES THE READER TO A NATIVE OFFICIAL.

THE mishap which befel one of the members of the committee appointed to select a site for the barracks at Budgepore, as related in the last chapter, did not in any wise damp the ardour of the other members of the committee, or prevent them from doing their duty. There were, in fact, only two sites in the neighbourhood at all suited for the purpose. One was a plateau of high ground, well drained, and well raised above the level of the surrounding country, to the north of the city. The other was a piece of waste land, that is, common land, to the south of the city, which was of a much lower elevation, and consequently during the rainy season very much in the condition of a marsh.

Dr. Tincture and Major Wrangler preferred the northern site: the latter, on account of its elevation and drainage; the former, because it was a bare waste with only one tree upon it. The other members of the committee preferred the lower site, on account of the vegetation, but being outvoted, the committee was directed formally to assemble at the spot selected by Dr. Tincture and Major Wrangler; and Mr. Wasilbakee, the Commissioner, was requested to attend.

I have said there was only one tree on the spot. That tree was a large peepul, that threw its ample and refreshing shade over a hut, and a pretty shrine, the one inhabited, and the other tended by a Hindoo fakir of great repute in the neighbourhood for sanctity. The hut was a small shanty, with mud walls and a roof of thatch. The shrine consisted of a small heap of stones, built up in the shape of something of a Jewish altar, upon which stood the sacred symbol of the most debased feature of worship in the degenerate Pooranic religion of the Hindoos, called the "lingam."

The whole was surrounded by an enclosure, a thorny hedge about two feet high. The tree grew in the centre, and at the foot of it was a deep well of masonry, down which if you looked you might see at a little distance the roots of the peepul, every now and then appearing from between the stones that lined the sides of the well; many of them had been loosened; some had been displaced altogether, and had fallen down. The water was sweet, and the fakir drove rather a thriving trade by selling the water, a brass lotah full at a time, to travellers and wayfarers, who stopped to rest under the grateful shade of the spreading boughs of the old peepul during the heat of the day. But besides this source of income, the old fakir was constantly resorted to by the city people and others of both sexes, who made him their confidant, and entrusted to his safe keeping many family secrets which were told in confidence, under the seal of confession, as it were, by those who wished to consult him on some affair of importance.

Women particularly resorted to him for advice, when suffering from the curse of barrenness, and many a childless parent had become the possessor of a full quiver, from, it is said, the prayers of the old fakir, and the blessings that followed upon a devout adoration of the small piece of stone that formed the object of attraction to so many devotees.

It so happened, that on the morning when the committee went to inspect the proposed site for the barracks, Shekh Futtoo had mounted his cob and ambled down to the hut to consult the fakir. A wonderful cob was that. Its body was white, it had red eyes and a pink tail, and its legs below the knees were green. The English reader may feel inclined to be sceptical, and to scout the idea of a horse having a coat of so many different colours as the skin of a chameleon. I can only say that as India is a country of marvels, so have I often seen horses of all colours, white, red, blue, green, and pink and yellow. It is not at all uncommon. How they become so is another matter altogether, the investigation of which belongs to a natural philosopher or physiologist, not to me.

Nor need the reader quarrel with me because I have related that a Mahomedan gentleman went to consult a Hindoo fakir, for so renowned for sanctity was this fakir, that Mahomedans very frequently resorted to him for advice, although of course they held in righteous abomination the idolatrous symbol that had such charms for the Hindoos.

Shekh Futtoo was in great trouble. Troubles will befal the most prosperous; and, although the Shekh's cup of prosperity was very well filled, and had been so for many years, yet of late he had been very heavy at heart, and felt as if evil fate had already marked him out as a victim for her malignity. And the Shekh's cause of trouble was this, that for the first time in twenty years he had failed to twist round his fingers the master whom he had throughout that time nominally served, but in reality ruled. Was he about to shake himself free from the trammels? Was he about to break the web that had wound so skilfully round and round him that he could move neither hand nor foot? Forbid it, fate! For the Shekh well knew that the day he fell from his post would be an evil day for him. Twenty years he had grown fat and wealthy upon corruption and bribery. For twenty years he had kept the avenues to his employer's ears and eyes. For Mr. Wasilbakee, the Commissioner of Budgepore, had been twenty years in India. As a writer in Writers' Buildings, he had engaged the Shekh as a moonshi. When he became an assistant, he had put him in the office, in a subordinate position at first, but soon managed to get him promoted. As a joint-magistrate and a collector, he had employed him as his factotum in different capacities, and finally, as Commissioner of Budgepore, he found the Shekh as useful, intelligent, honest, and faithful a servant of Government, as serishtadar, as he had ever been in the other capacities in which he had served. When he became Commissioner, he brought the eminent services of his dependant to the notice of Government, and begged that he might be rewarded with a title, and the Governor-General had consented, and at a durbar held at Agra in 185—, the Honourable Mr. Byewilwuffa conferred on the fortunate recipient the honorary title of Sirdar Bahadoor.

When luck first threw the Shekh in the path of Mr. Wasilbakee, he was a poor man, an adventurer, seeking his fortune in the Presidency. He was now a wealthy man. I don't suppose he could have counted up all his wealth had he tried. He had purchased land and villages in almost all the districts of the province. He had two lacs of rupees in Government paper. He had horses and carriages, and well-built houses in Agra, Delhi, Meerut, and half the great cities in those provinces. All his family were well provided for, one of his sons was a "talookdar," another was a serishtadar in the Sudder Court, and his brother was the confidential moonshi of Mr. Khas Mouza, the Secretary to Government. But the Shekh had not been unmindful of the claims of more distant relatives. His uncle and nephews, his cousins, were all in Government employ, in one capacity or another, and I need hardly add that he was held in much esteem by the natives. You need not suppose for a moment that Mr. Wasilbakee had any idea that his friend and confidant was so wealthy and influential as he was. Had he known it, seeing that when he entered his employ he was a poor man, glad to take service for twenty rupees a month, he might have pondered over the strange metamorphosis, and his reflections might have led to some inquiry as to how the man amassed such enormous wealth. But Mr. Wasilbakee had no more idea that Shekh Futtoo Sirdar Bahadoor was a wealthy man, than you had before I told you. Men of Mr. Wasilbakee's mental calibre seldom do know anything at all, except what it suits their factotums to let them know, and what comes to them through "the usual channel." Had they known more about the people, we might have been saved some trouble and expense in 1857.

Now that I have told you of this, you will understand why Shekh Futtoo was so much disturbed and alarmed at the otherwise apparently unimportant fact, that for the first time for twenty years Mr. Wasilbakee had proved unmanageable. Divers ways of management had Shekh Futtoo; divers were the arts he employed to gain his ends. You must not suppose that he ever officiously volunteered his advice when unasked, that he ever presumed to differ outright with his employer, much less that he ever ventured to disobey him. No, the Shekh was far too clever to go to work in any such clumsy method, nor did he ever interfere in any matter beyond his province. But enough matter was there within his legitimate province to occupy his attention, and prove a source of ample revenue. If opportunity was slow in coming, he waited, and it always came. A word, a gentle hint, that he was aware of the secret springs of action in such and such a case, that he could give explanation if asked for, that he had sources of information which he could develop, and he was sure to be applied to.

Not once during the twenty years did Mr. Wasilbakee ever for a moment dream that the Shekh was anything but the pink of honesty. To him, he was a faithful servant, an honest, upright, zealous, indefatigable assistant, and I do not exaggerate in the least when I say that Mr. Wasilbakee would rather have taken the Shekh's opinion upon any matter of law, revenue, and executive duties than that of any other living person. He came at last to consult him on every occasion, to refer to him on every point, to discuss with him every matter that came before him in his official duties. Most unconsciously, he always followed his advice. Once, only, during all that time had he differed from him, and that was what caused the Shekh so much uneasiness, that he determined to consult the Hindoo fakir.

But the reader ignorant of India will be at a loss to understand why the mere fact of Mr. Wasilbakee for once proving unmanageable in the hands of the Shekh Futtoo, upon a matter of such trifling importance that I have not thought it necessary to break the thread of my story to relate it here, why should that have given the good man so much anxiety? It was because the Shekh knew what would happen if he fell into disfavour. If it was once mooted abroad that Shekh Futtoo had been frowned upon by the "great sahib," there was the greatest probability that someone out of the many thousands of those upon whom he had been forced to trample in his career to greatness might raise his head from the dust, and tell the story of his wrongs. While in favour with Mr. Wasilbakee, the brittle fabric of his fair fame and good fortune untouched, no one dared to throw the first stone. There was hardly a central jail in the whole province that did not contain five or six wretched victims of the Shekh's scheming, men whom it was necessary for him to destroy, to crush, in order to secure some prize that he coveted, men who had paid him handsomely in former days for some service he promised to render, suitors probably in some case before his employer, whose cause he promised to win for them. The bribe had been paid, and either because the opposite party had bribed higher, or the cause was not to be won, the disappointed suitor deprived of what he thought his right, and robbed of the money he had paid in bribery, had in an evil moment threatened, unless the money was returned, to disclose the fact to the "sahib." In an instant tbe Shekh resolved on action. The next day the discontented client would be in the hands of the police, charged with some criminal offence, tortured till he confessed, and then consigned to jail, from which the head jailor had been well fee'd never to let him pass out alive.

There was not a record in the revenue office of Budgepore that had not been tampered with, provided that it was of such a nature that any tampering with it could benefit anyone who was willing to pay handsomely for that benefit. All this was not accomplished without much risk. Jailors, police, witnesses, chuprassees, all recipients of bribes, were so many trains laid to which the match might at any moment be applied. Two, at least, of the native subordinates of the Commissioner's court were cognizant of the fact of the records of the office being tampered with. Widows whose husbands, orphans whose parents had been put to death by the slow torture of "jail discipline" for the sake of removing a witness, or silencing a complaint, might at any time have poured the tale of woe, oppression and crime into the ear of some European official who would have seen justice done. So you would suppose, reader, if you had never lived in India, never taken the pains to look below the surface, where corruption, and infamy and crime lurk beneath the fair exterior presented to your view. But in reality the truth was this. Not one of these people, who might have revealed the true state of things, dare utter a word, for to breathe a word against the Shekh was almost certain death to the man bold enough to utter it; and not only death, but death in its most revolting form, and disgrace and ruin to his family.

So have you seen the monarch of the Bengal jungle, the lordly tiger, walking proudly in his domain. At his approach the herd of jackals skulk away into the depths of the forest, and hide themselves lest the eye of the tyrant should flash upon them and mark them out for his prey. No one of that countless host of meaner beasts that haunt the wide domains which the bounteous hand of nature has granted to them all in common, dare even to show its face in the tiger's path. But, one day, the rifle of the hunter wounds the lordly beast. He retires to his fastness to die, to die alone in his majesty, that his craven-hearted subjects shall not see him whom they feared, at whose approach they trembled, lying humbled, weak and powerless. His limbs almost refuse to carry him, but he has reached his lair, and there, weak and exhausted, he lays him down to die alone. But, hark! the scent of the hungry jackal has found him out, the shrill, prolonged yell echoes through the jungle and calls together the skulking confederates by tens and twenties. Then first one, and then the other approach the majestic form of the wounded monarch of the forest. Unable to resist, he sees the creatures gather round him whom his very look would ere while have scared, and he is torn to pieces while his mangled limbs quiver with vitality in the very jaws of the devourers. Shekh Futtoo Sirdar Bahadoor, well knew that his word was law. But he knew that if once only the meanest part of the glittering fabric he had built up for himself was to be assailed, the birds would gather from the four winds of heaven to feast on his living carcass. So he was careworn and anxious, and went to consult the fakir.

He knew all this without reading history, but if he had read it, he would have learnt some lessons which would have taught him that his fears were not unfounded.

While the committee were discussing the advantages of the proposed site, the Shekh was consulting his adviser. The coloured cob was tied up to the trunk of the peepul tree, and neither of the European officers on the ground observed it. But the astute Mussulman observed them, and having of course heard of the project of erecting European barracks at Budgepore, he at once guessed what the officers were about, and communicated the result of his observations to his companion. The latter naturally was not very well pleased at the idea of barracks for European soldiers being erected so near his abode, and he foresaw the not very improbable result of the removal of his hut and his shrine, to make way for swine and beef-eating unbelievers in the sanctity of the lingam. This removal must be prevented. He and the Shekh easily understood one another, and when the latter mounted his many-coloured cob to ride home, he had engaged to use his influence to prevent the removal, with the promise of a handsome present if he succeeded, and armed at the same time with one or two potent charms in the shape of iron and brass lockets, enclosing "muntras" or charms, and unintelligible hieroglyphics, which he was directed to wear as an armlet, and which he was assured would have the effect of restoring the confidence of the "sahib," and preventing any ill effect from accruing from the blow already given to his influence.

The committee decided upon the site, the Brigadier having yielded an unwilling consent; it only remained for the Commissioner to enquire if the land was available, and if there was any objection to its being taken up for the purpose. That enquiry he promised to make, immediately upon going to office. With Mr. Wasilbakee "enquiry" meant consulting his serishtadar.

What came of that enquiry will best be learnt from the following letter:—

No. 733.

"From

"THE COMMISSIONER OF

"*Budgepore*,

"To

"BRIGADIER HAVERSACK,

"*President of Special Committee*,

"*Budgepore, February* 18, 185—.

"SIR,

"With reference to the site selected by the Special Committee, of which you are President, for the erection of barracks, I have the honour to inform you that there are very grave objections to the ground being taken for the purpose specified. I have received a memorial signed by upwards of a thousand of the most respectable and influential natives resident at Budgepore, praying that the spot in question may not be given up to Government for the erection of barracks, as it is the site of a shrine of great sanctity held in much veneration by the people. The erection of the barracks there would be incompatible with the maintenance of the shrine in its present site, and the removal of the latter would cause a great deal of dissatisfaction among the natives, and I shall feel it my duty to remonstrate strongly against it.

M 2

"The other site to the south of the city, equally eligible for the required purpose, will be much more easily available, and I should recommend the Committee to settle upon that as the site for the proposed barracks.

"I have the honour to be,
"Sir,
"Your most obedient servant,
"JUMMA WASILBAKEE,
"*Commissioner.*"

There was some more correspondence on the subject, all of which went up to the Lieutenant-Governor, who endorsed Mr. Wasilbakee's views. The Governor-General, without reading the papers, endorsed Mr. Byewilwuffa's views, and the barracks were ordered to be erected on the south side of the city, much to the satisfaction of the Brigadier, who told everybody how he had disagreed with the other members of the Committee, how the correspondence had gone up to the Governor-General, who had acted upon his, Brigadier Haversack's, opinion and recommendation.

Tenders for contracts for bricks and building materials were then called for, and the 15th of May was the day fixed upon which the sealed tenders were to be opened. The advertisement calling for these tenders was published in the *Mofussilite,* which none of the people likely to contract, that is to say the rich natives of Budgepore, ever saw. But the matter got mooted abroad, and five men offered. I have their names before me, but I shall be better understood if I call them contractor No. 1, contractor No. 2, and so on up to No. 5.

Contractor No. 5 offered to furnish the bricks at three rupees a thousand, No. 4 at three rupees four annas, No. 3 at three rupees twelve annas, No. 2 at four rupees, and No. 1 at five rupees. Of these, Nos. 2, 3, and 4 failed to furnish the required security. No. 1 was a rich man, a nephew of Shekh Futtoo, who very easily persuaded No. 5 to withdraw, promising to give him the sub-contract for the whole at thirty-five per cent. more than the rate he had tendered for. The agreement between them was drawn out and signed. No. 5 withdrew, No. 1 was accepted, and his tender went on to the Superintending Engineer for confirmation.

On the evening of the same day that the contract was accepted by Lieutenant Stuart, Doolchund, his head writer, received from Contractor No. 1 four bags containing two thousand five hundred rupees each, for which he gave the following receipt:—

"Received on account of Captain James Stuart from Noor Khan, contractor, ten thousand rupees.

"(Signed) DOOLCHUND,
"*Head Writer,*
"*Engineer's Office.*"

"Who has been with you all this time? dinner is quite cold," said Mrs. Stuart to her husband, as he came in to dinner on the evening the tender was disposed of.

"Doolchund has been with me about these contracts. I am sorry I have kept you waiting. An excellent man that Doolchund is; I am very fortunate to get him just as I was setting up my new office here."

"Who recommended him?"

"Old Shekh Futtoo Sirdar Bahadoor, the Commissioner's serishtadar, brought him to me."

"I don't like the look of the man," said his wife.

After which they sat down to dinner and discussed other topics.

THE HISTORY OF THE BARRACKS.

CHAPTER VI.

THE DANGER OF INTERFERING WITH NATIVE CUSTOMS.

About a week after this, as Stuart was returning very early from a morning ride in the country, he had occasion to pass a small police chowkee or station. As he rode by, his attention was attracted by the sound of low, continuous moaning, varied by an occasional half-suppressed shriek or cry, uttered in a shrill voice, but apparently stopped either by the effort of a strong will or violence. As the gate was shut, and there was no one visible outside, Stuart, thinking that perhaps there might be someone very ill inside, and wanting assistance, dismounted, and tying his horse up to a neighbouring tree, went to the gate, and by a sharp and vigorous effort pushed it open and entered. He found himself in a small, square courtyard, surrounded with low, mud-built walls, and a row of huts on the further side against the opposite wall. In one corner of the courtyard two wooden posts had been erected on the ground, with a cross-beam on the top, connecting them like a gallows. Upon this cross-beam was suspended the body of a man, hanging by his two thumbs, which were tied tightly by thin cords to the beam in such a position that while his body, hanging with all its weight from the thumbs, was stretched to the utmost, the points of the toes were just the least bit above the ground. The man was stark naked, with the exception of a cloth round his loins. The expression of agony in his features was most painful to witness; and the low moaning sound which had attracted Stuart's attention proceeded from him. Unable to support in silence the intolerable torture occasioned by suspension, for a length of time, of the whole weight of the body hanging by the two thumbs (in reality a species of crucifixion), the poor wretch every now and then uttered a shriek, which was, however, speedily supressed by a threatening gesture from one of two men who stood by him, and who, as Stuart afterwards learnt, had prevented their victim from allowing himself a louder vent to his feelings by giving his body a push every time he commenced uttering the piercing cry.' The swinging motion thus imparted to the man's frame aggravated his sufferings so intensely, that even in the extremity of his anguish he had presence of mind enough to suppress the shriek and confine his expression of suffering to a low moan. When Stuart entered and advanced towards the group, the two men who were standing by the instrument of torture glanced at one another, and then turned angrily upon the intruder. Stuart was not likely to be influenced much by any gesture of impatience on their part, and at once ordered them, with the voice of authority, to release the man, and demanded by whose orders they were committing this atrocious outrage, and who they were. Seeing them rather disinclined to acknowledge his right to order the man's release, he took his penknife from his pocket, and standing upon a low stool he found close by, he speedily cut the string that was fastened round the man's thumbs, and released him. Exhausted by the suffering he had endured, he was unable to stand, and fell senseless at the young officer's feet.

Again Stuart turned angrily upon the two men, and demanded who they were, and by whose authority they had been inflicting those tortures. By this time they had leisure for reflection. Detected *flagrante delicto,* it was useless to take refuge in a denial. Their only course was to confess the truth. And so one of them, to whom Stuart had principally addressed himself, as he appeared to be the senior of the two in age as well as rank, replied, that he was jemadar of the police, and that the prisoner was in custody on a charge of rape and murder, and he had been subjected to the usual process to induce him to confess, according to the custom of the law in like cases, and in this especial instance by the express order of Shekh Futtoo.

After obtaining this information from the jermadar of police, Stuart turned his attention to the prisoner, and calling for cold water, which the other policeman rather officiously brought, endeavoured to restore him to animation. After a time he succeeded so far that the man was just barely able to speak, and Stuart, leaning over him, asked him who he was, and what he had done. The man replied, his name was Beharee; that he had unfortunately incurred the enmity of Shekh Futtoo, because he had sent in a contract for the bricks, which contract had not been taken; but he had subsequently taken a sub-contract from the man whose tender had been accepted. This person was a relative of Shekh Futtoo, and he had offended both him and his powerful relative by threatening, if he was not paid certain moneys then due to him, to send an urzee or letter to the "sahib," informing him that he had been one of the original tenderers for the contract, but had found it remunerative enough to take the sub-contract, under the man whose contract had been accepted; thus showing that, in taking this contract, Government were paying fifty per cent. more than they ought to have paid. Two days after this threat had been made, Beharee had been arrested by the police and taken before the magistrate on a charge of rape and murder. The magistrates had ordered him to be retained in custody of the police, pending further investigation; and the result Stuart had witnessed.

"This," thought Stuart, as he rode home after giving the poor wretch what encouragement he could, bidding him be of good cheer, and if any further violence were offered him, he, Stuart, would take signal vengeance on his persecutors, "this is the way which we English take to enlist the affections and sympathies of the people of India. Here is an accidental revelation made, one instance of the diabolical practices pursued over the whole country brought to light, by the exceptional circumstance of my happening to be riding this morning past the police station. How infamous is the system that allows of such practices as these! How tremendous the guilt incurred by those European officers who tacitly permit the enactment of such atrocities. At any rate there will be an exposure now. I will go to the magistrate directly I get home and tell him all. And, by Jove, if he does not get the perpetrators of it properly punished, I'll report it to Government, and, better still, send it to the papers."

So ruminated Stuart on his way home. What came of the report and the exposure will appear in the sequel.

"I have had a very extraordinary communication from Stuart this morning," said Mr. Dakhil Duftar, to Mr. Wasilbakee, as he sat down in the room where the latter was enjoying his after-breakfast cheroot, on the same morning that the occurrence took place. "I have come over straight to tell you about it, as I don't see very clearly what to do. He says as he was riding home this morning, and passing by the Palampore station, he heard groans inside; he went in and found a man in the last extremity of torture tied up by the thumbs. He cut him down, and the man fainted immediately. There were two of the police there, a jemadar and a man whose name he does not know. The jemadar, whose name was Soorut Singh, told him that they had been torturing the man to confess to a charge of rape and murder. I remember the case. It came before me the other day, and was remanded for further inquiry. One of the most curious parts of the story, however, is that the jemadar told him he had received orders to inflict the torture from your serishtadar, Shekh Futtoo. The man himself said that he had been charged with this crime immediately after threatening to divulge the fact that he had tendered for some contract to the Public Works Department, and that his tender had been refused, but he had taken the sub-contract and was actually furnishing the articles supplied to Government at fifty per cent. less than the price paid by Government for them."

"What a rigmarole," was Mr. Wasilbakee's rejoinder. "However, it is a serious charge against my serishtadar. I think it will be only fair to hear what he has to say about it. You know there's a deal of bosh talked about this torture. What, after all, is it, tying a man up by the thumbs? I don't see anything so very shocking in it. That fellow Stuart is just the kind of chap to find a mare's nest; he is an enthusiastic young man, rather addicted to psalm singing, I believe. Such people, you know, sometimes, are subject to mental hallucinations. We'll see what the Shekh has to say about it. I'll bet any money it is some trumped up story. It is astonishing how many enemies that man has. Every good native always has. Did you ever observe it, whenever you get a really good man to serve you faithfully and honestly, you may be sure there will be intrigues and plots against him."

"What do you think I had better do about the man?

Suppose he were to be tortured to death, and the papers get hold of it, or Government."

"The papers be d——, and as for Government, why, all they will do will be to call for a report, and if you don't know how to write a report by this time, Dakhil Duftar, you ought to, that's all I know. Have a cheroot?"

"But if the poor devil has really been tortured in this way," said Dakhil Duftar, lighting his cheroot, "surely we ought to make an example of the police."

"Fiddlestick—tortured to death! A nice nest of hornets you will stir up if you punish the police for torture; why, not an officer in the whole district will have a day's peace for the next five years. At least a thousand cases of 'tortured to death' will be reported at once, and will have to be investigated. No, no, Dakhil Duftar, take my advice, don't stir muddy water. We are bid not to interfere with the established institutions of the country, and if torture is one of them, what is it to us, we didn't introduce it?"

"We sanction it, though."

"No we don't, we simply obey orders, and don't interfere with an established custom of the country."

"It seems to me deuced like sanctioning it, if we don't punish for it when it is brought to our notice."

"Here comes the Shekh, now let us hear what he says."

The serishtadar's portly figure had just made its appearance in the verandah as Mr. Wasilbakee pronounced these words. He usually called at the house on his way to office to have a little private conversation with his master and take orders, for Mr. Wasilbakee seldom went to his office, as he transacted most of his business at home.

Dakhil Duftar watched narrowly the serishtadar's countenance as Mr. Wasilbakee was recounting to him the story, and thought he detected a curious expression passing over his features. It was very slight and very momentary, for the Shekh was not in the habit of allowing men to read his thoughts in his countenance. Still there was a change in expression, a change which Dakhil Duftar felt sure would not have occurred if he had been listening to the details of a story with which he was really unconnected in any way. When Mr. Wasilbakee came to that part of it where the Shekh's name was introduced, he smiled slightly, but said nothing. When Mr. Wasilbakee had finished, he said—

"Those who serve great men faithfully always have enemies and backbiters. Doubtless this is a shocking outrage, and, of course, the sahib speaks the truth. As we know, sahibs are not like the natives of this country in this particular. But still it is very strange that such a thing should happen in the Budgepore district where all the world knows the police are so honest and so well looked after by the collector sahib and your honour. Your servant does not think anything of his name being used; that is so often done that your honour will not require him to bring any proof that the whole thing is a fabrication as far as your servant is concerned. But if your honour would send for the man who has been tortured, and ask him about it, perhaps that would be the best way. We shall then hear all about the affair at once."

Both Wasilbakee and Dakhil Duftar were completely persuaded, by the Shekh's manner rather than his words, that he had been very badly used by having his name mixed up with the affair at all. The former, indeed, had adopted this conclusion from the first, being led thereto from sheer force of habit.

"You are right," replied Mr. Wasilbakee; "we'll send for the man, and have him here at once."

Saying this, the Commissioner called out to a servant, with the view of giving the order to have the man brought.

"Pardon me," said the Shekh; "there is no need of haste in the matter. I will become answerable that no more injury is done to the poor man. There is a case of the very utmost importance requiring your honour's immediate attention. I have the papers with me, here; and if your honour will attend to it at once, I will, with your honour's permission, go on to the court and get over the current business there and return here in the afternoon, when the man can be brought up and examined."

"As you please," said the Commissioner; "don't be later than three o'clock. I have an engagement at four. Meantime, what's this important case? I don't recollect it."

"Your honour has forgotten the application from the villages of Meeanpore and Akalabad for remission of revenue. The zemindars are very impatient, and they are a very discontented and disaffected set in those parts; and your servant heard yesterday that some agrarian disturbance was inevitable.

The only thing to pacify them is to attend to this application for remission."

"Indeed; are they so rebellious as that? But don't let us have a disturbance—that would go to the ears of Government. I hate a disturbance, of all things; there is no end to the trouble, reports and despatches, and statements; and the troops have to be called out, and the crops get trampled down, and then there are compensation claims, and the very devil. Where are the papers?"

The Shekh went out to fetch the papers, which were in a large bundle his attendant carried. From the position the papers were in, and the time it occupied to rake up that particular bundle out of the mass, it certainly would not have occurred to a bystander that the serishtadar had anticipated the necessity of this case being called for so promptly.

The serishtadar waited till Mr. Dakhil Duftar had left the Commissioner's house and repaired to his office, where he knew he would be closely occupied all day till five o'clock. Then, after having given the papers to the commissioner, he set out himself on the road towards his own office. Instead, however, of going there, he stopped at a turning in the road, despatched his attendants to the court, desiring them to say he would be there himself shortly, but had some private business to transact elsewhere. Having given these instructions he got his many-coloured steed into a brisk amble, and jogged away in the direction of Palampore police station.

What took place there I cannot exactly tell. But I know that he had a few minutes' conversation with the police jemadar, after which he went away.

In the evening of that day Stuart received the following note from Dakhil Duftar:—

"My dear Stuart,

"You must have been strangely mistaken about the story you told me to-day. The man Beharee was sent for by the Commissioner and examined by him, and he denied ever having been subjected to any torture at all, nor had he any marks of it upon his person. He said he had seen you. He is the same who was in custody upon a charge of murder, which turns out now to be unsubstantiated by any *primâ facie* case against him; and he is now at large.

"Yours sincerely, "Dakhil Duftar.

"*Budgepore, May* 25."

Before writing that note Dakhil Duftar had received the following from Mr. Wasilbakee :—

"My dear Duftar,

"Wonders will never cease. I was right. Your friend Stuart must have been labouring under some strange hallucination this morning, or mental aberration. The man Beharee was brought to me this afternoon. I carefully examined him. He denies most positively ever having been subjected to any ill-usage; on the contrary he says he has been particularly well treated ever since he has been in custody.

"He has no marks on his person of any ill-treatment, nor do even his digital appendages show the faintest trace of having supported the whole weight of his body, as represented. If you think you can suspend a man by his thumbs for twelve hours without the latter showing any signs of having been put to such abnormal uses, I recommend you to try the experiment upon yourself.

"He states, however, that he did see your friend Stuart, who came into the police station this morning in a most excited state; that he spoke to him, but could not understand what he said, and thinks it very possible Stuart sahib, as he calls him, misunderstood him. I examined both the policemen separately, and they both gave the same account of Stuart's appearance: their statement does not vary in the slightest particular. The serishtadar and the police jemadar are both very hot upon prosecuting Stuart for defamation, but I advised them not. I certainly think, however, that a man subject to such fits of mental aberration is hardly fit to be at large, much less to be entrusted with such important duties as he now has in charge; and I shall send a private report of the circumstances to Government, with a view to his either being removed or closely watched. I have, however, heard some strange things about him, with reference to his accounts and money matters, which have set me thinking.

"Yours sincerely,

"Jumma Wasilbakee.

"*Budgepore, May* 25."

On receipt of Dakhil Duftar's note, Stuart was fairly puzzled. He was the last man in India to justify the

Commissioner's opinion and suggestion of mental aberration. Cool, clear-headed, and practical in all the ordinary concerns of life, no man was less likely to have been deceived. What he had described he had seen with his own eyes, and heard with his own ears, and yet there was arrayed against him such a mass of evidence, that for a second or two he was almost startled into a disbelief of his own identity. A few moments' reflection, however, convinced him that the Commissioner and the magistrate were dupes in the hands of their subordinates, no rare phenomenon, and he resolved at once to investigate the matter further. With this view he ordered his horse, and rode out to the village where he knew the man Beharee lived. He did not find him, but he learnt from the neighbours that he had been released and had been to his house, but had gone out again with some relatives, who had come to congratulate him on his escape. Leaving word with his next door neighbour that he wanted to speak to him, when he had leisure to come into Budgepore, he rode back, after vainly endeavouring to procure an interview with Mrs. Beharee, who, being a "purda nasheen," or a woman who will not show herself to strangers, refused to see him.

"Have you any dispute with the Wasilbakee's or the Duftars?" asked his wife of Stuart, when she came in from her evening drive.

"No; why do you ask?"

"Because I saw them at the band, and Mrs. Dakhil Duftar and the Commissioner, who is usually so polite and friendly, both seemed as if they wanted to cut me. I thought you must have had some quarrel with them."

"No, I have had no quarrel with them, but a very curious thing has happened to-day, which may possibly have made them feel ill-disposed towards me; but yet I can hardly think so, it must have been your fancy."

"No, I'm sure it was not fancy. I don't take such fancies into my head easily. But what is it that has happened?"

He then told her what he had been too much occupied during the day to tell her before, the strange story about the man Beharee.

Nothing more happened that day, but the following night, just as Stuart was preparing to go to bed, his servant came and told him that there was a villager outside, who had come in from the district, and wanted to speak to him.

He went out, and found a lad of about fifteen or sixteen years of age, who told him that he was Beharee's son, and that his father had been taken very ill that evening with terrible pains in the stomach. His wife and the neighbours were very much alarmed about him, and he had desired that the sahib might be sent for at once, as there was something he wanted to tell him before his death, which he said he felt sure was near at hand. Stuart immediately ordered his buggy, and taking the boy with him drove out to the village. It was past eleven when he reached the place, and leaving his buggy in the road, he walked across the fields to the village where Beharee's house was situated. On entering the house, or hut, as we should call it in England, he found Beharee stretched upon a rude bedstead, by the side of which his wife was seated on her haunches, with her head resting on her knees, swaying her body to and fro, and uttering a low moaning sound, indicative of the agony of despair. A few of the neighbours stood round the bed, where the almost lifeless form of Beharee lay, the dismal scene lighted up by a miserable oil lamp, that emitted as much smoke as light.

As he advanced to the bedside, the natives respectfully withdrew. He merely glanced at their faces, but among them was one that seemed familiar to him. At the moment he did not call to mind where he had seen him before, but he recollected afterwards that the features he recognised were those of the second policeman, whom he had seen in the courtyard of the police station. He took the dying man's hand in his, and asked him how he felt. At the sound of his voice the man opened his eyes, and when he saw who it was, a gleam of recognition and an expression of relief passed over his pallid, agony-stricken features. He attempted to speak, but his voice was so weak that his visitor had to put his ear close down to his lips before he could distinguish what he said. And what he did say was uttered in broken sentences, and at times almost inarticulate words.

The substance of his communication may be paraphrased into something like the following :—

"I sent and begged you to come and see me before I die, that my wife and children may have someone to take care of them. It was you, sahib, that delivered me from the tortures of hell! worse than hell! but it was only that I might die by poison; and when I am dead, the enmity of those who hate me, because I escaped their hands and got them into trouble; will fall on my helpless widow and orphan children."

Stuart then elicited from him by a number of questions, that he had been taken ill with vomiting and violent pains in the stomach that day, immediately after eating his dinner, at a sort of feast or convivial gathering, given in celebration of his escape, by his uncle. There were no strangers, none but members of his own family present, except, and this only came out after rather a close examination of the dying man, one person, the policeman whose features Stuart had noticed but not recognised, and who had been especially invited, on account of his sympathy with Beharee.

"But," asked Stuart, noticing the swollen appearance of the man's thumbs, and the nails blackened with the blood that had been forced under them, and the marks where the cord had cut into the flesh, "how came you to tell the Commissioner sahib that you had not been tortured or ill-treated at all?"

"I never told him so," was the substance of the man's reply.

Again Stuart asked him if he had not been to the Commissioner's house the day before, and he declared most positively he had not; and "if I had," he added, "could not the Commissioner sahib have seen this?" intimating, by a slight motion of his thumbs, that it was to them he was referring.

It was impossible to continue the conversation further. The substance of what I have related, so far as communicated by the dying man, was elicited with much patient painstaking by his questioner, and the process occupied a considerable time, for the man's strength was failing fast, and latterly Stuart had had to make a long pause before he could get any answer at all from him. He remained by the bed of death till all was over, and then, leaving the sorrowing widow and orphan children to utter their lamentations alone over the corpse of the husband and the father, he drove home in melancholy mood.

The next morning, early, he drove over to Dakhil Duftar's house, in order to find him before he went out for his usual morning ride, and told him what had passed. That gentleman admitted that the affair looked suspicious, but could not believe that so respectable a man as Shekh Futtoo could lend himself to so deep a plot as to take a substitute for Beharee before the Commissioner, which Stuart declared he must have done. However, the result was, that Dakhil Duftar promised to see Mr. Wasilbakee about it that morning; and meantime the body of Beharee was brought into Budgepore, where a *post mortem* examination was made by the civil surgeon, who reported that the deceased died of inflammation in the bowels, brought on by natural causes, and that there was no appearance of any mineral poison having been used. Vegetable poisons the doctor declared himself unable to detect. He would have sent the viscera to the Chemical Examiner at Allahabad; but as the order from the head of the Medical Department directed that in such cases the substances requiring examination are to be put into old tart fruit bottles, and as there were none at that time to be had at Budgepore, he did not consider himself justified in assuming the responsibility of sending them in any other way.* There were no external appearances of violence or injury that could have resulted in death. The only marks were marks upon both the thumbs, which might have been caused by cords being tied tightly round them, or, what was more likely, by the deceased having bitten his thumbs very violently during the agonies he suffered from the disease of which he died; and this, the doctor added, he had learnt from careful inquiries, was the case.

The careful inquiries consisted in his asking the policeman who came in with the body, how the deceased got those marks on the thumbs; in reply to which the policeman told him, the deceased had bitten both his thumbs constantly ever since he had been taken ill.

Dakhil Duftar went up to the Commissioner's after breakfast, and while he was there the medical report of the results of the *post mortem* examination came in. Mr. Wasilbakee listened to all Dakhil Duftar had to say, and then replied:—

"I don't see anything in it, Duftar. It is not at all likely Shekh Futtoo would lend himself to such a dangerous plot,

* The chemical examiner having represented that a supply of glass jars or bottles were required for the purpose of sealing up and forwarding subjects for examination, in cases of suspected poisoning, the head of the Medical Department directed that in all such cases *old tart fruit bottles* were to be used.

and deceive me in a matter in which there must be at least fifty witnesses to the truth, any one of whom has him in his power. Besides, what object could be served? what has he to gain by it? Admitted that he is a knave, for the sake of argument, yet he is no fool; on the contrary, he has a deuced long head of his own. And do you mean to tell me he would ever do anything so foolhardy as to put his neck in a noose for nothing? No; it is a great deal more likely to be true, as the doctor says, that this man did bite his thumbs till they bled, in the agonies of his last sickness.

Dakhil Duftar did not look convinced. He did not know what to think. And the Commissioner, after a pause, went on:—

"However, it is a matter very easily settled. If there is truth in Stuart's story, the only way the affair could have been managed was, that they must have substituted someone else for Beharee, and brought another man here the day before yesterday instead of him. It is exceedingly improbable; but that all doubts may be cleared up, we'll just call three or four of these chuprassees that are here now, and see what they say. At any rate they are not under the influence of Shekh Futtoo, and he is not present."

This conversation, together with the determination of Mr. Wasilbakee, had been listened to by the jemadar of that gentleman's chuprassees, who understood English, reader, pretty nearly as well as you do, but who assumed a blank, stolid look of utter indifference, as long as the English language was being spoken when he was present. Quick as lightning he vanished from the doorway, where, ensconced behind the curtain, he had posted himself directly Mr. Duftar made his appearance, as it was likely that the Collector sahib had something of importance to communicate to the Commissioner sahib by his coming at that rather unusual hour to his house. I need hardly tell you that every chuprassee and servant in the establishment of Mr. Wasilbakee was the creature of Shekh Futtoo, whom any of them would as soon have offended as he would have walked into a tiger's den. The consequence was, as you may readily guess, that when Mr. Wasilbakee called the chuprassees and asked them if they were quite sure that the man brought to his house two days before, was really Beharee, and not someone substituted for him, they were not *very* likely to deny his identity, seeing they all knew what had been going on just as well as you do after reading these Chronicles.

So Dakhil Duftar went away quite satisfied that Stuart's suspicions were altogether unfounded. As for Mr. Wasilbakee, he had never been of any other opinion.

It was extraordinary how Stuart's popularity declined. By degrees the strangest rumours became circulated about him—no one could say definitely what there was against him, no one could tell whence the rumours came. The result was apparent enough in cold looks turned upon him and his wife, and bitter words behind their backs. Nobody knew exactly what to say or what to think, but no one in the whole place had the moral courage to associate with the Stuarts as formerly; they were regularly under a ban. The officials took their cue from Mr. Wasilbakee, who shook his head gravely whenever Stuart's name was mentioned, and used to "pity his poor wife." Mrs. Dakhil Duftar had no pity for Mrs. Stuart, she had always disliked her, she said, and thought there was something very odd about her, and that it was very strange she, a subaltern's wife, should be the best dressed lady in the station; her dresses and bonnets came out direct from Paris, and could not cost her less than two or three hundred pounds a year.

A bad calculation, that of Mrs. Dakhil Duftar, and showing how the head is likely to be influenced by the heart, for I knew the Stuarts intimately, and I know that all she had to dress herself upon was fifty rupees a month.

The officers of the different regiments at Budgepore followed the general example. They ceased to ask Stuart to dine at their messes on guests' nights, and treated him so coldly at the bath and the racket court, that at length he declared he could bear it no longer, and absented himself. His wife was in weak health and quite unable to get about, so that they did not feel the want of society so much as they might otherwise have done; and Stuart, who was conscious enough of the general feeling towards him, but totally unable to divine the cause, kept his troubles to himself, and would not let his wife be worried about them. He was a man of rather reserved character, fond of reading a great deal and thinking, and not at all disposed to court popularity. He was zealously devoted to his work, in which he laboured assiduously to do his duty. He put down the treatment he met with abroad to his own want of geniality of disposition, and the quiet and, to a certain extent, unsociable character of the life which his wife's state of health rendered incumbent on him to observe. He used to say the world always treats you as you treat it: they could not entertain nor go into society, and so they avoided the world, it was no wonder the world avoided them and left them to themselves. All would come right in the end. His wife would, doubtless, regain her health and strength, and be able to go out more, and they should be able to ask friends to their house, and matters would right themselves.

One very curious effect of the Indian climate has never received the attention it deserves. Elsewhere, so long as a man or woman gives no colour to a scandalous report, the thing dies out generally, and people cease to believe ill of one whose outward conduct is irreproachable. But in India there seems to be some evil principle at work, or some noxious moral disease that infests the whole tone of society, such a proneness to speak ill of your neighbour, to encourage ill-natured tittle tattle, such a shameless indifference to truth, such a pitiful eagerness to take advantage of another, as if in every walk in life, in the social as well as the official circle, every man and every woman was a rival to every other man and woman, that society seems to catch at the idea of a scandalous report, however infamously unjust, as if it had found a prize. It is a wonder that the blistered tongue has never been set down in the list of Indian diseases.

One reason of this may be, I think, that in India, like everything else, religion is a Government institution. The chaplain draws his pay for reading service every Sunday and preaching his sermon. Were he to open his church on a week day, or to intimate that religion was a thing ever to be taken note of except on Sundays, or that people were to have regard to its principles in their conduct in the drawing-room, the cutcherry, the parade ground, and the battle-field, "Indian society" would regard him with a stare, and inquire if he was a missionary.

I was astonished one day to hear that charges would be sent in against my friend Stuart of a serious nature connected with his professional duties.

Much as I dislike being the bearer of bad news, I drove over to his house as soon as I heard it. But bad news travels quick, they say, and prompt as I had been, the news was there before me. I found him just leaving his wife's room in company with the doctor. He attended him to the door, then returned and took my hand; tears were in his eye.

"I know it all," he said, anticipating from my look what I was about to say. "I know it all, but I do not understand it. God knows, I have laboured and striven to do my duty conscientiously. I know that, somehow, that man Shekh Futtoo is at the bottom of all this, but the threads he weaves his net with are too deeply hidden for me to trace their course. Thank God she is ignorant of it, and"—here he fairly broke down, and added, as he sobbed like a child, "she will remain so till the end."

"Is it indeed so?" said I. "Has the doctor given such a bad report? While there is life there is hope."

"No, no—it is not so—I cannot speak of it just now—I shall be calmer by and by. Sit down and wait here a little, there is a good fellow. I will come in again when I am calmer, and tell you all. This double blow, that has fallen upon me all at once is too much, I can scarce bear it, I cannot bear it now, but I shall be better by and by."

So saying he left me, and I waited. I heard his voice lowly murmuring in the next room, as he whispered consolation to his pain-stricken wife, he, alas, more needing consolation to be spoken to him.

By and by he returned. "She is better now," he said: "more easy, and will, I think, get a little sleep. But the doctor has warned me to anticipate the worst. Yes, it is God's will, but oh! how difficult to understand! Wifeless, childless by the same blow, I shall stand alone to confront the world's cold heartlessness and treachery! Do you know the Brigadier-Major has been here, and I am under arrest, and a general court-martial assembles as soon as possible. I hope it will not be till I am relieved from duty here. I do hope, I pray that I may be spared to tend her, to soothe her last moments. If I am away she will not understand it, and it would break her heart to hear of it. Oh! I hope that the secret may be kept from her to the last."

"But she will not believe it. Her faith in your unsullied honour will not be broken."

"No, no; but it would be so difficult to make her understand, and the shock alone would be so sad to witness. Oh! have men no mercy for one another? Do men never pause to think while heaping misery on others, that they themselves may cry out for mercy and relief and not be heard?"

"But tell me more about it. What charges could they possibly bring against you?"

"A trumped-up charge of receiving money from contractors, and conspiracy to defraud the Government, supported, I suppose, by some lying evidence. Truth I do not fear, but now as I am, broken-hearted, crushed, with only half my usual faculties about me, how am I to confront cunning and malice by skill, patience, and perspicuity? One thing is, if I am only spared to support and console her in the last trial, I do not care what becomes of me. Even honour stained by false calumny seems to me a light thing, compared with this great sorrow that looms before me. And what I dread most of all is, that sometimes under all this I feel as if my faith in God would almost be shaken."

"No, not that, Stuart," said I, shuddering as the shadow of despair for an instant threw a deeper gloom over his saddened features. And I added in a low voice, half speaking to myself: "What I do thou knowest not now, but thou shalt know hereafter."

Soon after this I left him, promising to return on the morrow, and wondering as I drove home how it is you so seldom meet an Indian chaplain in the house of sorrow, where you would find an English clergyman with words of consolation on his lips.

Mrs. Stuart lingered on upon her bed of death much longer than the doctor had expected. Stuart gave himself almost wholly up to her, and seldom left her bedside, or took any interest in the preparations for his approaching trial. Thoroughly imbued with an idea of his guilt, which had by dint of long acceptance of it as an undoubted fact (though it rested only on the baseless foundation of the purest slander malice ever invented) become familiar to their minds, the members of the court-martial had to go through what was in reality a form, viz., hearing the trial. The case for the prosecution rested on Doolchund's evidence, who swore that he received 10,000 rupees from the contractor in hard cash the day the contract was signed, for Stuart. The men who brought the money to his house came forward and deposed to the fact, and other native witnesses swore they had taken the cash to Stuart's house and counted it out before him. The contractor produced Doolchund's receipt given in Stuart's name, and showed that he had sublet the contract, though the sub-contractor, who was Beharee, was dead: yet there was plenty of evidence to prove that the articles contracted for had been supplied at fifty per cent. less than the sum tendered and accepted.

Even Stuart's own domestic servants were with meanness (I was going to say unparalleled, but that would be wrong) called to show that his monthly expenditure had far exceeded the income derived from his pay.

He met it all with a simple denial. He could not prove a negative, and he was too broken-hearted to cross-examine the lying witnesses with any effect. He saw that the court were against him from the first, and seemed indifferent to the result. The sentence, of course, was not immediately made known, but he felt morally certain what it would be.

The thing that grieved him most was his enforced absence from his wife, during the time the trial was proceeding, but happily, she was generally in an unconscious state, and I was there all day in case she revived, to minister what consolation I could, and disarm her fears and suspicions. At last the farce was over, and Stuart could remain at home to face the reality.

The day that the sentence was promulgated was the last day of his melancholy duties. I went to the house, and finding the drawing-room as usual empty, advanced on tiptoe to the bedroom door. Not a servant was about the place. It seemed as if every living creature had deserted this sorrow-stricken man. I heard no sound, and, anticipating events, lifted the curtain (which it is the custom frequently in Indian houses to suspend across a doorway, so as to ensure privacy without preventing a current of air from entering), and looked in.

He knelt by her bedside with her hand clasped to his lips. As I entered he raised his head, his features almost as wan and pale and worn as hers upon which death had laid its icy touch. He rose and grasped my hand.

"I know it all," he said, "I know the worst, thank God my prayer was heard, and she knows it not! Now welcome poverty, welcome disgrace, I can bear it all,—and more—since she is spared the bitterness."

Stuart was cashiered. Soon afterwards he left Budgepore, intending to seek his fortunes in Australia. He gave me a commission, which was to see that a young cypress tree and some rose bushes close to a grave in the cemetery were kept watered and tended during the dry season, and that was the last I have heard of him. Yet there was no one in Budgepore who could be made to see through the plot and understand that the whole case against Stuart was a false one.

Such things will, I suppose, one of these days be inquired into.

The barracks were completed under the superintendence of Stuart's successor. They cost seven lacs, that is £70,000, in building. They were not, however, occupied, for when the Commander-in-Chief came round on his tour of inspection, he condemned the site as unhealthy, and summoned a special committee of superintending surgeons, who, it is needless for me to add, quite concurred in His Excellency's opinion.

Being found unhealthy for troops, the barrack-rooms were divided into separate apartments, and made over to the families of the uncovenanted servants of Government attached to the civil offices at Budgepore, each family having to pay ten rupees a month rent for the accommodation.

THE HISTORY OF THE BARRACKS.

CHAPTER VII.

THE FATE OF THE FAKIR.

At the conclusion of my last chapter, I told you that the barracks, after all, were never used for the soldiers. The site was found unhealthy, which is not much to be wondered at, seeing it was selected just in front of what for four or five months in the year was a pestilential marsh. So the buildings were abandoned by the military authorities, and another range of barracks built where you now see them on the high ground to the north of the city.

You will recollect that this was the site originally selected by the committee, but not adopted in consequence of objections raised on the part of the Commissioner, objections which were in reality founded on the existence there of a Hindoo fakir's hut and his shrine, and how was it that they were removed to make way for the beef-eating European?

It happened in this wise. You may readily suppose that the events which preceded Stuart's misfortune made some little impression on an inquiring nature like mine. They set me thinking. Was that man, Beharee, poisoned? And if so, who poisoned him, and what was the motive?

I dare say you have observed how sometimes ideas cross your mind whose association you are utterly unable to trace, but which are, nevertheless, fraught with important consequences, perhaps to yourself, perhaps to others. Very often the most momentous actions of our lives, or conduct that eventuates in some momentous decision influencing much of our future fortunes, is undertaken upon some sudden impulse, some idea or suggestion that comes we know not whence. It seems like inspiration. Perhaps in those cases when really momentous and important consequences are the result, it would not be far wrong to call it inspiration. When less important consequences are involved you call it "a happy thought." Well, it was a happy thought, I suppose, that crossed my mind one day shortly after the events related in my last chapter occurred, as I was riding past the fakir's hut. It came athwart my mind like the shadow of a cloud that suddenly and for a moment obscures the sunlight on a summer day, the suspicion "that man is concerned in this poisoning business." The idea would not leave me. I turned it over in my mind, I criticised it, I endeavoured to persuade myself it was a baseless, groundless, unjust suspicion; why should I harbour it? "No matter," the idea said to me, "you may treat me just as you please, ridicule me as much as you like—all your mental logic won't affect me in the least. Here I am, and here I intend to stay, till you choose to act upon me."

And the idea did say, I couldn't get rid of it. I acted on it. Later in the day, after meditating over my folly and trying in vain to talk myself out of it, I summoned a faithful domestic of mine by name Sookha.

"Sookha," said I, taking my cigar out of my mouth (it was the third I had smoked that morning, but the "idea" was solely answerable for that excess), "Sookha, I have an idea."

Sookha folded his hands in an attitude of prayer and replied, rather illogically, that "I was his father and mother."

Then, thought I, in that case, your relation to me is very like that of my idea. "But listen," I said aloud. "Do you know that old fakir's hut under the peepul tree on the common, near the Toghluckabad road?"

"Why shouldn't I know it?" answered the illogical Sookha.

"Very well," said I, "now I'll tell you what you must do. You are a clever man" (a very low salaam followed the abrupt announcement, and a second assurance that I was his father and mother), "you must go and play a little trick for me upon the fakir. Dress yourself up like a villager from your native country, Oude, take a pack on your back and old clouted shoes,"—such as the Gibeonites wore when they went to take in the Israelitish host, I added, mentally—"and go and get into conversation with that old fakir. Tell him you come from a distant part of the country, where in your own village there resides a man who has done you a mortal injury, upon whom you wish to take your revenge. Make up a story, and then get the fakir to sell you exactly as much poison as will kill a man and leave no trace behind. Do you understand? There are some poisons that can be traced in a man by certain devices, which the doctor sahibs, who are very clever, know how to employ, and some that don't leave any trace at all. Make a bargain with the fakir, pretend you are very poor, and get the medicine for as small a sum as you can, and bring it to me."

Sookha made a salaam, and having received his instructions, departed to carry them out.

It was tolerably late that evening, when Sookha returned with a small packet containing a little whitish-grey powder, which he told me the holy man had assured him was quite sufficient for the purpose, and for which, after some bargaining, he had parted with for eight annas,* or one shilling.

"Very good, Sookha," said I, "now go out and tell the sweeper to catch a pariah dog."

A pariah dog was very easily caught.

I put about a tenth part of the powder on a piece of bread and gave it to the animal, which devoured it eagerly.

I watched it, and in half an hour it was seized with a shivering fit. This was followed by dreadful spasms indicating great pain, vomiting and purging. This was succeeded by a state of collapse, under which the animal sunk, and in two hours it was dead.

So, thought I—the idea was not unreasonable in its importunity. Now for the connection between the fakir, Beharee, and this Shekh Futtoo.

The next day I did a foolish thing. "Nemo omnibus horis sapit," which means that a man must make a fool of himself sometimes. And in this case did I, Old Mortality, behave like one bereft of reason. Instead of confiding in my own idea, I outraged the sensitive feelings of that good and trusty

* This same thing occurred at another place besides Budgepore the story was related to me by an officer who had done exactly as I did, and whose suspicions had been aroused by having a valuable horse poisoned close to a bunnea's shop on the road-side. This happened near Amritsur a few years ago. The officer who told me the story is now dead.

friend. I went to consult—I can hardly find it in me to register my own weakness and folly—yes, I went and consulted Dakhil Duftar, of all the people in the world! my idea was so ashamed of me for this act of folly that it completely abandoned me and left me to reap the result of my conduct—failure.

Dakhil Duftar was in his court. He received me most courteously, as he always did, made room for me to seat myself by him on the bench, and stopping the business that was going on, turned to me with an inquiring air.

Most of the amla, or native subordinates about the court, left when the cessation from the current business of the day took place. I was all the better pleased at this, and took no note of the chuprassee who was standing behind Dakhil Duftar's chair brushing away the obsequious flies from his master's head with a chowry. A chowry is a sort of thing like the tail of an animal, with a wooden or ivory handle, used in India to drive away flies from a dinner or breakfast table. Some people who affect state have a man with a chowry always behind their chairs keeping off the flies when engaged in reading or writing. The best instruments of this kind are made from the tail of the yak, the hairs of which are very long, silky and fine. You might make an excellent chowry with the silken tresses of your lady-love, and a very pleasing and sentimental souvenir it would be. And I dare say an ordinary chignon, unravelled or combed out, would answer, that is, if chignons do unravel, a little matter upon which I could not speak with certainty, as I am not sufficiently intimate with any lady friend to borrow one to try.

In a few words, I told Dakhil Duftar of my idea and its results. He seemed fully to apprehend its importance, and said he would at once have the fakir's hut searched.

"Would it not be better," I said, "to conduct the search yourself. I can take my servant down there, who will show you the spot and how the poison was concealed."

"Yes, yes," said he, "that will be the best way; one is so much in the power of the amla, you know, that I always like to do these things for myself. I never trust them on a delicate inquiry of this kind, never."

So it was arranged that as soon as the day's work was over, we should drive down together to the fakir's hut and conduct this investigation.

Was it by accident or coincidence that just at this juncture the chuprassee, who had been doing the chowry business all this time, found it was necessary that he should be relieved? At a sign from him, another man stepped up to take his place; he resigned the instrument of ease into his successor's hand, and disappeared.

"Does that man understand what we have been saying?" said I, uneasily.

"Who?" said Dakhil Duftar, rather astonished. "What, that chuprassee? My dear fellow, what an absurd question! No, we are not quite so surrounded with spies as all that. He is one of the dullest and stupidest men in the whole establishment—understand English! he scarce understands his own mother tongue, let alone English."

Nevertheless, that stupid dull man understood English just as well as I, and if he had not he would not have been where he was. Conceive the opportunities a man has who is always present, always looking over the collector's shoulder, hearing his private conversation with friends, his remarks on cases *sub judice!* He ignorant of English! of what use would he be? No, it is not so the machinery is managed by which the wires are worked that make the dolls and puppets dance.

When I got home and told Sookha he was to go with me to point out to me and the collector sahib where the fakir kept his store of poisonous drugs, he was as much affected as if he had himself taken some of the poison. He threw himself at my feet and grovelled in the dust; he besought me with tears in his eyes to spare him, he pleaded in the most piteous tone, he asked what fault he had committed that he should be subjected to such punishment; he called to mind his faithful services to me, extending over many years, his devotion, his zeal, the very identical service of the day before which had brought him into all this trouble. In vain I expostulated with him, reasoned with him, persuaded, scolded, commanded;—he retained the same attitude, grovelling at my feet like a criminal who had just been condemned to death by my mandate. My heart is not made of stone, and I could not help feeling for the man's distress. But why all this fuss?

The day he accompanied me on such an errand would be

his last, he said. The fakir would be taken to prison, perhaps punished, and upon his, the informer's, head, would fall all the odium of that deed; besides, it was well known that the fakir had powerful friends—he had friends in the police, among the jail establishment, in the court amla, and some said that even the Commissioner sahib's serishtadar was numbered among his adherents. Finally, the principle of combativeness or antagonism, which even in the most abject animals may be developed by despair evinced itself. He declared he would not go. I might beat him, torture him, hang him, but go he would not, and if dragged to the spot he would declare he knew nothing and had seen nothing.

I tried the motive of avarice. I offered him as much money as would make him comfortable for life, but he rejected it. I assured him of protection, of the ægis of the very collector sahib himself, the man shook his head and would have none of it. The case was hopeless. I turned away in despair, angry with Sookha, but still more angry with myself, for lo! my idea flashed across my brain again, and said to me almost as plainly as if it had spoken out in so many words, "Bah, couldn't you have foreseen this?"

I need not occupy much time by relating how after this Dakhil Duftar and I had a fool's errand. The fakir expected our visit with as much certainty as old Mrs. Tabby expects her friend whom she has invited to tea, when the tea is made and the muffins are being kept warm at the fire. Search! We might have as well searched Budgepore for an honest man as have looked for poisonous drugs in the fakir's hut, or anywhere near it.

It's an ill wind, however, that blows no good. And this miserable failure of mine, nevertheless, resulted in poetic justice being done. A few months more and the fakir was on his way to a penal settlement, and his shrine had been removed by the Department of Public Works! For Shekh Futtoo now perceived that the hounds were not far from his scent. The fakir knew a good deal too much. At any moment the secret of his dealing in poisons might be out, and then there was no doubt about it, the disclosure of his, the Shekh's, complicity with his guilt would inevitably follow. He knew human nature pretty well, did the Shekh, and the nature of the men he had to deal with. The slightest accident—a straw blown by the winds of heaven—might at any time reveal the whole story of the fakir's guilty trade. There were at least a hundred men in the city of Budgepore who were cognizant of it. But the fakir ever since the great Shekh had let himself fall into his toils, felt perfectly secure. No harm could happen so long as he was befriended by him. But once in danger, and that influence not exerted to befriend him, and he had hinted as much, he would reveal the whole story of the death of the man Beharee, and the circumstance that led to it, the purchase of the poison by the Shekh, and beyond this the fakir cared not to know.

It was not an easy task the Shekh had now to accomplish. The fakir was respected in the city, and held in repute pretty well all over the district. He was no ordinary foe to be trampled upon at once—no ordinary prey to be entrapped in the usual stereotyped manner, by a formal charge, and perjured witnesses and confession to police under the influence of torture. The blow, if struck at all, must be a grand *coup*—a blow that would annihilate the fakir's reputation for sanctity, at the same moment that it laid him low at his rival's feet. And it was a grand *coup*—a master-piece of amla audacity.

An examination of the jail records showed the Shekh that about ten years before, a man whose descriptive roll was among those records, and which answered in every particular with the external appearance of the fakir, allowing for changes consequent upon lapse of time, had been sentenced to transportation for life for an attempted murder. There were hundreds of others who had been transported also from Budgepore within the period embraced by that bulky file of records, which the Shekh so cautiously scanned. But there were two reasons why this particular one was selected. One reason was that the descriptive roll answered to the fakir's appearance, and the other was that in this particular instance it was recorded that the prisoner who had been transported had died at the penal settlement. So far, well.

One day, shortly after this, a petition was presented to Dakhil Duftar, from a jermadar of the police in the Budgepore district, which set forth that the writer, having recently been promoted, and being moved thereto by his zeal for the Sirkar, or Government, wished to rectify a great error he had been the instrument of many years ago. When engaged in the duty of escorting a prisoner condemned to transportation, from Budgepore to Calcutta, whose name was Sungram Sing, the party of police in charge, which consisted of himself and three others, had allowed this particular prisoner to escape. It had happened one night, when the escort with the prisoners under their charge, of whom there were ten, in irons, were bivouacked under a tree near the village of Makampore, in the Ghazeepore district. When the writer of the petition and his comrades were asleep, a rush was made upon them by several men. Sungram Sing was seized, and his irons being struck off, restored to liberty; and he escaped, but one of his liberators remained behind after the rest had run away, and told the discomfited police that they need be under no apprehension of suffering for their negligence, for that he, being inclined thereto for divers weighty reasons, which it did not concern the police to scan too closely, was ready and willing to go into transportation in place of Sungram Sing, and to undergo that worthy man's sentence as deputy. The number of prisoners they had to deliver up to the authorities in Calcutta would thus be complete, no inquiry would be made, and all parties would be satisfied.

Sungram Sing having fairly escaped out of their hands, the police had consulted their own interests, and consented to the arrangement, putting the substitute into the irons that had so recently impeded the free action of Sungram's limbs. And this very identical Sungram Sing, the petition went on to say, was now to be seen in the guise of a fakir living under the peepul tree, on the common outside the city of Budgepore, on the Toghluckabad road.

After hearing the petition read to him (it is the custom in India for all documents to be read to officials, whether they are petitions, or statement of cases, or depositions, or death warrants, or what not, so that the official hears and signs, if the document be for signature, what the reader wishes or chooses to make him hear; for of the document itself in the vernacular, he could not, if he tried, read one word), Dakhil Duftar passed an order summoning the writer to his presence.

He made his appearance in due time, and was examined by Dakhil Duftar as to the facts stated in his petition. His answers were consistent, and the story he told seemed plausible, and a warrant was issued for the arrest of the fakir.

I was a good deal surprised to hear of it, for from what little I have been able to gather about the fakir's influence with the amla, I did not expect he would meet with any molestation from that quarter. After thinking over it for some time, I began to see a glimmer of light breaking in upon the affair. What motive had Shekh Futtoo for wishing to compass this man's destruction? A very obvious one; my suspicions became then more confirmed.

"The villian is caught in his own net," was my remark to Dakhil Duftar, after he had told me about the discovery of the escaped convict, though I had of course heard of it before.

"What do you mean?" said he.

"Why, that although the man is altogether innocent of this charge, he deserves the fate that is impending over him."

"Innocent! What a fellow you are. How can he be innocent? Why here's the very man who had him in charge, who went with him half way to Calcutta, from whom he escaped, who must have seen him every day—he swears to his identity."

"Very likely," said I, "and what does the man say himself?"

"Oh, as a matter of course, he swears he has been there for the last twenty years under that tree, as if that were likely, you know. As if it were likely that he could be there all the time, and not a single soul in all Budgepore can be found to say he ever saw him there more than five or six years back. Why, if it were true, there must be a thousand men and women at least in Budgepore who could have recognised him."

"And will no one come forward?"

"No; I tell you the thing's absurd. Here is the descriptive roll answering exactly to his appearance. Here are three police constables who took him down in charge, from whom he escaped, and seventeen other witnesses, who all swear he is Sungram Sing and no one else!"

I will not detain you over this story. The fakir was committed for trial, upon the charge of having escaped from custody, when under sentence of transportation. The seventeen witesses all swore to his identity, so, of course, did the policemen. He was found guilty and sentenced to transportation, and did not *escape* this time. At least half the city of Budgepore knew the truth, but not a soul would come forward. Perhaps they did not do so for the same reason that I did not, for I knew perfectly well that the old fakir had been there certainly for five-and-twenty years, as I had seen him scores of times off and on during that period. But I was determined to leave the old villian to his fate, for I had found out that he made a practice of dealing in poison, and I am sure he was guilty of Beharee's death.

So he met with his deserts, but not in the way intended. And had he been really an innocent man, as I suspect very few of these fakirs really are, it is dreadful to think of the ease and simplicity with which he was got rid of, for of course nothing that he might say now about the sale of poison to Shekh Futtoo or anyone else, would be believed.

So the old fakir went to end his days at Penang, and the shrine and hut were removed, and the beef-eating European smokes his pipe over the spot erst sacred to the lingam. The well has been walled in, to prevent the children from the barracks falling in, but it is still used for the soldiers, for the water is as sweet and wholesome as ever it was.

CHRONICLE V.

THE LIEUTENANT-GOVERNOR'S VISIT, AND WHAT CAME OF IT.

CHRONICLE V.

THE LIEUTENANT-GOVERNOR'S VISIT, AND WHAT CAME OF IT.

IT was a great day for Budgepore when His Honour the Lieutenant-Governor came to our station on one of his tours. He was expected on Saturday, and was to stay over Sunday, and leave on Monday morning.

Great preparations were made to give the dignitary a fitting reception, and Crawford, who was then our collector and magistrate, looked forward to getting a little "kudos," for the condition in which his district was. And I must say he deserved it. Crawford was an energetic man, straightforward, and wonderfully free from the prejudices which detract so much from the usefulness of most officials in his position. He was fully alive to the responsibilities of his office, and knew well what a curse to the country a magistrate and collector becomes, as soon as he allows himself to be made a tool of by his serishtadar and the natives about the courts. As far as possible he looked into everything for himself; and never allowed himself to be biased by the opinions, or guided by the intrigues of the amla or police. He was a man of active habits, and spent as much of his time as he could spare from other duties in his district. And his district was in first-rate order. It was commonly said, that as soon as you came into the Budgepore district, you were safe from being robbed. The fact is, Crawford carried things with a high hand sometimes, and not seldom set aside the law and regulations quietly, when he found they interfered with the public weal. If he caught a man out in a crime he would not unfrequently punish him on the spot, without waiting for the tardy process of even summary trial. But he never did this except he either saw with his own eye, or knew from his own knowledge, that he had the real culprit in his hands. All the badly disposed feared him. The police and amla hated him. The bulk of the native community liked him.

One little thing he did on the occasion of the Lieutenant-Governor's visit, illustrates his character. It got wind that there were several natives of a village called Hajeepore, who had been summarily punished by him for cattle-stealing, or some such crime, who had prepared and were going to present to the Lieutenant-Governor a petition, setting forth how unjustly they had been treated.

These men he clapped in jail, and kept them there till His Honour had left the district, when they were released. This stroke of policy was an effectual one. Had the Hajeepore petition been presented, some five hundred others would have followed. But no sooner was it noised abroad that the petitioners were thus taken care of, than the other five hundred petitions were as speedily as possible committed to the flames.

At that time we had an amateur choir in our little church. Our padre, whom I shall call Mr. Shanks, was a little spare man, with reddish sandy hair, and wore shoes. The choir was conducted by Mrs. Crawford, and by Mrs. Hamilton, the wife of our officiating Sessions Judge. When I say the choir was conducted by these ladies, I do not of course mean that they both conducted it together. That would have been quite as great a feat as squaring the circle, or discovering perpetual motion. What I mean is, that Mrs. Crawford usually managed it, and as she was not able to be there always (for she very often accompanied her husband into the district), when she was absent, Mrs. Hamilton took the duties. You will not forget that Hamilton was only *officiating* Sessions Judge, the difference therefore between the rank and standing of these ladies was not so very great.

Of course when so great an event as the visit of the Lieutenant-Governor was expected, all the residents were in the station, and the consequence was that the choir bid fair to be well attended.

There were, besides the ladies I have mentioned, other members—Mrs. Dickenson, whose husband was a Lieutenant in the 80th Native Infantry, then stationed at Budgepore. Dickenson married as an Ensign, under the impression that an officer could live more economically married than single.

He was very much in love, but I am sorry to say it is too true, that when poverty comes in at the door, love very often flies out at the window; and, before three years were over, poor Dickenson found himself with an increasing family, and he also made the discovery, that the notion of a man's expenses not being necessarily increased by his marriage was a sad fallacy. At the time I speak of they had seven children. It is true he had meantime got his lieutenancy and the adjutancy. But these aids came too late, he was hopelessly in debt, and what is worse, broken-hearted.

The following year he died, killed by his cares, if ever a man was killed by anything. And Mrs. Dickenson found herself one morning with nothing but a single change of clothes for herself and each of her children, and her husband's sword. The Committee of Adjustment put their seal upon everything else in the house. Dickenson was carried to his last home, and a subscription was got up in the station to help to pay his widow's expenses to England, whither she betook herself; and it was pleasing to find that what with her own and her children's pensions, she was more comfortably off and happier than she had been since the first year of her marriage.

But I am digressing. The rest of the choir was composed of one of the young officers of the 80th, and three or four of the Christian drummers, as they were called. "Christian" drummers, I have often thought that adjective a good illustration of the principle of derivation involved in the phrase *lucus a non lucendo*. I am not one of those who believe that the calamities of '57 should necessarily be regarded as a judgment of Providence. But assuredly if there was anything in the old system that reflected disgrace upon the officers of the old Bengal army, and represented responsibilities ignored, it was the frightful state of ignorance and immorality in which the so-called Christian drummers of the old native army were suffered to live.

One morning that week I got a note from Shanks, asking me to go over and breakfast with him. I went, and found him in a ludicrous state of perplexity. The fact was, he said, there was to be a choir-meeting at the church that morning for practice, and the ladies were anxious to have some special musical addition to the service in honour of the Lieutenant-Governor, who was sure to attend church, and Mr. Shanks was afraid there might be a little difference of opinion, tastes differed, and so on—in fact——well, in short, he was nervous, and asked me if I could accompany him and give the aid of my advice if necessary.

"Certainly," said I, "I will go with pleasure. But it seems to me that although it may be quite right and proper for civilians' wives instead of singing to 'the praise and glory of God,' to sing to the praise and glory of the Lieutenant-Governor, I think if I were you, Shanks, I should set my face against any interference with the usual services."

Poor Shanks! I knew him at Oxford. He belonged to Exeter, and got a third the year Mandamus, who was lately Attorney-General, got his double first. Mandamus knew him too, and used his influence to get him an Indian chaplaincy. He was a bachelor, and dreadfully shy, timid in ladies' society, and very much in awe of the two fair beings who had taken his church by storm.

That shyness which most men feel in ladies' society, and which seems to be affected so much by the dress, is a curious characteristic of human nature, and worthy a deeper study than I have time to give the subject. A man who is fearfully shy and timid in the presence of a well-dressed woman, will be comparatively bold and forward with a badly-dressed one. What is the reason?

It would seem that the act of dressing elegantly and tastefully has some of the properties of magnetism which repels as well as attracts. For you see some men repelled just in proportion as others are attracted by that indefinable something, I suppose I may call it "force"—force means anything you like now-a-days, from an arm-chair to an invisible atom of infinity—which indicates the presence of a well-dressed woman.

It is the rustling of silk and muslin, or the fragrance of "Early Spring Flowers," or any other of Piesse and Lubin's productions, or the combination of colours, or the loveliness of the bonnet of the latest Paris cut, or the edge of an embroidered or frilled petticoat peeping out from underneath the dress, or is it the quiet self-possession and graceful demeanour of ladies accustomed to move in good society, that makes the heart of a man constituted like Shanks' sink within him as a stone, when he comes under the influences which to men of another stamp are so attractive? Shanks would have gone to a funeral quite cheerfully, but to meet Mrs. Crawford and Mrs. Hamilton—poor wretch, he was afraid. I call him poor wretch rather with reference to his subsequent fate, than his present fears. Unwilling, because too shy, to find a wife from among his equals in birth and education, he got caught, when on furlough, by the daughter of a lodging-house-keeper in London, and married her, and didn't he lead a life of it!

There was a great consultation at the church. Mrs. Crawford had some high church tendencies, and was bent upon having an anthem in the proper place, of course in the middle of the prayers. Mrs. Hamilton with a like object in view, but opposite tendencies, insisted on having "From Greenland's icy mountains," after the sermon instead of the anthem. I did not myself see the aptitude of the selection, but I thought I would not expose my want of taste by asking. Perhaps the "icy mountain" might have some reference to Nynee Tal or Simla.

Shanks of course was referred to, and he, as weak men always do, tried a middle course. My opinion was asked, and I recommended Brady and Tate, Ps. 15, not with any special reference to the present occasion, but because I thought it ought to be sung by order of the Governor-General in Council in every church in the Mofussil once every Sunday, and twice on Sunday in all hill stations, the 3rd verse being repeated. You recollect it of course?

> Who never did a slander forge
> A neighbour's fame to wound,
> Or hearken to a false report
> By malice whispered round

I need hardly add that after making my suggestion, I basely deserted Shanks and left him. The result was a compromise, and the Lieutenant-Governor had both the anthem and "From Greenland's icy mountains."

On Sunday evening we all dined with His Honour. This state ceremony was not marked with that funeral gloom that distinguished the state camp dinners of one of his successors (the late Lieutenant-Governor) where you hardly knew which was the coldest, the plates, the dinner, the reception, or the reception tent. Still, it was stiff enough. It was a cold winter evening, and one did not feel a pleasant change from the comfort of one's "ain fireside" to the "cold blast" of a large double-poled tent, though that was the Lieutenant-Governor's. When I got there all the other guests had arrived. The ladies were sitting in a semi-circle, the gentlemen standing about in groups, no one saying a word, but ladies and all looking exactly as if they had all come there to be wigged. Indeed, I thought the whole scene would have made an excellent group for Madame Tussaud. His Honour was standing with his back to a stove in the centre of the tent, conversing slowly, as if anxious not to exhaust the subject too rapidly, upon the weather, with Colonel Sungeen. No one else spoke a single word.

The duties of an aide-de-camp, except in the field, are not those which call into play the noblest parts of man's nature. Still I have always thought it very unreasonable that a man should grumble at having no more onerous or responsible duties to perform than to dress well and sit all the morning in a nicely furnished drawing-room, and hand ladies to and from their carriages and pass them through the ceremony of introduction. Anyway, whatever a man is paid for doing he ought to do it, as Solomon says, with all his might. Now, his Honour's aide-de-camps, I am bound to say, did not bend the undivided energies of their minds to the performance of the duties which their destiny had allotted to them. I am rather afraid they thought, or affected to think it beneath them, the consequence of which was, on the present occasion, that they managed the introduction so clumsily, that they left the impression on His Honour's mind that Mrs. Crawford was Mrs. Hamilton, and that Mrs. Hamilton was Mrs. Crawford.

It was a great relief when dinner was announced. But I doubt whether if an earthquake had set all the tables and chairs dancing, there would have been as much consternation as now took possession of the Budgepore *monde*. For His Honour, on dinner being announced, walked slowly and with dignified mien up to where the ladies were seated, passed quite close to Mrs. Hamilton, and offering his arm to Mrs. Crawford, led her off. Ten thousand thunders! Had the earth opened at Mrs. Hamilton's feet, and the dark mysteries concealed beneath the roots of the everlasting mountains been revealed in the depth of the yawning abyss, it would have been to her, comparatively, an incident of slight importance. For a whole month after that, whenever any two of the residents of

Budgepore met together, that event formed the sole topic of discourse. Every conceivable motive and many inconceivable motives were ascribed to the Lieutenant-Governor, who, as you know, had merely acted under a mistake. Crawford, as you may easily gather from the little I have said about him, was no favourite with his brother officers. A man who will choose out his own course of action instead of walking in the beaten track, never is a favourite with his fellows. If he succeeds in life, they envy him, if he does not succeed, they hate him. The Lieutenant-Governor had spoken highly in praise of the state in which he found Crawford's district, and now every one took for granted he was to be promoted immediately over the head of his seniors. Mrs. Hamilton's feelings did not recover the shock they received from His Honour's extraordinary disregard of the laws of society, all the evening. Nor were they at all softened by an unfortunate remark he made in the evening. With the best intention in the world, and acting still as Lieutenant-Governors sometimes, but *very rarely* do, on incorrect information, he went up to Mrs. Hamilton and complimented her on the success of her efforts in the choir, and especially on the beauty of the anthem.

Next day the camp took its departure, and Budgepore was left to chew the cud. The Hajeepore petitioners were soon afterwards released, for Budgepore was only two marches from the next district. Small-pox was raging in the jail where they had been temporarily confined, two of the petitioners died of the disease in jail, a third died of it in his village, and the disease having been thus taken into the district, it raged for several months, till whole villages were nearly depopulated. It was so bad that Dr. Macbole was sent to write a report, which he did, filling therewith twenty sheets of foolscap. The report was sent to the Secretary to Government, North-West Provinces, who had it docketed and tied with red tape and safely placed in a box.

The hot season of that year Mrs. Crawford spent at Mussoorie. Mrs. Hamilton was there also. I had a great regard for Crawford and his wife, and was much pained to hear various reports unfavourable to the character of the latter. All my letters from Mussoorie, written by gossiping correspondents, contained some allusion to the way Mrs. Crawford was talked about. I need hardly say, that knowing so well as

I do how often reports of this kind have no foundation whatever, except in malice, I put no faith in them whatever. But they reached Crawford's ear and he was exceedingly indignant.

He refused all explanation, he would not even ask for any. His wife, conscious of her innocence, resented his unworthy suspicions, and an angry altercation ensued between husband and wife, who had hitherto lived together on the most affectionate terms. There are few things more painful to see than a quarrel between husband and wife, both of whom love each other dearly and would give the world, if they could be reconciled, yet neither will be the first to offer to make amends. Bitter thoughts and angry feelings take the place of warm affection, and grow in intensity from the very necessity each is under of justifying the course they are pursuing to their own consciences. So the breach grows wider and the heart growes sorer, till at last, in desperation, one or the other takes a decided step and resolves to banish from the heart all former feelings of attachment. If it is the husband who takes the first step, he becomes a misogynist and rails against all the sex. If it is the woman, she not unfrequently gives colour to all the previously unfounded suspicions against her, by engaging in real and dangerous flirtation. Such, I am sorry to say, was the case with Crawford and his wife. Both had been warmly attached to one another till the demon jealousy, aroused by scandal, came between them. They were, each, too proud to acknowledge their faults, or to seek to make up the quarrel. Without returning to Budgepore, she made arrangements to go to England, and as he coldly intimated his acquiescence in the plan, and tried to persuade himself that he saw in it a fresh proof of the suspicions he entertained, she went straight down from Mussoorie to Calcutta and sailed for England in the *Hindostan.* They never met again.

I felt for Crawford, but he was too reserved a man to admit even me very closely into his confidence. I, however, went up to Mussoorie, determined to worm out the affair, and trace the unhappy scandal to its source. It was not till the following year I succeeded in doing so, and then I found it had originated entirely with Mrs. Hamilton, who, actuated as I cannot but believe by unworthy motives, and with deliberation, spread a report injurious to her old friend's character. What she said was, speaking of Mrs. Crawford to a lady notoriously fond of tittle-tattle, and to whom you had only got to breathe a word in confidence with a request that it might go no further, to ensure its being all over the station by the next day—what she said was, that she went into Mrs. Crawford's one day, and found her with Captain Smith, "and she saw—well, she would not like to say what she saw." That was all. The seed was sown, the snowball was set rolling, and the happiness of two loving hearts was marred for ever this side the grave.

Crawford, I am sorry to say, did not bear up against his troubles. Perhaps he wanted that alone which could have borne him up against them,—religious principle. He tried to drown his grief by intemperate drinking, and while he was to the last degree bitter against the opposite sex, he nevertheless adopted habits which showed how little independent he was of them. Thus, when people heard of his domestic troubles, they used to pity Mrs. Crawford, and say, "No wonder she had to leave a man who led the life her husband did." So you see, the Lieutenant-Governor's visit to Budgepore was followed by some rather important consequences.

CHRONICLE VI.

THE OVERSEER.

CHRONICLE VI.

THE OVERSEER.

I HAVE already given some description of Budgepore, its locale, society, etc., and shall therefore say no more on that head here.

In 183— there was an overseer in the Public Works Department stationed there, named Thomas Clarke. He had been a private soldier, and had taken his discharge and obtained employment in the department, in which he remained till his death, which took place under the most distressing circumstances, so distressing that it is painful for me to recall them to memory, and put them down in writing.

It happened that the head native in the department under Clarke, named Omichund, embezzled some public money. This Omichund was a sharp man, one of a type very commonly met with. He was an eminently useful man, and he knew it, and, native-like, took every pains to get into the good graces of the officials. If any of them wanted anything done to their houses or gardens, Omichund was sent for. He of course never took a contract himself, that would have been improper as he was in Government employ, but he always brought a man to take the contract, and the work was always well done, and on reasonable terms, Omichund himself superintending so far as to see that the interests of the "sahibs" were well looked after, and the "sahibs" themselves put to no trouble. He was a wealthy man, and kept a number of horses, and whenever any of the "sahibs" wanted to lay a dak to a neighbouring station, or to the foot of the hills, which was only about sixty miles off, Omichund's horses were always promptly lent. In this and a thousand and one other ways, which I need not particularise, this man managed to worm himself into the attachment of the local authorities, especially the

P -

magistrate, whose wife went to the hills steadily every year, and who was accordingly glad to get up to the hills himself once or twice during the season, on which occasions Omichund's horses were found very convenient.

Poor Clarke was a good, honest, quiet sort of fellow; he married when he got the appointment, and at the time I speak of had six children, his pretty wife still retaining her good looks. She was a neat, nice little body, the daughter of European parents. Her father had been an old pensioner, and Budgepore being a favourite station, with a number of little bungalows and gardens all about in the outskirts of the town, a good many old pensioners made it their place of residence. Mrs. Clarke's house-keeping was perfection, as, with their narrow means she managed to bring up her children and look after the house, which was always tidy and well kept, as well as the pretty little garden which surrounded it. Her children were always clean and nicely dressed, and she herself like a good wife, was very careful about her personal appearance, and was always ready to welcome her husband with a smile when he came back from his office or his work in the evening. They were very regular attendants at our little church, and altogether, though the great folk in the station troubled not their heads about them, I will be bound to say there was no happier home and no more decent, respectable family in Budgepore, than that of Clarke's.

Poor fellow! He was two conscientious to allow the misdeeds of Omichund to pass unnoticed, and though, as he told me afterwards, he had a presentiment no good would come to it, he thought it his duty to bring the charge he did against him for misappropriating the public money. He did not succeed in proving it, though there could have been no moral doubt that the man was guilty. However, Omichund asserted his innocence, and what with the extreme difficulty of getting any witnesses to come forward against a man of so much influence, and what with the good opinion always entertained of Omichund by the officers in the station, the charge fell to the ground, and Clarke incurred some odium for having brought it.

It was about a year after this that Mrs. Clarke came over to me one morning crying bitterly, to tell me her husband had been that morning arrested on a charge of murder, and the magistrate was then investigating the case. In reply to my question she told me that the night before her husband had been called out to speak to a man who had come to see him on some business connected with the roads. He went out, taking in his hand a little switch cane which he always carried with him, especially when he went out after dark, because their garden was infested with snakes, and once or twice he had narrowly escaped treading upon one. He came back rather disturbed in mind, and told her he had done what he very seldom did, struck the man across the shoulder with the switch, because he had been grossly insolent to him. He expressed regret for what he had done, but said he had never been so insulted before by any native or European. They shortly after retired for the night. After they had been in bed about half an hour, Mrs. Clarke, who happened to be awake, heard sounds in the garden, as if people were about. Apprehending thieves, she got up and looked out, and saw the figures of one or two men leaving the garden. As there did not appear to be any cause for alarm, and she supposed the men had come to steal a few flowers and shrubs perhaps, and as they had now left the place, and as there was very little prospect of overtaking them, she went to bed again and did not disturb her husband.

Next morning at day-break there was a great fuss. Some police came in and declared that there was the dead body of a man lying under the trees in the garden. Clarke was horrified and rushed out to see, and sure enough there was a corpse there, just on the very spot where he had stood the night before and had the altercation of which I have spoken. Well, the usual proceeding was taken, a *post mortem* was made, and the doctor declared the man had died of a ruptured spleen.

I did what I could to comfort poor Mrs. Clarke, and went down to the magistrate's cutcherry to see what was going on.

Two policemen had just been examined, who swore that the night before they had been on the road outside Clarke's garden and had distinctly heard an altercation between him and a native. They also swore they heard the sound of a blow, and a noise in the branches of the shrubs as of a body falling. In the morning they found the body of the deceased, and by it a garden hoe.

The case looked bad. I felt for poor Clarke, for I knew him to be a quiet, good sort of man, who would never intentionally

P 2

have done any harm to a fellow creature. A native woman, a prostitute of the town, next swore that she knew the deceased, and that he had told her the evening before that he had to go and speak to Clarke, and that he was rather afraid to go because he had reason to believe the sahib was angry with him. Clarke was thereupon sent to jail, and the case went down to Calcutta to go before the grand jury.

Never shall I forget the look of distress and misery on Mrs. Clarke's face that afternoon after she had taken a sorrowful leave of her husband. He said to her at parting, "Keep up your spirits, Annie, and look after the poor children. And whatever you do, never believe me guilty of this crime. I am innocent of it, as innocent as you, but it is a plot, I know, set on foot by Omichund, who vowed he would be revenged on me. Let us put our trust in God, and, whatever happens, submit patiently to His will."

This occurred in the month of May. A burning hot wind was blowing at the time, and as European prisoners were scarce in Budgepore, there was very little, in fact no accommodation for them in the jail there. Clarke was confined in a small square room, with but imperfect ventilation. A punkah was allowed him indeed, but it was pulled by the prisoners, who did not see why they should be made to work gratis for the benefit of a fellow prisoner, and you may be sure they did not exert themselves very much. The darogah of the jail was the son-in-law of Omichund, and this man did everything he could (and it was a good deal) to make poor Clarke's confinement as irksome and painful as it could possibly be. His wife was allowed to visit him daily, but the darogah took care that a native under-strapper should be in the room at the time, who insulted and annoyed them in every possible way. She used to send his meals to her husband, but they had to pass through the hands of the jail officials, who brought them to him in such a disgusting state, covered with flies and filth, that it was impossible for him to touch them, while the water given him to drink was more like soap than water, mixed with mud and all sorts of impurities. Of course Clarke complained to the doctor who regularly visited him, and the doctor reported his complaint to the magistrate, who sent for the jail officials and examined them; you may easily understand what sort of answer *they* gave. The darogah then complained to the magistrate of Clarke's violence. He said he was so abusive that he was afraid to go near him ; and once or twice he had threatened to use violence, and did on one occasion strike one of the jail officials. Again the magistrates examined the jail officials, and you may easily understand what they said. Poor Clarke was then put under constraint and kept handcuffed, in which state the police and jailors frequently jeered at him and spat in his face. All these things were repeated to me by Mr. Clarke, and I of course called on the magistrate and endeavoured to enlist his sympathy for the poor man. It was of no avail. He said Clarke's account of the treatment he was subjected to rested only on his own statement, whereas that of the darogah was confirmed by as many as a dozen witnesses. Neither I nor the doctor could do anything. Of course we understood how the case really was, but what could we say in reply to the magistrate's averment, which was in itself true, except that we believed Clarke's statement and disbelieved that of the natives. All he said was, that he differed with us, and believed the natives, and that as a magistrate he was bound to believe and act upon the evidence of a number of officials rather than the unsupported statement of a prisoner. Of course they took care that none of these outrages should be committed while any of us were by, but we could not remain with him all day, and no sooner were our backs turned, than the tormentors commenced their malicious work upon their victim.

It is a painful story. Mrs. Clarke, from going backwards and forwards to the jail in the heat of the sun, was prostrated with fever, and the consolation of her visits was thenceforward denied to her husband. This last blow proved too much, and I was one day called to go and see him in a hurry, for he was very ill. I went with the doctor, and found him in that stifling hot room stretched upon his wretched charpoy, with the shadow of death plainly darkening over him.

There had been one or two cases of cholera in the jail, and the depression caused by the painful circumstances in which he had been placed exposed him very much to the influence of that disease, which seems to affect the mental almost as much as the corporeal part of our frame. He was past recovery when I went in. I had put my prayer-book in my pocket as I left the house, a presentiment came upon me that something of the sort was the matter. He took my hand as I seated myself beside him, and in a very faint voice asked after his wife Alas! I had no good news to tell him. She was worse. He murmured, "It is the will of God." He said in answer to my question that he felt no pain, though he had suffered dreadfully during the night. He was calm and resigned. I poured into his willing ear the consolatory words of Holy Writ, and remained with him till the last, and so did the doctor, and when we both came away, we were so affected that it was long before we could speak. On our way home we visited poor Clarke's cottage. Alas, what a change was here! The little rooms which used to be so neat, and tidy, and cheerful, were all in disorder, the carpets unswept for days, the furniture untouched. The children had all been taken away by a kind neighbour, the wife of one of the pensioners, who lived close by. Mrs. Clarke was the only occupant of the once happy home, besides a sweeper woman who had been brought up in the family and remained with her in her hour of trial!

Why linger over these reminiscences?

The bereaved widow was herself sinking. The fever had left her, indeed, but she was too much weakened to rally. In a faint voice she asked after her husband. I was obliged to tell her. Poor soul! it would be a comfort rather than a distress to her to know, that he she loved had already gone before her and was even now waiting to welcome her with his old loving smile. She closed her eyes; my hand was still on hers. I felt a convulsive twitching of her slender fingers, and saw her breast heave with a stifled sob, and all was over. She had met her husband in a land where the cry of the widow, and the orphan, and the oppressed, is never pleaded in vain.

The house, and garden and furniture were sold the week after, and Omichund purchased them.

The next week the case was sent back from Calcutta. The grand jury had thrown out the bill.

Ten years afterwards I was talking one day to an old malee, or gardener, who had been three or four years in my service. His child had been ill of fever, and some quinine and medicines I had given the old malee for him brought the patient round. He expressed the utmost gratitude to me, and volunteered the following story, which he said he had long wanted to tell me, but had felt afraid. It was, that ten years before, he had been bribed by a present of six rupees to go one evening to the house of a "sahib" who lived there (pointing in the direction of what had been Clarke's cottage), and to be insolent to the sahib, so as, if possible, to induce him to strike him; he was then to go away to a village in another district several miles off, where, as long as he remained, he would receive two rupees a month. He did so, and had received the two rupees regularly for four or five years, when the payments suddenly ceased; and he then resolved, why he hardly knew, to come back to Budgepore with his family for work. He did not know what he was paid for, nor why he had been asked to insult the "sahib" and induce him to use violence. But as he left the garden that evening he recollected, he said, seeing two policemen on the road outside, and by them underneath the wall, there was something wrapped up in cloth, which looked like a man's body. He was afraid to take any notice of it or to say anything about it. But he had heard that it was Omichund who had supplied all the money which was paid to him.

CHRONICLE VII.

A LAW-SUIT.

CHRONICLE VII.

A LAW-SUIT.

"I HAVE been unfortunate enough to be involved in one or two law-suits, during my residence at Budgepore. One of them resulted from my having foolishly invested a little money in the purchase of a native house in the city. I did not live there, of course, or intend living there, but I let the house for a very decent rent. I had not been in possession long, before a rich native built a brick wall up within two feet in front of the door of the house. This, as you may easily see, was inconvenient to my tenants (one of whom was rather stout), and they all immediately vacated. I was obliged to bring an action against the trespasser. It was filed in the court of the native Civil Judge, of course, that being the court of first instance in which all original suits must be tried, unless the European Judge can be prevailed upon by having good and satisfactory cause shown, to send for any particular case, and try it in his own court. My case was numbered 35, and a day fixed for first hearing. Well, I went there on the day fixed, and then found I was mistaken; the number of the suit was 135, and not 35, and another day was fixed. I went, and to my astonishment found the suit was not numbered 135 at all, but 235. Again a postponement. But I cannot tell you how many times I went, only to have to go away again. At last I did what I ought to have done at first, inquired into the cause, when I found that the defendant was a creditor of the serishtadar, or head clerk of the Court, who owed him a thousand rupees.

"I then applied, and had the suit brought into the Judge's court. But here I was destined to no better success. I engaged a native advocate, to whom I entrusted all the papers in the case. This did not improve matters: the defendant easily bought him over, and he lost all the papers, and I had the trouble and expense of getting fresh ones. At last the case came on for settlement of the issues, when what was my astonishment, to hear the pleader for the defendant suggest in the first issue, whether there was any door at all. I lost my temper and got very angry, but I found, sure enough, that their first plea was, no door at all. It reminded me of the American case about the kettle, which the plaintiff alleged the defendant had borrowed, and returned without the spout. 'I shall prove,' said the counsel to the jury, 'that in the first place the kettle had no spout when it was borrowed; secondly, that it never was borrowed; and thirdly, that there was no kettle at all.'

"As soon as the day's business was over, I got into my buggy and drove down to look at the premises, and to see what the man could possibly mean by saying there was no door, when I had seen it scores of times. To my utter astonishment, I found he was correct; there was no door, and to all appearance there never had been one. No vestige of such a thing could be traced anywhere on the wall, so adroitly had it been built in, and the place concealed. I got in through one of the windows, and examined the inside wall, and found that it exhibited no more trace than the outside wall. I asked the neighbours if they could not swear there had been a door there, but they all denied ever having seen one. I went to the kotwal, and he said he had already promised the defendant to depose to the fact that the house never had had a door. In despair, I went to the man from whom I purchased the house, and he calmly assured me that this was the very reason why he had sold the house, because it had no door, and he had found residence there inconvenient in consequence. That was the state of my case, and now tell me, for you have had some experience in these matters, what do you think of it?"

"Well, OLD MORTALITY," said I, "your chance of a decree was not worth much. Why didn't you get proper legal assistance in the first instance? Why didn't you get a barrister from Calcutta?"

"I did try, but I found the expense too great. My attorneys in reply to my letter, asking what Mr. Small Talk would take up the case for, intimated it would be necessary for me to pay the fees beforehand—that of course I knew, but when they said that Small Talk would not come for less than ten thousand rupees down, and a thousand rupees an hour from the time he left till the time he returned to Calcutta, I thought it was too much. So I determined to be my own lawyer, and set to work to study the decisions of the Sudder Dewany from 1857, and I conducted the case myself. I have brought you the judgment, which you can read."

"*In the Court of the Civil Judge of Budgepore.*

"OLD MORTALITY *versus* SALIG RAM.

"Claim, 3,000 Rupees.

"JUDGMENT.

"The plaintiff in this suit purchased a house in the city of Budgepore a short time ago. He claims 3,000 Rs. damages from defendant, who, he alleges, erected a brick wall two feet from the door of that house, thereby destroying its utility as a place of residence, and in fact ruining the property. The main difficulty in this case is the fact, that the existence of the door, the approach to which is said to have been blocked up by the erection of the brick wall by the defendant, is disputed by the defendant. The evidence on this point is all in favour of the defendant. But I find certain admissions in the evidence of some of the defendant's witnesses, that go far to shake the confidence I might otherwise feel in a train of testimony so well substantiated by witnesses of the most respectable character. The principal witness for defendant, Jootharan, who built the house, and from whom the plaintiff purchased it, declares he built it without a door. This in itself is a suspicious circumstance. For of what use could a house be without a door? The witness himself says his object in having no doorway was to keep the cats out; but it is in evidence that he built a window, and it seems inconsistent to built a house for human habitation with a window, by which the ingress and egress of cats could be accomplished, and at the same time to put no doorway, by which the ingress and egress of its occupants could be affected. Had there been neither a window nor a door, then the original design of the builder would not have been inconsistent with the course he alleges he pursued, because the Court cannot but see that the object of keeping cats out would be effectually accomplished by the construction of a house without doors or windows. But to erect a dwelling-house with a window, by which the cats might undoubtedly effect an entrance, and yet to put no door, by which the occupants of the house could go in and out, seems to the Court so extraordinary an act, that the assertion of its commission must be received with great caution.

"The city kotwal, a man of undoubted veracity and most respectable character, deposes that the house never had a door; yet he admitted that he knew certain parties who resided in it. When asked how, in the absence of any door, these parties went in and out of the house, he replied, that they were not in the habit of going in and out.

"The Ameens appointed by the Court to examine the premises, report that there clearly never was any doorway, but at the same time they put in a list of articles that they found inside, among which I observe a cot included, which could not by any possibility have been taken in through the window.

"Although, therefore, the testimony of the defendant's witnesses is absolutely unimpeachable, the whole of them being men of the highest respectability and undoubted veracity, yet I find myself totally unable to adopt their conclusion, in face of the very strong presumption raised on the other side, viz., the presumption of the existence of a door.

"As the defendant had rested his whole case upon the denial of the existence of the door, and does not attempt to show that he did not build the brick wall in front of it, and so block it up, I find both the first issues for the plaintiff.

"The question of damages remains only to be considered.

"It is quite clear to this Court, that, whatever may have been the previous condition of the house, its present condition is not such as to allow of occupation by any tenants but such as can find ingress and egress through the window. Such tenants would no doubt principally, if not wholly, belong to the class the exclusion of which was contemplated by the witness Jootharam, when he constructed the edifice. There are no data before the Court by which the Court can derive any accurate idea of the probable rental derivable from that class of tenants.

"The value, however, of the bricks and material used to construct the wall erected by the defendant, is in evidence, and the Court considers that it will meet the equity of the case by awarding a decree to the plaintiff of the amount expended by defendant in constructing this wall, or 200 rupees. This decree will carry with it the costs of the suit.

"(Signed) BASIL MOOLTAWEE,

Judge."

CHRONICLE VIII.

THE VISIT OF OUR SPIN.

CHRONICLE VIII.

THE VISIT OF OUR SPIN.

OH, it was a great day for Budgepore when—I must really be excused for using that horribly vulgar Anglo-Indianism—the spin arrived. *The* spin, did I say? Yes, for you know there had not been one at Budgepore within the recollection of the oldest inhabitant! I say, before she arrived, the excitement was at boiling-pitch. We heard of her expected arrival a month before she came. A month's notice was rather a short notice, and when viewed in connection with some circumstances that transpired subsequently, which I shall detail all in good time, I may say it was a suspicious circumstance. Because, you see, in those days—I am speaking of 1840—you generally heard of the expected arrival of so important a personage as "a spin" a least three months, sometimes six, before the event happened. For before the young ladies left England it was always known to their friends to whom they were coming, when they might be expected, and they, of course, would naturally enough spread the report abroad. So that, in fact, Miss Smith or Miss Jones was expected at Muddlepore, or Hotchpotchabad, even while the interesting girls were engaged in shopping in London, selecting silks and muslin, laces and cambrics that were destined to commit havoc among the hearts of the male dwellers at Muddlepore and Hotchpotchabad.

"I say, old fellow, have you heard the news?" said young Anderson, coming into my room one morning.

"No, what news?"

"She's to be here to-morrow."

"You don't say so! Who told you?"

"Mrs. Gregory—I've just met her."

One word about Mrs. Gregory and her worthy husband. The Gregorys were the jolliest couple I ever knew. They had married early in life; they seemed to have no cares, enjoyed good health, and never dreamt of going the hills. At the time I speak of he had reached the rank of Major, and was enjoying the *otium cum dignitate* of that very easy birth, a Major in a native regiment commanded by a Lieutenant-Colonel, with little to do but to draw his 750 Rs. a month.

Mrs. Gregory, though a good many summers, and those Indian summers, had passed over her head, had lost none of the freshness and vivacity of youth. She was acutely sensitive to the ridiculous, and no one understood or appreciated a joke better than she. Perhaps, for a lady, she was a little too fond of jokes, even practical ones. I knew her so well that I could always tell by a peculiar twinkle in the corner of her eyes, when she was up to mischief, and took care to be prepared accordingly.

The next evening Robertson came in, as a small party were sitting down to dinner at my house, in a state of great excitement.

"I've seen her!" he said.

"Have you!" we all cried simultaneously. Not that I individually felt much interest in this young person, but I did not like to show indifference to a matter in which they were all so much concerned.

"What is she like?" two or three asked at once.

"Is she tall or short?"

"What colour eyes and hair?"

"How does she dress?"

"Where did you see her?"

"What about her paces?"

These and several more queries of a like kind were hurled at poor Robertson before he had had time to throw his cap on a chair, and draw another chair to the table.

Nobody had asked her name—that was left for me to do.

"Sophy Wilkins."

"Now I'll describe her to you," said Robertson when he had finished his soup, "and answer all your questions at once. Our new spin—she won't be a spin long, I take it—is the most angelic creature I ever set eyes upon. Her hair—well, I don't know what colour her hair is—I scarcely saw it; in fact, I think she has very little, but what there is, is light; her eyes are blue, her figure perfection, and her manners—"

A shout of laughter at this crisis drowned Robertson's voice, and prevented us from hearing the remainder of the description he was prepared to give. He blushed up to the eyes, and looked ashamed of himself. It was clear he was already head and ears over in love, and his friends had no delicacy in telling him so.

Sophy Wilkins was very pretty, there is no doubt, and Robertson's enthusiastic description of her did her but justice. I noticed that mischevous twinkling in the corner of Mrs. Gregory's eye when she introduced me to her pretty niece, and I said to myself, "You are up to some mischief, I know; perhaps you are anticipating the pleasure of seeing OLD MORTALITY in love."

Those were gay days for Budgepore. Budgepore hardly knew itself. It was the cold weather, and we had pic-nics, and archery parties and riding parties, balls and amusements without end. We mustered altogether about ten ladies, all of them, of course, except the last arrival, married. It is hardly necessary to say all the young men lost their hearts, and all were ready to propose to Sophy after she had been there a week. The first that did propose, and was accepted, too, was poor Robinson. The older officers shook their heads at the imprudence of such a match. I went so far as to remonstrate with my old friend Mrs. Gregory, for Robertson was only a lieutenant; but she merely gave me another malicious twinkle, and said it would be all right. I took her to mean that young ladies were proverbially fickle, and that the match would be broken off, or that Sophy Wilkins was a rich banker's or merchant's daughter, and an heiress.

At first all went well, Robertson was seen out riding with his affianced bride for two evenings, and they rode together round and round the band-stand. After a few days there began to prevail sinister reports about the engagement. Sophy was observed to bestow her favours upon Sharpe, the adjutant, and poor Robertson looked more and more crestfallen.

I don't know how these things are managed, never having had any experience of the world of matrimony myself, but I do know this, that Sophy Wilkins managed to jilt Robertson and took Sharpe into favour.

Of course everybody observed it, and Robertson got jealous; still, he could not believe that his goddess was faithless, and hoped on, though his rival daily grew in favour.

One evening we had a dance at the mess. It was the Thursday evening, the week after her arrival. I had just concluded a set of quadrilles with Sophy Wilkins, when she slightly pressed my arm with her taper fingers, and asked me to take her outside. She seemed suddenly depressed, excited, pained at something. Was she ill? No. As I turned to lead her out, I saw the cause of her discomposure. There stood her adorer (number one) the picture of sadness and grief, leaning with his arms folded against the door, and looking most woe-begone. Only that week she had confessed to him her love, and sworn to be true and faithful, and now she had been flirting all the evening with this fellow and that, and especially with Sharpe, the adjutant.

When we reached the garden, Miss Sophy seated herself upon a rustic bench underneath a magnificent peepul tree, whose leaves and branches the rays of the full moon were bathing in a flood of silvery light. She motioned me to seat myself beside her, which I did, at least as well as I could, for there was only a very little bit of the seat left just at the end, four-fifths of it being enveloped with the folds of her snowy tarlatan dress, a mass of dazzling drapery that shone in the moonlight, the emblem of virgin purity. I did not venture to remove it, much less to sit upon it, but placed myself respectfully at the edge of the seat, in a position that caused me very shortly to suffer from cramp.

I had begun to take a considerable interest in this young girl. She seemed at times so artless and innocent, one trembled to think of her being exposed to the temptations of the world, and at other times her genius would flash out in remarks and suggestions, that in one less child-like would have seemed like being *very* wide-awake. "Does she intend, I wonder," said I, mentally addressing myself, "to try it on with me—me—OLD MORTALITY? no, hardly that!"

"Are you unwell, Miss Wilkins?" said I, in my blandest tone, and most sympathetic manner.

She sighed.

"Worse and worse," thought I. "I hope she won't cry."

An awkward silence ensued—a very awkward one. What

was I to do? Did she expect me to take her hand, and press it with gentle sympathy! Yes; perhaps that will be the best way.

I took it. "My dear Miss Wilkins," said I, at the same moment, "Do tell me if you are unwell; is there any grief weighing upon your spirits, any sorrow you are longing for sympathy under? I am an old man, old enough to be your father; confide in me, if I can comfort you, I will; if I can advise you, you shall have my advice; if—"

"Yes, Old Mortality," she said in her sweetest tones. She had a sweet voice, and it seemed somehow in harmony with the soft evening air, and the bright moonlight.

"Yes; I have a deep sorrow—poor Gerard!"—(that was Robertson,) "his reproachful yet tender look cut me to the heart—how could I have been so cruel!"

And she put the loveliest cambric handkerchief, bordered with the loveliest Maltese lace, to her eyes. I knew she was weeping.

"Is it the case then? but excuse me, I have no right to ask the question; Gerard Robertson is jilted, is he? and Sharpe is the happy man?"

I had no sooner said the words, somehow, than I felt as if I had been a brute; and I wished the earth would open, or, what was much more likely of attainment, that a large cobra would open his mouth and swallow me up.

But she did not turn on me and spurn me. She withdrew her handkerchief from her eyes and raised those glorious blue orbs, still glistening with pearly drops, upwards through the branches of the noble old tree, to where the stars in heaven were sleeping in the calm moonlight.

Then she turned them full upon me, and said—

"You have saved me, oh, so much pain. You have expressed, curtly, it is true, but with manly vigour, what I was trying in vain to get my foolish woman's heart to say to you. Yes, Gerard and I must part. Our souls are not in unison. Were we to marry, and he has only lieutenant's pay, two hundred and fifty-six—ten and a company, we should be unhappy for life. I feel that I have wronged him, but do you think you could do me a favour?"

I am quite certain that if she had asked me to climb up to the top of the tree, I should have attempted it.

"I will do anything I can for you, Miss Wilkins," I said.

"Oh, thank you—thank you a thousand times. This is what I want you to do; to go and break it to Mr. Robertson —in the gentlest way you can. He is here to-night, go now and tell him."

I went upon the unpleasant duty, and performed it like a man, and returned to the garden seat to receive her thanks. She asked me if he seemed to feel it very much. I said yes, I thought he did.

She signified her intention of returning to the ball-room. Obedient as a slave, I rose and offered her my arm.

When we returned, Robertson was gone. Sharpe was, however, there, and the next minute she was whirling round with him in the dance, his arm clasping her waist and her head reclining gracefully upon his shoulder.

Next day it was given out that she was engaged to him, and they rode together side by side round the band-stand.

Sharpe was a pattern adjutant, the man of most influence in the regiment next to the native doctor. He was a well-made man, of about six feet one, with well-developed chest and muscular limbs. He had a great idea of the dignity of his office, and used to wig the junior officers as if he were commandant. He was generally to be seen, except, of course, upon parade, with a service letter in his hand, to the contents of which he would ever and anon refer, even while in conversation, as if the whole business of the administration rested upon him, and he had no leisure to attend to matters of minor import. That he should have cut out Robertson was not, we thought, to be wondered at, so much as that he should have condescended to accept the post of suitor No. 2.

As soon as the engagement was complete, he began, recklessly almost, to prepare his house for the reception of his bride. The verandah was thronged with a crowd of carpenters and work-people; he began to have his rooms painted, at least coloured, and bought a silver tea-pot and a pony-carriage.

I left Budgepore for a few days about this time, and when I came back I drove over to the colonel's. Finding Mrs. Sungeen alone in the drawing-room, I entered into conversation with her, as I was curious to hear the news. And she did not keep me long waiting. Of course Sophy Wilkins was the theme.

"What a girl that is, to be sure!" she said. "I never knew a girl behave so shamefully as she has done, upon my word I never did."

I supposed she was alluding to her having jilted Robertson, and said—

"Yes, but I have always understood it was a privilege ladies were allowed to indulge in. Robertson was foolish to make so much of it. I'm sure if it had been I, I wouldn't have cried my eyes out; stuff and nonsense, all women are alike, and—"

"All good for nothing, you think, Old Mortality, I know. No, it was not Robertson I was thinking of, but there's poor Sharpe, he's spent already three thousand rupees in furniture and horses."

Mrs. Sungeen, you observe, used to call the officers of her husband's regiment by their surnames. It was a common practice in those days, I don't know whether it is so now.

"Well," I replied, "it is not too much. Any man who marries such a pretty girl as Sophy Wilkins ought to have his house nicely furnished. If she was my wife she should have everything of the best."

I was pretty safe in saying that, and chuckled inwardly while I said it.

"Everything of the best! Then it seems you haven't heard."

"What?"

"Why, the last?"

"Pray do not drive me to distraction, Mrs. Sungeen," said I, irritated beyond endurance. "I really like this girl,—that s—I—take an interest in her—a fatherly interest, you know, —tell me, has anything happened to interfere with her engagement with Sharpe?"

"Anything happened!—Yes, a little. She's engaged to Cocker, that stuck up young assistant civilian, you know."

Now Cocker was not at all particularly "stuck up." He was a very good fellow. But Mrs. Sungeen hated a civilian as a wild bull does a piece of red cloth. In her eyes all the service were "stuck up."

I was so astonished at this communication that I actually jumped off my chair.

"Lawk a mercy! Old Mortality, you needn't be so much

astonished at that. It's just what I expected. I *am* thankful of one thing, at any rate, that the girl does not come into the regiment."

"But how did all this come about, do tell me, I am dying to know."

"Well, it was easy enough coming about. Young Cocker saw her at hand, and met her two or three times, proposed, and was accepted, and what do you think the heartless creature said? I spoke to her, I was determined I would speak to her, she shouldn't break the heart of all my boys this way, without my having a word with her. So I told her I thought she ought to have known her own mind better than to break poor Robertson's heart (the poor boy has hardly smiled since; he has been over to dinner every day, and I do my best to cheer him, but it's no use), and there's Sharpe, he has not only broken his heart, but he's furnished his house, which is a much more serious thing. Now what do you think she said; "You don't know, Mrs. Sungeen, how I hate myself for the way I have behaved to these young men; but a poor helpless orphan as I am, must take care of herself. Now Mr. Cocker is a civilian, and a civilian is £300 a year, 'dead or alive.' That's what she said, the very words,—'dead or alive.'"

"Upon my word, she is a cool young lady. But, do you know, I rather respect her for having the honesty to speak out her sentiments; and how does Sharpe bear it?"

"Oh, very well. He has sold all the furniture and carpets and the silver teapot to Mr. Cocker, who has taken them off his hands at cost price."

Cocker's engagement lasted long enough for Miss Sophy to lame both his horses, and for him to buy a new Arab for 1,200 rupees on the strength of a loan from the Agra Bank, which he sent up with a bran new saddle and bridle one morning to Gregory's house. After a short time, Molyneux, the Collector, who had been out in the district, returned to the station, and Cocker rather proudly introduced him to his affianced bride the first evening after his return.

There was something rather peculiar, I thought, about Miss Sophy. She never appeared except in the evening. If you called at the Gregory's house, you did not see her, though on one or two occasions, after keeping them waiting a long time, she had vouchsafed to gladden the eyes of her lovers with her presence. She never went to church. Was she a dissenter, I used to wonder? She used to enjoy dancing and riding, and the pleasure of her society in these two pastimes was the only one she ever allowed her lovers to enjoy.

The day following that of Molyneux's introduction, Cocker had orders to go out into the district and complete the work that his superior had left uncompleted. He went reluctantly enough, poor fellow. Mrs. Sungeen said she knew very well how it would be. But, then, it is very easy to be wise after the event. How it came about I do not know, but within a week of Cocker's departure Sophy had engaged herself to Molyneux. Cocker was very angry at first, and insisted on calling him out, but it ended in Molyneux paying the costs, that is, taking the furniture and the carpets and the silver tea-pot off Cocker's hands. They used to say at Budgepore that it was quite a common thing to see the carts laden with the furniture going from house to house, indicating the direction in which Sophy's affections had been transferred. But this was an exaggeration, because they, I mean the chairs, tables, &c., &c., had only been moved twice—once from Sharpe's to Cocker's, and once from Cocker's to Molyneux's.

Molyneux was now the happy man. And no sooner did it become noised abroad in the district that the Collector Sahib was about to take a wife, a wife with whom, moreover, he was desperately in love, than the affectionate and attached inhabitants of the villages, zemindaries and jageers round about Budgepore came in to pay their respects to the Collector's wife that was to be, bringing with them or sending before them such little offerings in the shape of fat kine, goats, baskets of fruit and vegetables, and other presents of a more costly nature, that Mrs. Gregory was put to her wit's end to know what to do with them.

Molyneux, in addition to *the* furniture, sent down a large order to Shearwood to the amount of 5,000 rupees, for spring-chairs, sofas, foot-stools, a cheval glass, dressing-tables, &c.

Alas for human hopes and human wishes! We were playing pool in the billiard-room, a lot of us, one afternoon, Molyneux being of the party, when a pink-coloured envelope was put into his hands. He took it into the verandah on pretence to get more light to read it by. Artful man. *I* saw him.

His back was no sooner turned and his face, as he thought, out of sight, than he pressed the seal, I mean the part where the seal ought to have been, to his lips, and then he opened it. Ah, he should have opened it first! And reader, do you learn a lesson from this. Never kiss a letter till you have mastered it's contents.

The note was as follows:—

"My dear Mr. Molyneux,—

"Before this reaches you we shall have parted for ever. Do not ask me why. Do not seek to follow me. Do not rend still further my broken heart by forcing me to explanations, painful because they will so forcibly recall the sweetness of the past, now fled from me—from us, for ever. Duty, more binding than the vows of an affianced wife, calls me elsewhere. Adieu. I am gone.

"Yours, heart-broken,

"SOPHIA WILKINS."

Molyneux turned deadly pale. He threw down the billiard cue, snatched his coat and rushed out of the house, jumped into his buggy, and drove off towards Gregory's. I followed, for I feared some catastrophe.

But what was the good of our going except to be laughed at by Mrs. Gregory? I do not mean that she openly ridiculed Molyneux's sorrow, but I saw by the twinkle of her eye that there was no real sympathy in her bosom.

Sophy Wilkins' sojourn among us and her sudden departure had had something the same effect upon the secluded little circle of Budgeporeans that the failure of a bank would have had. Robertson was the one of the victims to the fair enslaver who escaped without both an empty pocket and a broken heart. And in consequence, having only one sorrow to mourn over, he felt it all the more deeply. Molyneux soon got married, and Shearwood's consignment came up just in time. Cocker, who had manfully struggled against debt, and with success, hitherto, now being below the water, gave up the attempt to keep any longer above, and eventually became very heavily involved.

* * * * * * * *

About a couple of months after this, I passed through

Umballa on my way to the hills. The —— Lancers were quartered there, and I put up with one of them on my way through. It happened there was a theatrical performance by the officers the evening of my halt, and as I was to start for Kala at twelve at night, I willingly consented to accompany my friend to the regimental theatre. One of the pieces played was the "Lady of Lyons." What was my pleasurable surprise to see the principal part in the piece taken by my old though still young friend, Sophy Wilkins, or at least a young lady as like her as one pea to another. There were the same rosy cheeks, the same blue eyes, the same clear complexion, the same short hair, the same grace of manner, that had charmed us all at Budgepore.

Walking home with my friend Quartly and his chum Howard, they asked me how I liked the play?

"Very much," said I; "and it adds to the charm of a thing of this kind, where you get ladies to take part. I wish it was more generally the custom in India, as it might be in well-managed amateur theatres, where the actors are all gentlemen, and belong to one corps."

My sage remarks, to my surprise, were greeted with shouts of laughter from my two companions.

"What are you laughing at?" said I.

Quartly was about to say something, when Howard nudged him, and said in an under-tone, but not so softly but that I could hear,

"Don't tell him."

We had by that time reached the compound gate, and I found my palkee and bearers ready waiting. I was busy adjusting the contents of the palkee when my two friends passed me to enter the house. Just at that moment I heard a pony's hoofs clattering along the road, and by the time I had finished my arrangement, and had got inside the house, where supper was laid out, the pony had brought its rider to the door.

"Come in, Chaffers," said Quartly, going out of the verandah. "Come and have some supper."

"Well, I don't mind if I do. Those petticoats are devilish hot.'

"Oh! is that Chaffers?" said Howard, putting down a bottle of champagne he was just manipulating, and running out.

"Come in!—there's one of your Budgepore friends here."

The estimable Chaffers, whoever he was, had just reached the doorway, when Howard uttered the last few words. He turned like a flash of lightning, with a little scream you might have taken for a woman's just before a fit of hysteria, leaped on his pony, and in an instant almost, judging from the sound of the animal's hoofs, was out of the compound, galloping down the road at least ten miles an hour.

* * * * * *

When I returned to Budgepore in November, the cold weather had set in. There was a large dinner party shortly after my return, and as usual every one in the station was present. Now, thought I, I will pay her out.

It was during the awkward period, before dinner was announced. There happened to be a dead silence. No one spoke a word. I went and stood in the centre of the group, and addressed myself pointedly to Mrs. Gregory, who was a little distance from me, so necessarily everyone in the room heard what passed. This was just what I wanted.

"I had a very pleasant visit at Umballa on my way through, Mrs. Gregory," said I.

"Indeed!"

Everybody's attention was now attracted to us, not because they were particularly interested in my visit to Umballa, but simply because no one had anything else to attend to.

"Yes," said I. "I had the pleasure of witnessing a very pretty wedding."

"Indeed!" said Mrs. Gregory, not exactly understanding why I addressed such a pointless observation to her.

"And pray whose was it?"

"Your niece's, Sophy Wilkins, did you not know, she—is married?"

Mrs. Gregory's eye did not twinkle with mischief at me then. It implored pity, it prayed silence—it besought me for mercy.

I felt like an executioner—at least like what I suppose an executioner feels just as he adjusts the rope round the victim's neck, and thinks of the majesty of public justice.

"Dinner is ready," said the old khansama in Hindustani; and this saved her.

Mrs. Gregory is my friend for life. I can make her do my slightest bidding, and she dare not thwart my will, for I have something over her *in terrorem*. I don't know how her husband likes the relative position in which we stand, but then I never intend to ask him.

CHRONICLE IX.

THE REMOUNTS.

CHRONICLE IX.

THE REMOUNTS.

CHAPTER I.

A FAUX PAS.

The events which I propose briefly to chronicle in the following pages occurred at Budgepore in the year 18—.

I have already taken the measure of the society of Budgepore. There were, however, some important characters whom I have not yet introduced to my readers. When I say "characters" in the plural, I speak, perhaps, scarcely with grammatical correctness, for I intend to designate the famous firm of Cork, Screw & Co. That is to say, the Budgepore branch of that illustrious firm was represented by one individual only, and that was Screw Septimus, the seventh son of old Screw, and the nephew of the gentleman who, as one of the principal shareholders in the firm, lent his name to the partnership. One of these days, perhaps, I may chronicle the history, the rise, progress, and decay and ultimate fate of this enterprising house, how, beginning from small things they grew to great, then having reached the zenith of prosperity and fame they become transmogrified into a joint-stock company under the title of the "All India Europe Goods Association," how the shareholders fell out, and went to law, and the whilom prosperous concern flowed gently into the hands of a liquidator, who liquidated so successfully that after two short years there was nothing left for the shareholders to fight about any more, which, as you will easily see, was the most fortunate termination that the affair could possibly take, inasmuch as the shareholders were after that always contented and good friends, whereas before they had always been quarrelling.

The firm of Cork, Screw & Co. has elsewhere been described by an abler pen than mine, I have, therefore, no intention of dwelling upon it here. I merely allude to it, as their premises happened to be the place where I one morning picked up a piece of news.

There was at that time residing at Budgepore, Colonel Chugli, who having reached that stage of promotion where there was nothing left for him to get but a brigade command, took up his abode at Budgepore during the cold weather months, and always went to Simla in the hot. He had one of the best houses and nicest gardens in the place. He did not entertain, but he gave, or rather I should, perhaps, say, he held, for people do not "give" but they "hold," prayer meetings. He was a dissenter, and belonged, I believe, to one of the one hundred and seventeen sects of Independents. I do not know which, and I rather doubt if he did. However, that is nothing to the purpose. But he was always to be found at Screw's in the morning, meandering, or as it is less poetically, but more forcibly expressed, "mooning" about the shop, not buying anything in particular, but he went there, I fancy, as a great many others did, as a sort of morning lounge where you might hear all the news, *id est* the scandal and tittle tattle of the day before, which, after dripping through the minor channels of the coffee-shops, formed itself into a pretty large stream and ran merrily through the premises of the great dealer in "Europe goods."

The "coffee-shop" is an essentially Indian institution, and and a very estimable institution it is in its way. The habit of early rising, and of taking out-of-door exercise before the sun gets hot, necessitates a meal before the usual breakfast hour. And so the custom has grown up among us of meeting at one another's houses in the morning after parade is over, or on our return from our morning walk or ride. In a shady nook in the garden, or in a summer-house, these social gatherings take place, where from half-an-hour to an hour, or even longer, those who are very intimate meet round the breakfast-table, for so it must be called, discuss the news, open their letters or newspapers, talk gossip, and, when there are ladies, usually practise archery, or play some other game on the lawn.

I once asked young Screw if Colonel Chugli made many

purchases at his shop. I don't know what business I had to ask the question. But one does get into a bad habit of thinking and talking a great deal about one's neighbour's private affairs in India, you know. I suppose the reason is that peoples' "private affairs" are so often dragged before the public in the Commander-in-Chief's orders, that curiosity becomes involuntarily excited. And I had seen the Colonel so constantly at the shop that I imagined he spent a share of his income, proportionate to his time, there.

"Oh no, sir," said young Screw, in reply to my question, "he never bought anything but once, and that was at auction."

"Indeed! and what did he buy then?"

"Why, he made rather an unfortunate purchase; at least, it was a mistake; but the Colonel behaved like a gentleman, and there was no disturbance about. He bought a gross of green gooseberries."

"A gross of green gooseberries!" said I, much astonished.

"Yes, Sir, and he was taken very ill after it. It happened in this way, you see, Sir. We had an auction, selling off all the old stock to make room for the new. Among the old stock there was a gross of green gooseberry tart fruit. We put them up at two annas a bottle, and the Colonel thinking he was bidding for a bottle only, bought the whole stock at five annas a bottle. Wasn't he mad when they were sent home! He had them put out in a row in the verandah, like a regiment of soldiers, and walked up and down in front of them for full half an hour, as if he was inspecting them on parade."

"I wonder he did not send them back, you would not do me in that way, I can tell you."

"Well, sir, if he had sent them back we would have taken them back, of course, upon the mistake being explained. But the Colonel, he made a good thing of it."

"How did he manage that?"

"Well, sir, it is a curious story rather. But the way was this; about nine months before this occurred there was a chemical examiner appointed to Government. His business is, when it is supposed anybody has been poisoned, to get the insides of the persons that have been poisoned and analyse them."

"Analyse them?"

"Yes, analyse them, to see what they died of. A day after the appointment appeared in orders, Mr. Gerkin, Joint Magistrates of Ahmedpore, reported that seven children and the father and mother had all died under suspicious circumstances. The Civil Surgeon had made a *post mortem* examination, and all the insides were readily packed in separate parcels to send to the chemical examiner, Dr. Machnonochy, the same that had the harness depôt at Cawnpore. Well, Mr. Gerkin wrote an official letter to the Magistrate who wrote an official letter to the Commissioner, who wrote another to the Deputy Inspector-General of the division, who sent it back, recommending the Commissioner to apply to the Public Works Department for bottles or jars to put the insides into. The Public Works Department returned the application, and said the Commissariat was the proper quarter to apply to. So the Commissioner wrote to the Commissariat Officer, who referred him to the Deputy Commissary of Ordnance. The Deputy Commissary of Ordnance sent the letter on to the Deputy Inspector, who was travelling then upon a tour of inspection, but the letter reached him after about three weeks, and he wrote to say that he thought the Department could not interfere without orders from Calcutta; but he thought either the Clothing Agency or the Gun-Carriage Agency at Futteghur would be able to do what was necessary. Meantime the Civil Surgeon at Ahmedpore was almost wild with vexation and annoyance. He had been obliged to move out into tents with his family and abandon the house, and, indeed, not only was the house abandoned, but no one could drive along the road past the gate. For, you see, sir, the articles having been taken out and packed up under suspicious circumstances, couldn't be buried without being examined. The Doctor, he wanted to bury them, but the Joint Magistrate said if he did, he would be tried at the High Court on suspicion of having poisoned the parties himself. So he was determined to do something, and he addressed the Lieutenant-Governor on the subject. The Lieutenant-Governor sent the letter back, with a wig, saying, he was to address him through the proper channel, his immediate superior. So he wrote to the Deputy Inspector and begged that his letter might be forwarded to the Inspector-General. When the Inspector-General found what was wanted, he addressed the Government, recommending them to purchase in the bazaar a number of empty tart-fruit bottles,* and distribute them about the country among the different civil officers. So Colonel Chugli heard of it, and when tenders were called for, his was the lowest and largest. For no one else had a gross of empty tart-fruit bottles to spare, and he sold them at a profit of six pie on each bottle. And that is the history of the tart-fruit bottles."

I have rather digressed, however, from the main point of my chronicle, which was to relate what Colonel Chugli told me that morning.

He asked me if I had heard the news. I said no. Then he told me, at least I gathered it from his observation, that young Twemlow of the Stud had got into trouble.

The Budgepore Stud, I must tell you, was an institution of the class its names intimates. It was situated about twenty miles from the station. It was a favourite appointment, that of Superintendent of the Stud, and Twemlow had been considered very lucky to get it.

I must confess when I heard this news I was a little taken aback and conscience-stricken. I was taken aback, because I could not conceive how Twemlow, who I knew was the soul of honour and as upright a man as ever breathed, could have possibly done anything that was wrong. I was conscience-stricken, because the day he got intimation of the appointment he happened to be passing through Budgepore and putting up with me. If it had not been for my persuading him I do not think he would have taken it. Appointments in India are given away without the slightest regard to a recipient's fitness or unfitness for them. Twemlow's name was down in the Governor-General's list for the first staff appointment, and it happened to be a Stud appointment, and he got it.

"Do you know, Old Mortality," he said, after telling me what the letter contained—the letter that had brought him the offer of the appointment—"I cannot possibly accept this offer. It's very kind of Tudor to offer it, but it's deuced unlucky it was a Stud appointment that fell vacant."

"But why not," said I, "Why not take it? You must not

* Official instructions have recently been issued by the head of the Medical Department for the employment of empty tart-fruit bottles for these purposes.

fly too high at first. It is a great catch for you to get away from your regiment at all. You are the last one that can get away, you know, for they have their full complement of absentees. Besides, it is a very nice birth. You will be able to be married now, and it is a healthy place you live at, and a capital house and easy work, and very tolerable pay. Upon my word, Twemlow, I do think you are rather hard to please. Why, bless my soul, when I was at your age——"

"Oh, stop that, please. There's nothing I hate more than to hear a man saying, 'when I was your age,' as if every one that had not reached a certain age must be a fool. No, no, you misunderstand me. What I mean is, how can I have the face, the bare, brazen-faced impudence to take an appointment in the Stud when I should not know a horse from a cow, except for the horns. I hate the very smell of a stable, and only get on the back of a horse when I am obliged. I'm perfectly and utterly ignorant of all and every duty connected with the Stud. The idea of my breeding horses, and looking after mares, and stallions, and oats, and head-stalls! Oh, dear! Oh, dear! And yet if I don't take this appointment I'm done for. I shall never get another such an offer, indeed I shall never get another offer at all, for Stubbs, you know, has been promised, and if he gets away from the regiment then I'm shelved, and my marriage must be put off and the devil to pay."

"Don't bother yourself, my good fellow," said I; "take the appointment, and do your best. No man can do more. Ten to one, aye, a hundred to one, you will find some old baboo who has been in the office for the last thirty years, who will show you all the office work; and as for the horses and mares, why, if I were you, I should leave them pretty much to themselves. Any way your assistant, who will probably be a man who lives in a stable and understands the thing thoroughly, he'll put you up to it all."

"But I shall look such a fool, talking about things I don't understand."

"Then why talk about them? can't you listen? Why, I've known men to go through life with the reputation of being exceedingly clever and very deep, and yet they were dolts; only they had sense enough to keep their mouths shut, and Society put them down for philosophers. Depend on it, if you want people to be afraid of you, and to think you wise, you have only got to be always silent."

So Twemlow took the appointment, and was married on the strength of it.

I was determined to hear more of this, if possible, so I drove over to Mrs. Thwaites's house. Mrs. Thwaites was one of the gems of Budgepore. Her husband was at that time Civil Surgeon, and a very popular man he was, a good doctor, and a useful member of our little circle; always ready and willing to take a foremost part in any little piece of innocent gaiety, a dance or a picnic, or amateur theatrical performances got up *pro bono publico* for the good of our little commonwealth. Mrs. Thwaites, who was the doctor's second wife, was some ten years younger than her husband. She was pretty and amiable, attractive without being a flirt; with all that charming grace of manner and liveliness of disposition, and at the same time an abundance of good sense, that makes such a woman in the little coteries of Anglo-Indian society all powerful for good in the beneficial influence she exercises.

Her morning assemblies were extremely popular. She had a pretty little summer-house, and a very nicely-kept garden, with an archery-ground; croquet in those days had not been discovered. The greatest attraction, however, to these charming little *réunions* were the grace and vivacity with which the hostess herself presided over them, and made the occasion a pleasant one for all her visitors.

Her appearance in the morning was enough to refresh the spirits of a dry old bachelor like myself, and make my memory wander back down the vista of past years, to the time when youth gilded the horizon of life, and I could not help thinking how different an aspect that life would have worn, if it had been enlivened all through its course with the constant presence and society of one so bright, and innocent, and fresh as the peerless creature that cheered, like a beam of sunshine in an English house, the pathway of our friend Thwaites. Lucky fellow! But you did not feel envious or jealous of him, he had such a good heart, and was so devoted to his pretty lovely wife; and she was so fond of him!

Like a flower freshened with the early dew, she used to appear in the morning, with the hue of health upon her cheek, even in that climate, clad all in white, pure and spotless as her own soul, and perform all the little duties of her homely hospitality with as much innate grace and such winning ways, that half an hour spent in her society in the morning, seemed to give a pleasant, healthy tone to your spirits all the day.

The Thwaiteses did not entertain largely; his income would not allow it, for he had a young, rising family. But Mrs. Thwaites was immensely popular for all that; and, although they did not gather nightly a large assemblage round their mahogany, nor give their guests, when they did entertain, great feasts, yet you were always sure to meet at Mrs. Thwaites's at the hour when it was known she received visitors, pretty well everyone in Budgepore who was not kept away by duty from her charming circle.

One more trait in Mrs. Thwaites's character and I close my panegyric, and that was, that you never by any chance saw those beautifully chiselled rosy lips open to emit a single ill-natured remark, nor a word of scandal. That scandal was talked at her morning breakfast parties was a necessity, for did she not live and breathe at Budgepore? And was not Budgepore an Indian station? and did not everybody in Budgepore almost meet at Mrs. Thwaites's in the morning? But, though scandal was talked there, as indeed how could it not be? it was a sort of contraband. And whereas at other ladies' houses, and at other gatherings, it formed the staple of conversation, here the little choice morsels of tittle tattle were repeated or invented in almost an under-tone, and at odd times, between neighbours who sat close enough together to talk to one another without addressing themselves to the general public. When any scandalous story was repeated to her, or was mentioned in such a way that it would be affectation to pretend to ignore it, or make believe she did not hear it, she would always turn it off, or draw out the sting in her own pretty way, just as she performed all the simplest and most ordinary commonplace actions of daily life. Men adored her, women envied, though they could not help loving, while they wish they could imitate her, and with it all, she never, as far as I knew, and I did know most things that went on at Budgepore,—as far as I knew, she never gave her husband cause for one instant to be jealous.

I knew I should be sure to hear all there was to hear at Mrs. Thwaites's, because I knew I should meet Mrs. Cameltrunk there, and Mrs. Mountjoy, and Mrs. James, and Miss Graham, besides a whole host of bachelors—everybody; in fact the world of Budgepore; what need I say more? So to Mrs. Thwaites's I went.

"Oh, have you heard the news?" said Mrs. Mountjoy, as I took the only vacant chair by her side.

"What news?" said I

"Oh, about young Twemlow at the stud, such a shocking thing; and his young wife too!"

"Yes, indeed! I pity her," said I, "if anything has happened to her husband, they are so devoted to one another, and she, poor girl! so little able to battle with the world!"

"I don't see that she is to be pitied so much as all that. I do pity her, of course, as I have a woman's heart. But I cannot say I see her great beauty; and after all, if one does marry a swindler——"

"Mary, what's that you're talking about?" said Mountjoy, with his mouth full of muffin.

"Not about you, George."

"No; I should hope not, by gad. You ladies make use of strong words sometimes. Twemlow's as honest a fellow as ever breathed."

"Amen to that," said I, hoping that I should hear something by-and-bye to put me on the right track.

"Honest, you may call it," said Cameltrunk, who was the Executive Commissariat officer at Budgepore, "I don't call it honest. Though what the fellow can have been about I can't imagine. But it is just these things that give the service such a bad name. I say a black sheep should be marked and turned out of the flock, and every white sheep who does not want to be blackened too should help to turn him out."

"Even so," said I, "let every one try and be the first to cast the first stone."

"Stone, yes, stone him. I wish the old Jewish practice was in vogue in these days. It was a right good custom, that. Society protected itself by destroying the man that turned against it. Every member of the community that was wronged had a hand in the punishment, and so it ought to be now."

"It's your turn, Mrs. Cameltrunk," said Mrs. Thwaites, coming up just at this moment from shooting, with her bow in her hand. "I have got two reds, and a bull's eye, see if you can beat that. How do you do, Mr. Old Mortality?" she added, holding out her hand to me. She had heard what we were talking about, but she did not choose to notice. Mrs. James came with her, and I shook hands with her just afterwards. She also had overheard our conversation, for the two ladies had arrived at the spot where we were seated a second or two before, and we had not noticed them. As Mrs. Thwaites was there, of course it was the centre of attraction, and there were several people on the spot, as it were, by magic.

"Oh, yes," said Mrs. James, taking up the thread of the discourse, "James told me all about it. Captain Twemlow has ridden away with all the horses in the stud."

There was a little amusement caused by this remark, though no one seemed to know whether it was intended as a joke or not.

"How the devil did he manage to do that, I wonder?" said Major Carshore, who had a great dislike to Mrs. James, for he had loved her once, and she had snubbed him, having preferred a young civilian upon three hundred and fifty rupees a month to an elderly captain on four hundred and fifteen. And he very often had an opportunity for showing his contempt for his whilom mistress, for she was not very wise, and occasionally used to make the most absurd remarks, putting the cart before the horse without knowing it, or letting something dreadfully *malapropos* fall plump in the middle of your feelings.

I found that the little observation I have recorded, and several of the same tenor that I have not recorded, all being very much in Twemlow's favour, simply because I was determined not to prejudge my young friend's case, had made me for the time unpopular. They seemed suddenly to recollect that Twemlow was a friend of mine; so they let the conversation drop. The only one that kept it up was Cameltrunk, and he went on harping upon the old subject, "black sheep," and the necessity of expelling them from the flock less they should taint the immaculate. So finding I could get nothing here, I soon left and came away, determining that after breakfast I would go and ask the brigadier, and I knew the good-hearted old gentleman would not disappoint me. On my way home, however, I was intercepted by a messenger on an errand of some import, and I was detained at home all that day in consequence.

In the evening I was engaged to dine with Mrs. Forceps. This lady's husband was then Commissioner of Budgepore, and she was the Commissioner's wife. It may at first sight appear mere tautology to state this, as it would appear to follow from the premises. But I should not be doing Mrs. Forceps justice if I did not give her a sentence all to herself. If I had left it as it stood, it might have been perceived that she was Forceps' wife, but I wished to express a little more, viz., that she was the wife of the Commissioner.

Just a word about her antecedents. She came out to India when a young girl of two and twenty, good-looking, well educated, and with lady-like manners, as a governess in the family of the judge of Mamlukabad. Being the only marriageable young lady at that interesting place, where there were exactly fourteen young bachelors all eager to marry if they could find an English lady to lead to the altar, it is not very surprising that she had the prospect before long of a position, better, as the world usually regards such things, than that of a governess in a civilian's family, where she had every possible comfort, was treated in every respect as a lady in her situation should be treated, and enjoyed all the pleasures of society without sharing in its responsibilities and cares. So she was engaged to young Fairbrother of the 77th N.I., and as it was the hot weather and the chaplain was in the hills at Paharpore, he was written to and requested to come down and perform the marriage ceremony. The day was fixed, and the guests invited, and the breakfast ordered, when a letter came from the Reverend Mr. Freeman, saying that it was as much as his life was worth for him to come through the terai (the jungle at the foot of the hills) at that time of the year, and the young couple might wait. Young Fairbrother, who was hotly in love, was frantic. He became quite a poet in the sublimity of his indignation against "a mercenary priesthood," "pampered ecclesiastics," and "idle drones." The Colonel said it was a great shame, and took the matter up and wrote to the General, who wrote back to say he couldn't interfere. Then he wrote to the Commander-in-Chief, who forwarded the letter on to the Bishop, who sent it back, saying that the chaplains, as regards their movements, were under military orders.

While this correspondence was going on, young Forceps came down from Paharpore and put up with his aunt and uncle, saw Miss Fleetwood, and loved. He was an assistant, just then about to develop into a "joint." Emily Fleetwood was young and fascinating, and, if married, had a prospect of increasing expenses in her household. Fairbrother was a lieutenant and adjutant of a marching regiment. But, then, he was madly in love. The correspondence with the authorities seemed endless. He wrote and offered Freeman three hundred rupees to come down. Freeman, wise in his generation, wouldn't stir without money. The money was sent, and he came in time to unite in the bonds of matrimony—Emily Fleetwood and Charles Forceps.

Forceps gave him two hundred rupees more, and he returned to his flock at Paharpore. Fairbrother was saved from the cares of a young family and a straitened income. Freeman invested his five hundred rupees in the Budgepore Bank, which was formed before the days of "limited liability," and stopped payment one morning. He never knew an hour's peace after that for many years, and his five hundred rupees cost him as many thousands.

Mrs. Forceps filled to perfection the position fate had placed her in, she made a good wife and an excellent mother, and was at the time I write queen of Budgepore.

Like the famous minister who rose from a humble labourer to be ruler of a kingdom, and kept locked up in a room the soiled garments he had worn in the days of his poverty, in order that he might frequently, by seeing them, be reminded of his former state, she allowed the recollection of her past position to adorn the station she now filled as the first lady of Budgepore.

Among the official residents at that favoured station were a Mr. and Mrs. Thomas. Mr. Thomas was in every respect a good, worthy, upright, and honest man, but he had U.S., * the mark of the beast upon him. Still, as he filled a very responsible official position, he was occasionally visited, at least, I mean his wife was, by the civilians and the officers in the station.

* Uncovenanted Service.

Mrs. Thomas had been a schoolfellow of Mrs. Forceps, and they had both started in the world simultaneously in their careers as governesses. The one, fortune had led to India and wedded her to an embryo commissioner; the other, fate had kept at home, where Thomas one day, being on furlough, met and loved her. Mrs. Thomas, a sensible woman, neither courted nor shunned the opportunities afforded her by the position of her old schoolfellow, of entering into society, but took matters as they came, received with lady-like courtesy, but without any affectation, the visitors that chose to call, saved as much money as she could for her husband out of his hard-earned and slender income, and looked after her children.

Mrs. Forceps, had she been left to herself, would have allowed none of the artificial conventionalities of Indian life to interfere with her good nature and regard for her old schoolfellow, though the two girls as children had never been very intimate. But she was fettered by her husband's prejudices, and once or twice during their married life had provoked him into using unchivalrous and unmanly words, when, resisting her importunities to allow her to break through the barrier of social prejudice and renew her intimacy with Mrs. Thomas, he had forgotten himself so far as to taunt her with her position before marriage.

However, he was always ashamed of himself after these outbursts of temper, and her quiet, lady-like dignity of demeanour was much more than a match for his littleness of mind. So it came to pass that after one of these little exhibitions of domestic strife, his repentant feelings led him so far as to beg his offended wife to ask the Thomases to dinner. And it so happened that on this occasion I, with many other Budgeporeans, were invited and went accordingly.

The Forceps had a tolerably large family, and almost every five years Mrs. Forceps went to England with relays of children to be located with relations, guardians, and wives of clergymen on the sea-coast, who took charge of "Indian children." At present the eldest of the little ones who cheered their home with their bright sunny faces and merry voices, was rather a precocious child, Miss Lucinia. She was a little over five, a pretty girl with blue eyes, delicate complexion, and long flaxen hair that curled down over her alabaster neck and shoulders, for she always wore a low frock in the evening, and it was in the evening that I generally saw her.

There were the elements of a pleasant little party assembled when I arrived, and I was the last of the guests. I do not recollect now who there were particularly, some fourteen or fifteen in all. But I do recollect that the Thwaiteses were there, and the Mountjoys, and young Perkins the adjutant, whose soul was in his profession, and who looked on every being in a black coat as at least one degree removed below Perkins in a red jacket, in the scale of creation.

And of course there were the Thomases. Although no such thing was hinted at by word of mouth or in writing, yet one felt that *the* people of the party were the Thomases. There they were, heaven scaled at last! Mr. and Mrs. Thomas, bearing U.S., the mark of the beast, although there was no external indication whatever of it either in their dress, their demeanour, or their conversation! No matter, there was a feeling among that little group that Mr. Forceps had immolated himself on the altar of domestic peace, and sacrificed at his hearth the time-honoured prejudices of the traditions of a century.

No man could be more studiously and yet unostentatiously polite than was Forceps. Neither by word, nor sign, nor gesture did he let it be understood, that to-day, for the first time had the barrier of his officialised social circle been invaded by the mark of the beast. Nevertheless, in spite of all, there was a feeling there, that the Thomases were *the* people of the party.

My entrance apparently caused a break in a conversation, with difficulty sustained, about the weather, and after I had shaken hands and seated myself in a vacant chair by Mrs. Thwaites, there ensued one of those awkward and rather uncomfortable pauses in the conversation before dinner among a small party, where you feel the necessity of adopting the worst possible method of keeping up or originating a conversation, that is, thinking of something to say. When, among a number of people, there is a silence, no matter for how short a time, the first person who speaks, speaks as it were in public, and all men are not used to public speaking, so I suppose it comes to pass, sometimes, that before dinner you think of something to say and don't say anything, and at dinner you don't think of anything to say and talk a good deal. Anyhow there was a dead silence, till little Lucy,—Lucy she was called, though her name was Lucinia,—broke the silence and said,—

"Mammá, dear!"

She was standing then by her mother's knee.

"Yes, Lucy," said her mother.

"Do the uncovenanted go to heaven when they die?"

I suppose if a shell had fallen into the middle of us we should all have jumped up and run away. As it was, we were fixed to our seats. Mrs. Thwaites, who thoroughly appreciated a good joke (not the least pleasant trait in her character) was very nearly committing herself by a peal of laughter. She was covering as much of her face she as could with her handkerchief, but by the quivering of her bust I could see she was with difficulty stifling her merriment. No one exactly seemed to know which way look. There was an awkward pause for a second or two. It was Forceps's duty to fill the breach.

"What very silly questions you do ask, Lucy," said her father, taking her upon his knee; "of course, all people who are good go to heaven: it makes no matter, you know, when you die what you are so long as you are good, even soldiers ——"

There was a sort of stifled snort from Perkins, who was sitting on the other side of Mrs. Thwaites, at this second *faux pas*, and he gave an incipient wriggle in his chair at the same time. I was most afraid of my next neighbour, for she was literally shaking with subdued laughter.

"What a distressing accident that is to the Lieutenant-Governor," said I, acting under a sudden fit of inspiration, and perfectly desperate.

"What is it?" asked two or three at once. My purpose was gained.

"Oh, haven't you read it in the *Delhi*," replied I, seeing that, having accomplished my purpose, it was necessary for me to look out for a retreat.

"No; there is nothing that I see," said Mountjoy, with the paper in his hand.

"He fell into the lake while out fishing," I said, thinking that better than making his gun burst.

"Dinner is ready," said the khansama at the door.

I took Mrs. Thwaites into dinner. She had not stopped laughing when the salmon was taken round.

"Is this some of the fish the Lieutenant-Governor caught!" she said.

"Yes," said I; "just before he fell in. Never mind him, I thing you owe me something. Another second, and propriety would have been shocked by a peal of laughter."

The Lieutenant-Governor's dip into the lake had saved society at Budgepore. But I have forgotten all about Twemlow.

Later in the evening, after the ladies had left the dining-room, I found myself next to Appletree, of the 77th. He always went by the *sobriquet* of "Apples." And to him I addressed the question, as to the matter which was then uppermost in my mind, I mean what it was that had happened to my young friend, Twemlow?

"Oh, yes; of course, I know all about it," said Apples, directly I mentioned it. "I heard it all at Chugli's last night. Why don't you go there, if you want to hear the news? It's the best place in the station for finding out the gossip."

"You don't mean to say," said I, inexpressibly shocked, "that you would have me go to a prayer-meeting in order to pick up scandal!"

"Well, I don't know," replied Apples; "you have such a queer way of putting things; in that sense, perhaps, it is not quite the thing, but anyhow, that's where I always get the news, and I go regularly."

After this, we went into the drawing-room. I asked six different people that night the same question, and they all gave me different answers, and there was not one of them that could give the least clue as to the source of the information, or from what quarter the report originally came. One said, Twemlow had been embezzling money; another, that he had run away with the horses; a third, that he had purposely burnt his house down to destroy the accounts; a fourth, that he had been making money by the leases of the stud lands to cultivators; a fifth, that he had killed an overseer; and a sixth, that he had been giving bills on bankers or agents, with whom he had no assets.

As we were coming away, and were saying good-night to Mrs. Forceps, I happened to be the last in the room. So I said:

"Do you know, Mrs. Forceps, what is this about the Twemlows?"

"No, I do not," she said, "except that they are in some trouble. It is totally impossible to believe the accounts you hear. It was to-day I heard it, when I was out calling in cantonments. And some very unkind remarks were made in my presence. So, directly I got home I wrote to Mrs. Twemlow, and sent the letter out by a mounted messenger; and I told her I heard something was amiss, and that if they had to come into the station she would find rooms and everything ready for them here. I thought he might be obliged to come in here. You know them, don't you?"

"Yes, very well indeed. I am quite sure there is no truth in any report that attributes anything dishonourable to my friend Twemlow."

"Good-night."

"Good-night."

The gentlemen guests were lighting their cheroots under the porch; Forceps was standing at the doorway. They were talking about cheroots, and Forceps was just saying he had recently got a new batch up from Mackenzie Lyall's.

"Good-night, Forceps," I said, "you're a lucky fellow."

He thought I referred to the new batch of cheroots.

CHAPTER II.

SHOWING HOW A GREAT SOCIAL PROBLEM WAS SOLVED.

Next morning, after breakfast, I determined to hear the truth about my friend Twemlow, and drove over to the Brigadier's in time to catch the old gentleman at his after-breakfast cheroot, and before the Brigade-Major came for the day's orders. I found the Brigadier, as I expected, in his room. He was always glad of a chat, and invariably began, as it was observed, much to our amusement, with abusing his Brigade-Major. No matter to whom he was talking, he always, as it were, lifted up the sluice-gate and let off all his superflous spleen by a little hearty abuse of Baker, the Brigade-Major, and then he was comfortable.

"Do you know," he said to me in a confidential sort of whisper, as I sat down, "that fellow Baker's the d——est fool that ever was born." This superlative was a favourite expression with the Brigadier, who was not very choice sometimes in his language.

It was, as I say, his ordinary method of beginning the conversation to make some remark to the above effect, no matter whom he was addressing, and he always waited for a reply; it was necessary to say something—"indeed," or "I'm sorry for it," or "what a pity," or "he doesn't look so," meaning that Baker did not look such a fool or such a reprobate as the Brigadier always described him. On the present occasion he said, in answer to my commonplace "indeed," on hearing that he was "the d——est fool that ever lived;" "What d' you think he's done now!" I said I really could form no idea of the excesses into which Baker's folly was not capable of leading him. "Well," he said, "he's gone and ordered the brigade to parade to-morrow in quarter-distance column instead of in line!" And he looked at me as much as to say, There now, can it enter into the imagination of man's head to conceive such an unpardonable act of idiotcy as that? Then he added, "He's a fool, that's what he is, and so were his father and mother for begetting him."

I could not help thinking how much easier it would be to write three lines with a pencil on a scrap of paper, which would at once rectify the unpardonable folly which Baker had been guilty of in the Brigadier's eyes; but then it was a habit of his, and now that the surplus muddy water had run through the sluice it had left the reservoir behind it tolerably clear.

"Do tell me, Brigadier," said I, "the real truth about this affair of Twemlow's. I cannot make head or tail of what I hear."

"No, I should think not," he said, after a hearty laugh. "No, I should say not. Neither could I. So I got on my horse yesterday and rode out there. I have seen Twemlow, and he has told me all about it;" and again he went off into a hearty laugh.

"I am glad to see by the way you treat the matter that it is nothing serious. I felt sure Twemlow could never be guilty of any dishonourable conduct."

"My dear fellow," said the Brigadier, "I really wonder at you, with your reputation for wisdom and philosophy speaking in that way." He was quite serious now. "I was laughing at Twemlow's, story, and I'll tell it to you. But don't ever talk to me about a man not being guilty of dishonourable conduct, and therefore you know no harm can come to him. It doesn't follow, I can tell you. I could count them off on my fingers now—one, two, three, four, five, six—these six that I recollect now off hand, and if I were to sit down to think I should recollect as many more, I dare say—men that I have known in my time; *known*, mind you, and to my certain knowledge ruined, cashiered, reduced, transported, by gad, one of 'em was, when there had been nothing more dishonourable in there conduct than there has been in yours and mine. You don't know what a place India is."

"Is it true Twemlow is under arrest?"

"Yes, it is. I put him under arrest by order from the General," and here the Brigadier again burst out laughing.

"I'll tell you what he has done." he said, wiping the tears

from his eyes from excess of laughter. "Poor Twemlow, you know hasn't the least idea of his duty, at least when he went to the stud he hadn't. Not a single thing did he know about it. As ill-luck would have it, the overseer was laid up with fever, and the head baboo had gone away to be married, and there wasn't a soul there that could put Twemlow up to anything. He hadn't been there a day before in comes an indent duly passed from Fitzburr for a lot of remounts for his troop. The troop was just going on escort with the Governor-General, and Fitzburr was glad to get fresh horses, as he likes to cut a swell with his troop, you know. Twemlow, it seems had one idea, and only one idea, about stud horses, and that is, that they were always marked with an R., which he thought meant 'Remount.' So when this indent came in he got hold of the marking-iron, and he had them all stamped R. before he sent them off!"

The reader, who it is possible may understand almost as little about the custom and practice in the studs as did my friend Twemlow when he went to take charge of that establishment at Budgepore, must be told that Government horses, when they become unserviceable, are inspected by a committee and "cast," as it is called, that is, set aside to be sold by auction, when they are stamped on the buttock with the letter R.

When the horses reached Umballa, and Major Fitzburr went to see them, he gazed with horror and consternation at the fatal letter.

"'What,' he said to his Adjutant, 'have they sent me all castors! By George, I'll condemn them all instanter! Where's White?' White was the vet. White came. 'Mr. White, do you see they have sent us all castors?' 'Yes, sir,' says White, who, although he was 'Vet,' knew just as much about horses as horses did about him. 'Examine them,' says Fitzburr, 'and a regimental committee will assemble this evening.' So White drew up the report, and there every horse figured! one was spavined, another had a sand crack, one had this and another had that; he found out something the matter with them all, because, you know, he daren't expose his ignorance and report a castor sound" (here the old Brigadier laughed till the tears literally rolled down his cheeks). "There isn't a complaint or a disease that a horse ever had since the day they came two and two out of Noah's ark that some of these hadn't had. The regimental committee, of course, signed the papers, and then there was a station committee ordered. The President of the station committee was Colonel Crawfoot, who may be a good judge of a camel, but I'm blest if he is of a horse. Well, he went down to the parade ground, saw the Vet, who showed him the R., whereupon he signed the papers and went home. By-and-bye the two members of the committee came one after the other and did the same. So the remounts were in due time ordered to be sold by auction. And I don't know if it's true, but I hear the Vet bought some five or six for a mere song, and so I believe did each of the subalterns of Fitzburr's troop, and Fitzburr himself got a pair for his carriage. Well, of course, there was a deuce of a row about it, and the upshot of it is that Twemlow is under arrest."

"And what is he charged with?"

"I don't know. I haven't seen the charge, and I am rather curious to do so; for young Simmons knows just as much about military law and drawing up a charge as Twemlow does about breeding horses."

Shortly after this Twemlow came into Budgepore under arrest, and I learnt from him that the circumstances of the case were just as the Brigadier had told them to me.

There was a great discussion at Budgepore as to what should be done with regard to calling on the Twemlows when they came in. I happened to be present on most of the occasions when the thing was discussed, but I never let out that I was the only one that did know that Mrs. Forceps had asked them to put up at their house. I kept that to myself, and quietly watched the stream as it flowed along. I think nearly all the married ladies were together one morning when it was discussed, at least I recollect Mrs. Mountjoy, Mrs. Cameltrunk, Mrs. Smithies, Mrs. James, and Mrs. Fantail were there, and they unanimously resolved that society demanded of them to cut Mrs. Twemlow, because her husband was temporarily under a cloud. They each, I suppose, acted in conformity with the wishes and views of their husbands, and it was in vain for me to utter the commonplace remark about a man being innocent till proved guilty, and so on. The fair conclave pronounced their verdict and I said nothing more.

The Budgepore world, of course, bowed its head meekly to the decision of these august powers. And, in consequence, it is utterly out of my capacity to depict the consternation that overwhelmed society when, on the evening after the Twemlows came in, Mrs. Twemlow appeared in Mrs. Forceps' carriage at the band! It was a sort of moral earthquake, a bursting of a social shell right under their noses. Mrs. Mountjoy thought Mrs. Forceps was *so* eccentric, there was no knowing what she wouldn't do. Mrs. Cameltrunk said, what could you expect from a *ci-devant* governess. Mrs. Smithies confided to Apples at that evening prayer-meeting that Mrs. Forceps was known to have Popish tendencies, and that, as Apples knew, would account for a great deal. Mrs. Fantail, the Collector's wife, thought Mr. Forceps would be removed when the Lieutenant-Governor heard of it, and Mrs James said it would be very awkward for Mrs. Forceps, she thought, when Captain Twemlow was transported. However, they all made a secret compact that none of them would call at the Commissioner's while the Twemlows were there. In fact there was a sort of rebellion. Mrs. Forceps was voted "deposed" from her throne as the leading star of Budgepore, and Mrs. Fantail was elected, constitutionally to succeed to her place. I say constitutionally, because, if Mrs. Forceps was constitutionally deposed, it was quite right that Mrs. Fantail should succeed her. It was a difficult question to decide, however, and on the whole, I am of opinion that there was no change, that Mrs. Fantail never was legally promoted, because Mrs. Forceps never was legally deposed, and certainly she never resigned.

It happened that a short time after the revolution or the rebellion, for a revolution is an accomplished rebellion and I don't think this ever was actually accomplished, the disaffected were electrified at the astounding intelligence that the Lieutenant-Governor was coming through Budgepore and was going to put up with the Commissioner!

Now here *was* a pretty piece of business! Wasn't Mrs. Fantail in a way about it! The Lieutenant-Governor's untoward arrival just then, and his putting up with the Commissioner, would not only deprive her at once of the dignity she had acquired as the head of the malcontents, but it would condemn them all in their conduct towards the Twemlows, and worse than all, it was so vexatious that she was bound by compact and by honour not to call, and the Lieutenant-Governor and Mrs. Byewilwuffa would go through Budgepore without her paying her devotions at their shrine!

There is nothing I know of that so nearly approaches idolatry as the feelings which civil servants, from collectors downwards, as well as their wives, bear towards the Lieutenant-Governor. The Honourable Kist Byewilwuffa was no exception. I suppose it arises from their coming to view the Lieutenant-Governor as the impersonation of the spirit of the order. And assuredly in Mr. Byewilwuffa's case they were not far out. A man more perfectly useless in his position, it is impossible to conceive; yet they looked on him as a Solon in law, a Demosthenes in eloquence, a Socrates in philosophy, in short, as little less than divinity in everything. The fact to other eyes being that he was a very ordinary mortal with less than the average amount of intellect, totally void of every generous impulse, every good feeling, dead, in fact, to every consideration but the interests of his own service. All the routine work of the office which is generally dignified by the word "Government," was conducted by the Secretary, Mr. Khas Mouza, who went usually by the nickname Moses, among those who were profane enough to nickname one who stood so near to the object of adortion as did Mouza to the Honourable Kist Byewilwuffa.

Of course it was a crushing blow for Mrs. Fantail, the Lieutenant-Governor's arrival at Budgepore. She was not only condemned and stultified in the eyes of the faction, but she felt all the mental horror of a devotee, when his demon-god seems to frown at him for some act of disobedience. But if she could by any possibility get out of that foolish compact and go and call, it would not be so bad, because she would have the pleasure of dipping her wings in the sunbeams of official greatness, and if she was the only lady (oh, the pretty little traitress!) out of all Budgepore, who was asked to meet the Honourable Mrs. Kist Byewilwuffa, why it was not in nature that she would not be able to make an impression on the Honourable Mrs. Kist Byewilwuffa. There were only three days. They were to be there on Monday, and that was Thursday. She must call on Friday, or not at all.

Yes; she did! She ordered her carriage without even

telling her husband where she was going, and drove to Mrs. Forceps and paid the visit, the preparatory visit, that would be followed by an invitation to meet the Lieutenant-Governor and his wife on Monday. Oh treachery ! *O tempora ! O Mores !* Unworthy descendant of Boadicea ! The queen of the faction thus betrayed her cause !

The visit was paid. She had a ten minutes' chat with Mrs. Forceps and Mrs. Twemlow, and Captain Twemlow handed her to her carriage.

Not half pleased with herself, she was driving out of the compound when another carriage met hers. It was the Smithies' equippage. She leant back very far into the corner, among the morocco cushions, and squeezed in the flounces of her dress and her stiff embroidered petticoat, that peeped out from underneath, into the smallest possible compass, in the vain hope she might pass undiscovered, for she never dreamt that there was anybody but Mr. Smithies in the carriage, going, of course, to pay a visit upon the Commissioner. But Smithies would see her, and would be sure to mention to his wife her, Mrs. Fantail's, treachery. All these considerations, thoughts, movements, and artifices were the work of the two seconds that elapsed after the heads of the horses in the other carriage were within sight of Mrs. Fantail's pretty hazel eyes. Her heart seemed to leap into her mouth as she saw Mrs. Smithies in the carriage, sitting forward to see who it was in Mrs. Fantail's conveyance ! There was no doubt about it ! Both ladies blushed, but there was no one there to see them.

Mrs. Smithies on the way home met Mrs. James going, and the latter as she returned met Mrs. Cameltrunk and Mrs. Mountjoy, who went together. So they all were traitresses to each other, but each one, except Mrs. Cameltrunk and Mrs. Mountjoy thought the secret was confined to the other. But it soon came out, because Mrs. Smithies told Mrs. Fantail she had seen Mrs. James going, and the latter of course confided to her that she had met Mrs. Cameltrunk and Mrs. Mountjoy.

And so Mrs. Twemlow was visited.

It was all a canard about the Lieutenant-Governor's coming ! He never came at all, and was never expected ! It was Apples who set the report going from *malice prepense.* He had been taken into Mrs. Smithies' confidence, and heard all about the compact, and in the depths of his own moral consciousness he conceived the idea of circulating the report about the Lieutenant-Governor, on purpose to see if it would not produce the very results it did! Whether he learned it or not at the prayer-meetings at Chugli's house, he had a marvellous knowledge of human nature, had Apples.

At last a copy of the charge against Twemlow came. The original was sent up to headquarters for approval. The charge was as follows:—

"That he, Augustus Theophilus Twemlow, &c., &c., being a stud officer, serving 120 miles from Fort William, had committed an offence to the prejudice of good order and military discipline, in that,

1st. On or about the 27th Novomber, 18—, he passed into the service as serviceable, fourteen unserviceable horses.

2nd. That on or about the 27th November, he, &c., &c., stamped, or caused to be stamped, on the back, fourteen serviceable horses, the property of Government, with the letter R. against the peace of our sovereign lady the Queen, her crown and dignity."

The Judge-Advocate-General returned the charge with a slight alteration, he took out the words, "on the back," and inserted "fraudulently" in their place.

The charges, however, had to pass through the office before they went to Budgepore, and in the office they fortunately had to go through a purifying process in the hands of a head writer named Richelieu, who supplied all the legal knowledge required at headquarters, and so they eventually arrived in a proper shape, under which Twemlow was to be tried on two counts; one for fraudulently, the other for carelessly, stamping serviceable remounts as unserviceable and condemned horses.

The court-martial was ordered to assemble on the 15th of March.

CHAPTER III.

THE COURT-MARTIAL.

There was a good deal of excitement at Budgepore when the court-martial began. Colonel Sungeen was President. I need not detail the rest of the officers' names that composed the Court. Another officer, I forget his name now, was the prosecutor. Simmons, the Deputy-Judge-Advocate, delayed, that is to say, conducted, the proceedings. I have already stated that Twemlow was to be tried on two counts, one with having fraudulently passed unserviceable horses into the service in lieu of serviceable ones, and the other count was for carelessly and negligently allowing serviceable horses to be passed as unserviceable, condemned and sold. Deprived of the technical language in which the legal law of Richelieu, the uncovenanted head of the Judge-Advocate-General's office, had folded them, the above is the sum and substance of the charges.

The prosecutor commenced with making a statement which I will not weary you with, and then called his first witness Major Fitzburr, who stated that, when the remounts arrived at Umballa, he went down to the parade ground to see them, and found to his astonishment that they were all castors. He had directed the Veterinary Surgeon, Mr. White, to examine them, who had found them all more or less unserviceable, and committees having been assembled in the usual manner, and the horses having been condemned, they were sold by auction.

Major Fitzburr's evidence lasted till tiffin time. After tiffin, the prisoner proceeded to cross-examine.

Q.—(By prisoner.) Did you examine the horses?

A.—Yes, I did.

Q.—And what did you find the matter with them?

A.—I found them all stamped R., and consequently unserviceable.

Q.—Did you never see a serviceable horse stamped with an R. before?

The prosecutor objected to this question, and the Court was closed to decide.

Upon the Court re-opening, the President announced that it was the opinion of the Court that the question should not be put.

It being four o'clock, the Court adjourned.

SECOND DAY.

Cross-examination of Major Fitzburr was resumed.

Q.—(By prisoner.) Where are the horses now?

The prosecutor having objected to this question, the Court closed to consider.

Upon re-opening the Court, the President announced that the Court were unanimous that the question should not be put. The Court, at this stage of the proceedings, it being now one o'clock, adjourned for tiffin.

After tiffin, the cross-examination was resumed.

Q.—(By prisoner.) Have you got any of the horses in your possession?

The prosecutor having objected to this question, the Court closed to consider, and, on re-opening, the president announced that the Court were of opinion that the question might be put.

A.—Yes, I have.

Q.—How many?

The prosecutor having objected to this question, and the Court having closed to consider, decided that this question should not be put.

It being now four o'clock, the Court adjourned.

THIRD DAY.

Cross-examination of Major Fitzburr resumed.

Q.—(By prisoner.) How much did you pay for the horses you bought at auction?

The prosecutor having objected to this question, the Court, having closed to consider, decided it might be put.

A.—I paid twenty rupees for one, sixteen for another, twenty-five for another, thirty for another, and thirty-eight for another.

It being now tiffin time, the Court adjourned.

After tiffin the cross-examination of Major Fitzburr was resumed.

Q.—(By prisoner.) Which of the officers of your troop, besides yourself, purchased horses out of this batch at the auction?

This question having been objected to by the prosecutor, the Court was closed; on re-opening they decided it should not be put.

The Court then adjourned, it being four o'clock.

Fourth Day.

The cross-examination of the witness was resumed.

Q.—(By prisoner.) Did any of the officers of your troop purchase any of the horses out of the batch at the auction?

A.—Yes.

Q.—(By prisoner.) Will you be good enough to let us know their names?

The prosecutor having objected to this question, the Court was closed to consider, and, upon re-opening, decided it might be put.

It being now one o'clock, the Court adjourned to tiffin.

After tiffin the cross-examination was resumed.

A.—Andrews, Smith, and Jones.

Q.—(By prisoner.) Were any of these officers on the committee that condemned the horses?

Prosecutor objected to this question, and a long discussion ensued; after which the Court closed to deliberate, and on re-opening, decided that the question might be put.

A.—Yes, Andrews and Smith were.

Q.—Did they consider the horses really unserviceable?

A.—No, they did not.

Q.—How do you know?

A.—Because Andrews told Smith he thought there was nothing the matter with the horses except the R., and that when that was got rid of, they would be first-rate ones.

By Court.—Was that in your hearing?

A.—No, not in my hearing.

Q.—What was Jones's opinion about them?

Prosecutor objected to this question, and after a long discussion the Court adjourned, at 4 P.M.

Fifth Day.

The discussion of yesterday was resumed this morning. At length the Court closed to consider, and on re-opening, decided the question might be put; but as it was now tiffin time, they adjourned for half-an-hour. After tiffin, the cross-examination was resumed.

A.—He thought they were first-rate horses.

Q.—Were either of those officers on the regimental committee?

A.—Yes, two of them were members of the committee, and the third was president.

Q.—(By prisoner.) Which was the president?

The prosecutor objected very strongly to this question, and read several passages out of a number of formidable looking law books, to show why the question should not be allowed. It was referred to the Deputy-Judge-Advocate, who said he thought it really did not matter. The Court having closed to consider, decided that the question should not be put.

It being four o'clock, the Court adjourned.

Sixth Day.

Shekh Sachai Khan, Jemadar, Budgepore Stud, called and sworn (examined through interpreter).

Q.—(By prosecutor.) How long have you been in the Budgepore Stud?

A.—Forty years.

Q.—Are any of the horses in the stud marked with the letter R.

A.—Yes, all.

Q.—Are all the horses marked with R. when they are in the stud?

A.—Yes. All the Sirkar's (Government) horses are born with the mark upon them.

Prisoner declined to cross-examine.

Court adjourned to tiffin.

Jemadar Peer Bux was the next witness.

Q.—(By prosecutor.) Did you take a batch of horses, remounts, from the Budgepore Stud to Umballa in November last?

A.—Yes.

Q.—Were they stamped with the letter R. when they were made over to you?

A.—No, they were not. They were not stamped at all, either when they were made over to me, or when I made them over to the Major Sahib at Umballa.

Q.—What non-commissioned officer went with you?

A.—Havildar Ahmed Khan.

Prisoner declines to cross-examine.

It being four o'clock, the Court adjourned.

SEVENTH DAY.

Havildar Ahmed Khan sworn.

Q.—(By prosecutor.) Did you go on command with the Jemadar, the last witness, to Umballa, in November last, in charge of horses?

A.—Yes, I went on command with the Jemadar, the last witness, to Umballa in November last, but there were no horses with us.

The President of the Court here remarked that perhaps the witness had not exactly understood the question. Would the interpreter explain more clearly what was meant?

The interpreter, addressing witness:—Look here. When you went to Umballa, had you no horses at all with you?

A.—Not one.

The President thought perhaps the witness was confounding the word "ghora," a horse, with "gora," a European.

The Interpreter.—Look here, I am not asking you about white men, but about horses; do you mean to say you took no horses to Umballa?

A.—Yes, sahib.

The Interpreter.—Then what did you take?

A.—Animals, sahib.

Q.—What animals?

A.—Goats, sheep, buffaloes—

Q.—No horses?

A.—No, sahib.

Prisoner declined to cross-examine, Court adjourned.

Next witness, Lieutenant Andrews, sworn.

Q.—(By prosecutor.) Were you president of the regimental committee appointed in November last to report upon remounts received from the Budgepore Stud?

A.—I was.

Q.—In what state were the horses?

A.—I don't know.

Q.—Didn't you examine them?

A.—No, the Veterinary Surgeon did that, and reported them unsound, and the Major said as they were all castors they were to be condemned.

Cross-examined by prisoner.

Q.—Did you buy any of the remounts when they were sold by auction?

The prosecutor objected to this question, and the Court closed to consider it; upon re-opening, the Court ruled that it might be put.

It being 4 P.M., the Court then adjourned.

EIGHTH DAY.

Lieutenant Andrews gives reply to the question of the previous day.

A.—I did buy some of the horses.

Q.—What for?

The prosecutor having objected to this question, the Court was closed to consider it; before re-opening, as it was one o'clock, the Court adjourned to tiffin.

The Court having decided that the question should be put, witness replied.

A.—I bought them because I wanted them.

Q.—If they were unserviceable, what did you intend to do with them?

A.—I did not say they were unserviceable.

Q. Did you not report them unserviceable in the Committee Report?

A.—Yes, but that is a totally different thing from considering them unserviceable in the sense of useless for one's own purposes.

Q.—Then you consider these horses, though condemned, were serviceable?

A.—They were unserviceable because they had R. upon them.

Q.—How does the letter R. make them unserviceable, if in other respects they are serviceable?

A.—It makes them castors, and castors are unserviceable.

It being 4 P.M., the Court adjourned.

Ninth Day.

Colonel Crawfoot called and sworn.

Q.—(By prosecutor.) Were you President of the Station Committee that assembled at Umballa in November last to survey and report upon remounts from Major Fitzburr's troop?

A.—I was.

Q.—Did you examine the horses?

A.—No.

Q.—Were you not President of the Committee?

A.—Yes, but I was not directed to examine the horses.

Q.—Did you report them unserviceable?

A.—Yes.

Q.—Why did you do that without examining them?

A.—Because they were marked with the letter R., which made them castors.

Prisoner declined to cross-examine, and the Court adjourned to tiffin.

Next witness, Mr. Veterinary Surgeon White, sworn.

Q.—(By prosecutor.) Did you examine the remounts that came up from the Budgepore Stud to Umballa in November last?

A.—Yes, I did.

Q.—Was there anything peculiar about them?

A.—There was; they were all castors.

Q.—How do you know they were castors?

A.—They were stamped with the letter R.

Q.—In other respects, were they unserviceable?

This was the most important witness on the trial, and we, that is, all the spectators, were very anxious to know what answer would be given to this. The witness hesitated, stammered, and at last said,—

A.—I don't think I should have condemned them if they had not been marked.

Q.—Were they sound?

A.—No, they were not sound. In the Committee Report I entered every case and the description of attack from which the animal had been suffering.

Witness shown the Committee Report, and asked if it is his handwriting.

Cross-examined by prisoner.

Q.—Did you buy any of the horses at the auction?

The Court here adjourned for tiffin. After it re-assembled, the witness replied,—

A.—Yes, I did.

Q.—What for?

A.—For my own use.

Q.—Then the horses were serviceable?

A.—Yes, in that sense they were serviceable. For a private individual they were of use, for Government service not.

Q.—Why not?

A.—Because they were marked with the letter R.

Here the examination of witnesses ended, and the prisoner read his defence. I shall not delay you with recording it. It was a very able one.

We were all kept in suspense for three weeks before we knew the upshot of the trials, and then it came out, Twemlow was acquitted on the first charge, and found guilty on the second, and sentenced to be reprimanded. The following were His Excellency's (Sir Walter Grubb was Commander-in-Chief in those days) remarks:—

"His Excellency the Commander-in-Chief, while confirming, though, at the same time, taking into consideration, which is out of the question in the present case, although his approbation of the sentence has the effect which if circumstances arose similar to those under which that result recently arrived at by the members of the court-martial independently altogether of such considerations as are connected with and in some measure more or less directly dependent on other contingencies in the event of which the result that has now occurred might have been otherwise shown, does not wish to imply what it would seem if it is allowable in these cases to be guided by the ordinary rules in other instances, especially when analogy in circumstances may be looked for, the Court, might not have intended, so far as intention can be presumed or gathered, independently of that alternative, must be aware that in such cases which His Excellency cannot but consider called for considerable intelligence in the transaction more particularly as regards such duties with which the prisoner, in view of that position when under ordinary circumstances nothing less could have been expected does not understand what the Court evidently in respect of the other alternative might not, if the evidence which considering the character and position of the witnesses who if they had not possessed those advantages if as His Excellency assumes, those advantages to be, in the former alternative, peculiarly adapted, as will be seen by reference to the standing orders, trusts that for the future in circumstances where devotion to the interests of the state in duties connected with the Stud Department, will not yield to responsibilities that in all positions in life more particularly in that under consideration involved.

"This order will be read out to Captain Twemlow in presence of all the officers at present quartered at Budgepore. After which it will be translated and read at the head of every native regiment.

"By order,
"PAT GREEN,
"*Adjutant-General of the Army,*
"*Head Quarters.*"

Within a month from this date I noticed that five interpreters were sent to England on medical certificate; whether the task of translating the order had not something to do with it I do not know, but I have often thought it may have.

After this, Twemlow returned to the Stud, and I never heard of his ever getting into any other scrape through his zeal for the service.

CHRONICLE X.

BUDGEPORE COMMERCIAL INSTITUTIONS.

CHRONICLE X.

BUDGEPORE COMMERCIAL INSTITUTIONS.

A GREAT many fortunes have been made and lost at Budgepore in my time. This has been more especially the case since the joint-stock company mania a few years ago. My earliest reminiscences, however, go back to a much earlier date, to the day, for instance, when the Bank of Budgepore was set going, and which, by confining itself to true banking business, that is, in a Budgepore sense, lending money as loans in small sums to needy subalterns and spendthrift civilians, on two personal securities, at enormous interest, realised a good deal. If it was easy to lose money in those days, I am speaking of ten or twenty years ago, it was easy enough to get it.

Tom Pringle, an ensign on a hundred and ninety rupees a month, wanted a couple of thousand to buy a horse and a gun, to pay off a few trifling debts. Jimmy Hare, a lieutenant in the same corps, wanted the same. So did Stubbs, a captain, also of the gallant regiment. One day at tiffin, in comparing notes, the three made the discovery that they were each and all exactly in the same condition of impecuniosity. So the matter was easily arranged. Pringle got the loan papers first, and filled them up, Hare and Stubbs being his securities. The doctor of the regiment filled up the insurance papers, and Pringle was rich for the time. Then Hare went through the same formalities, Pringle and Stubbs being his securities, and last of all, Stubbs obtained his accommodation on the personal security of Pringle and Hare. As a matter of course, the instalments, after the first few months, when they were regularly paid, fell off, and finally stopped altogether. It was not the bank's business to complain, nor to warn, and so the interest went on accumulating merrily. Stubbs never paid his instalments, but he took for granted Pringle and Hare paid theirs regularly. Each of the two latter was under exactly the same impression with regard to the other two. Meantime, years passed on, the interest at 12 per cent., compound interest, too, accumulated formidably. Still, all were in happy ignorance. Pringle died after two years, Stubbs got into a scrape, and was obliged to leave the service, and Jimmy Hare found himself saddled with a debt of a little short of fifteen thousand rupees, running on at compound interest, which he had to pay out of his three hundred or less a month he received as lieutenant in command of a company. When he became junior captain the debt reached 20,000, and as his step was worth that sum to his juniors, they gave it to him, and he resigned after spending twelve years in India, without any pension, and having realised by his step just enough to pay off the bank debt.

This style of business, as you may understand, by easy multiplication, was very profitable, for the bank very seldom indeed drew blanks. Its business increased. Officers in the army took small loans and civilians large ones. The ready facility with which money could be obtained was too tempting a bait to young men who had been, perhaps, a little extravagant. They had but to get two names, names of brother officers, who very possibly were under similar obligations themselves to others, and the thing was done. So this infamous system grew and grew, till like a monstrous boa constrictor it threw its coil around three fifths of the members of the services.

Debt, debt, debt, was the burden of the melancholy song, the wail uttered from one end of the land to the other. The hard-won earnings of a life of toil and danger in a tropical clime were sacrificed to this; the princely salaries which might have cheered the years of declining life with ease and luxury, were squandered upon this. The portions of the widow and the orphan were snatched away to fill the coffers of the usurers. One small moiety of the service, who had taken shares in the Budgepore Bank, grew rich at the expense of their brethren.

It is an ill wind, however, that blows no good, and one advantage that accrued from these money-lending institutions, was that there was less need for judges and magistrates, and other official persons to go into debt with the natives.

Another of the institutions was the "Budgepore Fire Insurance Company." This Company was remarkably prosperous, and had accumulated a large reserve fund; when about the time that Sir Amethyst Jones was to retire, his period of command of the army having expired, he and his adjutant-general, and some others of the Staff, bought up a large number of the shares at a considerable premium. They then called a general meeting of shareholders, and proposed to wind up the company and divide the reserve fund. Having a preponderence of votes at the meeting, they carried their point, and the Budgepore Fire Insurance Company was wound up, and a division of the assets made among the shareholders.

Perhaps, altogether, the grandest speculation Budgepore ever saw, was the conversion of the famous firm of Cork, Screw & Co. into a joint-stock company. This scheme was projected after Mr. Cork had retired from business, when Mr. Screw was the only one of the original partners in the house.

Messrs. Cork, Screw & Co. were dealers in "Europe goods," and did a large business. Shop-keeping or store-keeping, as it ought more properly to be called in India, is a very different thing indeed from similar business in England. There is, at least in Upper India, so little competition, that the ordinary relations between customer and vendor are reversed, and it is a favour rather than anything else for the latter to attend to a customer's requisitions.

It was generally believed that Messrs. Cork, Screw & Co. had been doing a very thriving business, and when the senior partner retired, which he did one day, to Cheltenham, where he set up a large house and establishment, and called himself Major-General Cork of the Indian army, a proposition was put forward to purchase the good-will, stock, and business, a joint-stock company being started for the purpose.

There were at the time one or two old gentlemen at Budgepore who had saved a little money, and wanted a good "investment." There was Sergeant Kunkur, who had been road overseer through six generations of executive engineers. He had the best furnished house in the place, everything from Shearwoods. There was not a chair in his drawing-room that cost under seventy rupees, as he has often told me. He knew a thing or two about the Public Works Department. He has gone home now, and bought a little estate in Ireland. Then there was Colonel Moodle of the 46th N. I. He held rather a curious position in the army, by the way, did Colonel Moodle, which illustrates practically the operation of the amalgamation rules. I call him colonel, but he was properly only lieutenant-colonel, that is by brevet. He was, however, in reality a subaltern, doing subaltern's duty with the corps which was commanded, would you believe it, by his own nephew, Captain Kummerbund! After being thirty years in India, I suppose the Colonel found that a subaltern's duties were too confined a limit for his abilities and intellect to range within, and he sighed for something better. He sought and found it in speculation. Then there was the Reverend Erasmus Chillblain, baptist minister at Budgepore. He was not averse to a little speculation. He had saved a little money out of his stipend, and he must needs jeopardise it, not that anyone ever thought of jeopardy in connection with the joint-stock company. Oh, no! We were all to be rich, so rich we should not know what to do with our money. I say we, and you will ask, "What! did you, too, Old Mortality, takes shares?" "*Certes* I did, and wherefore not? Am I not also mortal?" And how should I have been able to write my chronicle about it, if I had not? More than that, I was a director—yes, on the board of directors."

We called our company the "All Over India Europe Goods Association." The managing agent was called "The Secretary;" the deputy shop boy, "assistant secretary;" the book-keeper, "The cashier;" the shop was "The Rooms," the "All-Over-India Europe Goods Association's Rooms." The little den adjoining the shop, where the books were kept, was the "Secretary's office," and so on.

The first meeting was attended by Colonel Moodle, Sergeant Kunkur, Erasmus Chillblain, myself, and Screw. The only one of the whole lot who knew anything about business being of course Screw. Kunkur, it is true, understood business of a certain kind, but it was the business of the D. P. W., which you know is not at all like business in other branches.

Colonel Moodle was asked to take the chair out of respect to his rank, and Mr. Screw proceeded to lay before the meeting the prospectus. There was to be a capital of three lacs, raised by three thousand shares of a hundred rupees each.

The accounts were drawn out in ship-shape order, and laid before the meeting.

This is an abstract of them from memory :—

Capital	Rs. 3,00,000
Outstanding credits	50,000
	Rs. 3,50,000

Paid to Cork, Screw & Co., for stock and good-will, business premises, &c. . . .	Rs. 1,78,000
To liabilities, purchase of stock, &c., &c.	1,00,000
Reserve	72,000
	Rs. 3,50,000

This looked all right. There was no doubt that the stock and good-will were remarkably cheap at a lac and seventy-eight thousand, and then Cork, Screw & Co. guaranteed the shaseholders twelve per cent. for the first two years. This bait took immensely; Erasmus was appointed officiating sectary, and he had applications for shares from all quarters of India. Private soldiers, sergeants with large families dependent on them, retired officers, hundreds of every rank and position of society invested, or wanted to invest their money in the concern. Cork, Screw & Co.'s reputation was good, and their guarantee was looked on as making the thing as safe as a church. And so it was—quite safe.

The first day, on examining the prospectus and the statement of accounts, I did not like to be too inquisitive. It would look as if I suspected Screw, and I was unwilling to hurt his feelings in any way. It did occur to me, however, that the 72,000 rupees "reserve" required some explanation.

However, no one said anything about it, and the matter was passed over. The next day, however, I did call on Mr. Screw, to ask him to explain that item about the 72,000 rupees.

"Oh, Mr. Screw," I said, after I had sat with him for about five minutes; "I just wanted to ask a question about a little matter in that prospectus, you know. It is not for myself that I want any explanation. I am perfectly satisfied myself that everything is all right, but as I am a director, you know, I might be called upon by some intending shareholder to explain matters; it is just as well that I should be in a position to answer any question that may be asked of me."

"Certainly, my dear Sir, your desire is most reasonable. I shall only be too happy, I assure you, to give you any information in my power."

"Well," I said, "it is that item, 72,000, that I don't understand."

"Oh, indeed! that is very simple. It is the interest. You see, twelve per cent. on the three lacs comes to thirty-six thousand rupees a year, or seventy-two thousand in the two years. Well, the interest, you know, is guaranteed for the first two years, and it is always customary to set apart a sum to meet the interest. Suppose the profits the first two years were not to be sufficient to meet it, it would be very awkward, you know, guaranteed and all."

"Certainly, I see," said I, and went away quite satisfied, and feeling rather sorry that I had given so much unnecessary trouble.

So the company was launched. Screw took his lac and seventy-eight thousand and went home. We got our interest regularly for the first two years, "Twelve per cent. per annum," how fine it looked in the prospectus, and the report of the half-yearly meetings. At the end of the two years, however, the Secretary resigned and went home, and after that everything went to the bad. Some said the Secretary could not show a clear balance-sheet; some said this, and some said that. All I know is, that the company went into liquidation. I believe myself the chief reason why it broke down was, because every shareholder considered himself entitled to take goods and never to pay his bill. And when I came to examine the ledger, I was a little surprised to find that there were no other customers except shareholders.

It is now a year and more since the All-Over-India resolved upon liquidation. There was a meeting at Budgepore about it. Colonel Moodle was in the chair. There were all our old friends present—Mooltawee and Dakhil Duftar, Dr. Golee, Fitzmisl, myself, Sergeant Kunkur, Erasmus Chillblain,

Captain Kummerbund, and some three or four officers of the 150th, whose names I do not recollect; and last, though not least, our respected Secretary, Fancy Goods, Esq., and several others. You know, matters had not been going on quite as they should. It was in liquidation a very long time, but it never seemed to be any nearer being liquidated. At least all the men who had been appointed liquidators left the country and went home, and the affair was brought into court. Well, the Judge, Mooltawee, asked me if I would undertake the office of liquidator, and, as I had more time to spare than the others, and moreover, as I had a very good legal adviser at hand in my friend Watson, you know—he has the law at his fingers' ends—I consented. Would you believe it! such was my Ill-luck, that very day Watson was taken ill, and went away to Simla, and thence to England, and I never saw him again. Still, I knew Mooltawee would give me every assistance in his power, so far as direction and advice went, and I was not deterred from undertaking the office. Fancy Goods, Esq., sent over to my house all the books, ledgers, letters, bills, &c., &c., which filled two carts, and I stowed them away very carefully, taking every precaution, as I thought, to prevent them from being eaten by white ants, and next day I went over to Mooltawee's court to get my first lesson in my new duties.

"'Your duties?' said Mooltawee, as soon as I had communicated the object of my attendance at his court. 'Yes, I'll tell you what the duties of a liquidator are. They are very simple. First, you have to pay the debts of the company.'

"'Pay the debts!' and my breath almost went out of my body—'why, they amount to somwhere about four lacs.'"

"'The amount does not make any difference,' said Mooltawee. 'Here you see, it is laid down in paragraph 10, section 149 of the Act, 'the liquidators shall pay the debts of the company.' That's clear, isn't it? Then, the next thing you have to do is to find the contributories.

"'But they have been trying to find the contributaries for the last year or two: and have not succeeded. The contributaries have all vanished into thin air. The most subtle gas, a shower of rain in a gale of wind, are but feeble representations of the facility for dispersion and disapperance evinced by the contributaries.'"

"'No matter,' said Mooltawee, 'you must find them.'"

I returned home disconsolate, to talk the matter over with my friends, co-sharers, and creditors.

We determined to get counsel's opinion, and under the idea that in the multitude of counsellors there is wisdom, we laid the case before two eminent barristers of Calcutta. In due course of time the opinions came, when what was our consternation to find them diametrically opposed to one another. We had another consultation, and it was proposed to get the opinion of a third. We did so; and you may imagine what our feelings were when we found the third differed essentially from the other two. I had already expended 2,500 rupees in law expenses. But there was no help for it, we felt ourselves forced to lay the case before a fourth counsel. To make a long story short, we got altogether opinions from six different counsel, each of which differed from the other, and the whole presented such a mass of complications to our unprofessional minds that we were fairly bewildered.

As there really seemed no way out of the labyrinth of difficulties that had accumulated around us, and as my interests were to a great extent concerned in a rapid and easy solution of these difficulties, I volunteered to set out, like Cœlebs in search of a wife, or Keeper in search of his master, in quest of contributories. And as the name of the Company is the All-Over-India Europe Goods Association, so is its nature.

I have visited in the course of my travels almost every large town from Peshawar, in the north, to Hyderabad, in the south of India, but without much result, for you will be able to gather from this judgment of Mooltawee's, in a case that came before him, to establish the liability of a contributary, that it is not so easily done even after you have found your contributary.

Mooltawee's judgment is interesting, apart from the ability and ingenuity with which he deals with the legal subtleties of the case, as it gives a sketch of the rise, progress, and collapse of the company, and affords a very fair insight into the history of commercial speculation at Budgepore. Here is the judgment *in extenso*.

In the Civil Court of Budgepore.

In the matter of the All-Over-India Europe Goods Association, Limited, the Liquidators, plaintiffs, *versus* Kissa Khan, defendant.

This is a suit brought to establish the liability of the defendant as a contributary to the company in liquidation, represented by the plaintiffs as liquidators.

The company, as it appears from records before the Court, was established a few years ago, and subsequently undertook to purchase the stock, business, outstanding debts, and goodwill of the firm of Cork, Screw, and Co., formerly general merchants and traders in Budgepore.

The affairs of the firm appear to have been in a very prosperous condition up to the period when the senior partner, Mr. Cork, sold out and retired to England. The remaining partner, Mr. Screw, then appears to have entered into several very heavy speculations. He established an All-Over-India Dawk Company, intended, as far as one can judge by the prospectus, to convey travellers to and from any spot between Peshawur and Cape Comorin. But this failed. He then entered into a contract to supply a million sleepers to two or three railway companies. But the railway companies being under the control of directors in England, some of whom were large iron masters, just about that time came to a resolution, grounded on accurate data received from India, that there was no wood in the country suitable for railway sleepers, and it was necessary to ship from England iron sleepers. Mr. Screw, it seems, had contracted with the railway for five rupees a sleeper, and had also entered into certain arrangements with sub-contractors, by which the sleepers were to be cut and delivered in Budgepore for three rupees eight annas per sleeper, and had advanced these gentlemen twenty thousand rupees to meet current expenses. The railway authorities in England, having decided upon adopting iron sleepers, refused to ratify the contract with Mr. Screw, and he was forced into a court of law to recover what he considered due to him as damages for breach of contract and compensation for losses. In the Court of First Instance Mr. Screw lost the case with costs, but on appeal the judgment was reversed, and Mr. Screw gained a decree for the whole amount, with costs, in the lower, as well as in the upper court. The proceedings, however, occupied two years, and the railway companies then carried the case to the Privy Council, but the record was lost on the way to England, the papers having been accidentally consumed in a fire which destroyed the mail when in course of transit to Calcutta. A fresh set of papers had to be prepared from the originals which were in the court, and were transmitted by another route; but they did not reach England, owing to the mail by which they were being conveyed to Bombay having been robbed by dacoits in the Gwalior territory. The record had to be transcribed a third time, and on this occasion it reached England safely. This occured three years ago, since which nothing more has been heard of this case, but it is supposed to be nearly ready for hearing by the Privy Council, and may possibly be heard two years hence.

By this time Mr. Screw's losses had been so heavy that he was unable to meet his engagements, and he resolved upon selling his business to a joint-stock company; this company was at first called the "Budgepore Joint-Stock Company, Limited," and had been got up as the prospectus sets forth, for the purpose of purchasing anything that might be offered for sale, and selling by auction anything anybody could be induced to buy. This company undertook to purchase the business, stock, outstandings, and goodwill of Mr. Screw's firm, but they had no money to pay for it. This difficulty was, however, obviated by a resort to the Budgepore Bank, a new bank got up mainly by the directors of the "Budgepore Joint-Stock Company, Limited," assisted by Mr. Screw. This gentleman and the directors each took one share in the new bank, but the other shares were rapidly sold, the principal purchasers of them being military officers and members of the civil service. The bank having been thus formed, their first transaction was a loan of three lacs to the Budgepore Joint-Stock Company, Limited, for the purpose of purchasing the business, stock, outstandings, and goodwill of Mr. Screw's business; upon the security of the stock then in hand, valued at one lac, and some house property belonging to Mr. Screw at Budgepore and elsewhere, represented as worth three lacs. When the transaction was complete, Mr. Screw made over his property to the Budgepore Joint-Stock Company, Limited, upon payment in cash of one lac and a half of rupees, and an equal sum in shares in the company, which now changed its name to the "All-Over-India Europe Goods Association, Limited."

After paying Mr. Screw a hundred and seventy-eight thousand rupees, the company had still in hand remaining from the original sum borrowed from the Budgepore Bank, one hundred and twenty-two thousand rupees. This would appear from the account books of the company to have been thus disposed of :—

To Mr. Screw, the promoter . .	Rs. 5,000
Bonus to six directors . . .	6,000
Interest at 12 per cent. for three years, guaranteed to shareholders at 36,000 per annum . . .	1,08,000
For working expenses . . .	3,000
Total . .	1,22,000

The affairs of the company seem to have been conducted for many years on the most approved (Budgeporean) commercial principles. An account was opened with all shareholders, who were allowed their goods at cost price, an additional twenty per cent. being added to the price of articles sold to the general body of constituents to compensate for the loss on sales to shareholders. The three thousand rupees which had been set aside for working capital was expended in defraying the travelling expenses of Fancy Goods, Esq., who came out from one of the first London houses to take charge of the company's affairs as General Manager. It is due to this gentleman to state that at the first annual meeting of shareholders he brought to their notice the financial prospects of the company, and represented that nine-tenths of the constituents were shareholders who were allowed a heavy discount on purchases: that in the nine months which had elapsed between the purchase of the business by the company and his, Mr. Fancy Goods', assuming charge, there had accumulated a lac of rupees of outstandings, of which seventy-five per cent. would have to be written off to profit and loss, while a large sum was due in England for stock which had been supplied, amounting to £12,000. An extraordinary general meeting of shareholders was shortly afterwards held, and the condition of the company's affairs laid before them. Two alternative courses were suggested, either a fresh call of five hundred rupees a share, or the payment of the debts then due by shareholders for purchases effected. The meeting unanimously rejected the latter course, but consented to a call of ten rupees per share.

The business was carried on for another year, when at the annual meeting it was resolved that as the original debt to the Budgepore Bank with interest had now risen to 4,020,000 rupees, they should apply to the bank for another loan of six lacs, out of which the original debt was to be liquidated, and the balance paid by instalments of 10,000 rupees per annum. The directors of the bank being most of them shareholders in the company, the proposition was favourably entertained, and the loan was negotiated.

The guaranteed interest of 12 per cent. having been paid regularly from the fund set apart for that purpose, the shares had risen considerably in value, and had been purchased by many persons at a distance, who were, no doubt, induced to make the investment by the regularity with which so handsome a dividend was annually declared.

The affairs of the Bank of Budgepore, however, were not altogether satisfactory to the shareholders, and at the next annual meeting, which was held subsequently to the negotiation of the loan of six lacs, some of the shareholders pressed the directors for explanations, which, after a threat to resort to legal proceedings, were at last offered, and the result was that a new manager was appointed, and steps taken to obtain regular payment of interest from the All-Over-India Europe Goods Association, Limited. It will be sufficient to add that these proceedings resulted in the company being put in liquidation.

It now remains to be seen how far the defendant is fixed with the liability of a contributory. The plaintiff asserts that he has been from the first a shareholder in the company, that his application for shares was duly entered in the register, that scrip was issued in accordance with that application, and that dividends to the extent of 12 per cent. have been made to him regularly as well as to other shareholders. The plaintiff adds, and supports the statement by a large amount of evidence, that he is unable to produce parol vouchers, or the register showing the entry of defendant's application, and the issue of scrip and his receipts for the yearly payment of dividends, because these documents have been destroyed by white ants.

Defendant denies his liabilty on the following grounds:—

1st.—Because he is a Massulman and has been circumcised.

2nd.—Because he behaved with exemplary loyality in the disturbances in 1857, in support of which he files the originals of certificates from the Commissioner of the division.

3rd.—Because in a suit brought by one Gunnee Lall, for the recovery of the purchase-money of certain villages, he is not described in the plaint as a shareholder.

4th.—Because in seven other suits all brought subsequently to the period at which it is stated by the plaintiff he became a shareholder, he is not described as such either in the plaint or in the decree of the court, or in any other document connected with the proceedings.

5th.—Because there is no entry in any of his (defendant's) books to show that he ever purchased shares or received any dividend.

6th.—That on the day of which it is alleged he made an application for the shares he was away at his brother's wedding at a place thirty miles distant from Budgepore, and did not return for a week.

7th.—That he had to defray the expenses of his brother's wedding, and was not in funds to purchase shares.

8th.—That the plaintiff has not adduced reliable evidence to establish his liability.

At the first hearing of the case the following issues were drawn.

1st.—Is the defendant as he alleges a Mahomedan, and how does that effect his liability?

2nd.—Is the defendant the person alluded to in the certificate of loyalty in 1857?

3rd.—If the facts as stated in the 3rd and 4th pleas are correct, in what way do they effect defendant's liability?

4th.—Similarly what is the effect of the allegations, in paragraphs 5, 6 and 7 of the defendant's statement, and are the facts as there stated?

5th.—Has the plaintiff adduced satisfactory proofs of defendant's liability?

At the second hearing of this case, both parties being represented by their respective pleaders, the evidence was recorded.

As the 5th issue lays the burden of proof upon the plaintiff, it will not be necessary to enter into a consideration of the evidence on the other issues until this has been disposed of.

The plaintiff ought to have produced vouchers for his statement, but he accounts for the absence of this all-important evidence by the fact of the documents having all been destroyed by white ants. These insects, it is true, are very destructive, and particularly so in Budgepore. And although it is quite possible that valuable records should be destroyed in this manner, because it is known that white ants' destructive faculties are indiscriminately applied, that insect not being able to distinguish between what are and what are not valuable documents, yet it is a very remarkable coincidence indeed that in this case the ants should have made a selection of documents and devoured only those which were applicable to this case. There is no exception to be taken to the parol evidence which the plaintiff has adduced. Three witnesses of the utmost respectability depose to having seen the defendant write the letter forwarding the application for the shares. Three others of equal respectability depose to having seen the application received and entered in the register, and the scrip signed and despatched in accordance with the application. These witnesses are all all native clerks in the service of the plaintiffs, for the rejection of whose testimony no good reason has been adduced by the defendant. The most conclusive evidence of all is that of witness No. 7, who deposes to having seen the white ants in the act of destroying the very documents alluded to. Witness No. 8 says he himself despatched the various sums which it is alleged were paid to defendant as dividends on his shares; but he does not produce the receipt, for the same reason that the other vouchers were not forthcoming, viz., because they were devoured by the white ants along with the other papers. The defendant seeks to impugn the veracity of the plaintiffs' witnesses on the ground that in the course of his business as money-lender or banker the plaintiffs' witnesses have become indebted to him, and he has at various times sued them at law and got decrees against them.

Although I do not consider that the defendant has succeeded in his attempt to impugn the testimony of these witnesses, yet as I consider that the plaintiffs were bound to put the vouchers in a place where white ants could not reach them, and that the production of them (the vouchers) is necessary to support the plaintiffs' case, and as they have not been produced, I shall dismiss the claim.

The decree will carry costs.

Signed,

BASIL MOOLTAWEE,
Judge.

CHRONICLE XI.

THE BUDGEPORE POLITICAL AGENCY.

CHRONICLE XI.

THE BUDGEPORE POLITICAL AGENCY.

CHAPTER I.

A THING OF BEAUTY IS A JOY FOR EVER.

THE English reader will not see anything worthy of remark in the heading of this chapter, but the Indian will immediately say to himself, "Political agency of Budgepore! How comes there to be a political agency there?"

But there really was a political agency at Budgepore. And this is how there was one. I have already chronicled the political history of Budgepore, and traced its destinies from Warren Hastings' time downwards. The Nawab of Budgepore was still an independent prince. The capital and palace were situated about twenty-seven miles from the military and civil station and the native city of Budgepore. But the whole province went by this name. The political agency was an average one in point of emolument, and a very desirable and coveted appointment it was. It was at the time I write held by Captain Kummakl. Kummakl was the son and grandson of two old Bengal civilians. The family name was Carmichael, but the natives always pronounced it Kummakl, and the grandfather, after he retired from the service, wishing to perpetuate the fond associations that gilded the horizon of his memory in the sunset of his days, left all his money to his son on condition that he should change the family name to Kummakl. There were several of the family in the different services, and Captain Lionel Kummakl was, as I have said, political agent of Budgepore. He lived in one of the Nawab's palaces, and a very beautiful residence it was, in the centre of a large garden which bordered on a lake. In the middle of the lake there was an island partly natural and partly artificial, in which stood the picturesque ruins of an ancient Hindoo temple, whose rugged edges of brown stone peeped here and there from underneath the foliage of the peepul tree and the luxuriant creepers that almost overwhelmed it in their embrace. There was a boat on the lake, and plenty of good fishing and good shooting in the neighbourhood. You will say Kummakl ought to have been happy in such a place. And so he would have been, but for one thing. He was like Adam alone in paradise—he sighed for an Eve to keep him company, and enjoy life with him.

Julia Congreve was the prettiest girl that ever came to India. This is saying a good deal, I allow, and I have reflected a moment whether I ought not to qualify the assertion. But when I re-call to mind her figure, her exquisitely shaped head and hands, her dark grey eyes, "fringed," as a novel writer would say, but it is more philosophical to call it "protected" by long eye-lashes: her complexion, which Madame Rachel might have taken for a model; not sickly white, but pure and translucent, like alabaster, coloured with nature's loveliest tint, which she has given to the rose and reproduced in the bloom of youth and beauty; I say when I recall this image to my memory I find no reason to modify my statement, sweeping though it is. In this brief allusion to a few out of her many charms, I must not forget her hair. In those days that peculiar tint of ladies' hair which was lately in fashion and has now gone out, was not generally admired. I have heard monsters with no taste and no eye for the beautiful speak slightingly of her hair and call it red. Red! well, it was red in the same sense that that deep golden-tinted cloud at sunset all glowing amid a blaze of rosy light may be called red. What would you think of the man who pointed to such a sunset scene and remarked, "Look at that red cloud?" Why, you would feel the same as I felt when I heard men remark on Julia's hair and call it red. She was just seventeen when she first came to India. Her father was a civilian, and at the age of five Julia had been sent home to school. Her mother died a year after, and Julia remained at school and under the charge of her friends till she was sixteen and a half, during which time she had never seen her father, and then came out to India. He was not at Budgepore, but she was then on a visit at her aunt's, Mrs. Mooltawee, who was a good woman enough, but rather too fond of match-making. The night after Julia's arrival there was a ball, and she made her first appearance in the Budgepore world on that occasion. Her beauty was striking anywhere, how much more when enhanced by the accomplishments of an elegant and tasty toilet. Ah, me! what havoc she made among the hearts of bachelors. Poor Kummakl was there. I don't know why I should call him poor except for the condition in which he went home that night after dancing twice with Julia. He had to return next day to the agency, but he managed to find time to call at Mrs. Mooltawee's, and there he saw Julia more beautiful, if possible, in her simple morning attire of glistening white than in all the glories of white satin and lace flounces. Her manner was perfection, her conversation sprightly and cheerful, and Kummakl returned to his solitary palace in the garden by the lake in a mood bordering on distracton. He thought to himself what bliss it would be to see that fairy creature seated opposite to him at the dinner table, to see her in the drawing-room, to hear her light foot-fall on the carpet and the rustling of her dress, to ride with her, to walk in the garden with her, to gather flowers for her, to row her on the lake, to be her slave, in short, and wait upon her everywhere from morning to night. It seemed to him as if his palace would be a palace, indeed, graced by the presence of an angel.

When a man is addicted to intellectual pursuits, or immersed in business, that all day long absorbs the utmost powers of his mind, a fit of love may do him no harm ; on the contrary, it may do him a great deal of good. But love is fed by fancy, and lives on imagination. A very busy man, as Bulwer somewhere remarks, has no time to be in love. Now Kummakl was not a busy man. Few political agents are, and if they are, it is generally in doing mischief, and then trying to undo it. A political agent of long experience, much longer experience than any of the political agents of the present day can boast of, once remarked to me, in reply to an observation that So and So did nothing, that that was the best thing he could do. And that had reference to a critical time too. How Kummakl's fit of love would have ended I don't know. He might have drowned himself in the lake, or shot himself ; he was just mad enough for either, till one day the idea struck him, why not marry Julia? That would be better than killing himself out of love for her, or dying by inches. He looked round at the handsome suite of apartments in which he lived, and thought that with a little outlay they might be made worthy of such a goddess. Then he got up and looked at himself in the glass; and that did not dissatisfy him. He was a good-looking fellow enough, tall, well-built, with dark hair, and a neat moustache. What, if Julia could be brought to love him one tithe, one millionth part as much as he loved her! The thought was maddening, but the idea after simmering in his excited brain for half an hour, resulted in a call for his servant.

"Pack up my things," he said: "I shall go to-morrow morning into Budgepore, and remain there——a week—no, a fortnight, perhaps more."

On reaching Budgepore, Kummakl went and called on Mrs. Dakhil Duftar, who was a great friend of his, and took her into his confidence. Mrs. Dakhil Duftar was delighted to be consulted in a love affair, what lady is not? and entered into the thing with much interest. Her advice was consolatory to Kummakl's feelings.

"Why should not you try, Captain Kummakl? Julia's a sweetly pretty girl and well educated, and will I dare say look a little high, but I don't see why you should not succeed. You've a capital appointment, and live at a delightful place; —it is true I know her aunt wants her to marry in the service, but I don't think in your case that would be an insuperable objection. You are not so good as a district, but much better than a joint.* I advise you to try. There are a good many already in the field, I hear, Isteefa for one; but he has no chance. Julia can't bear him. Don't be too shy. Faint heart, you know, never wins fair lady; and don't be too spooney, girls like Julia don't like men to be too spooney."

"I'll try," said Kummakl, getting up to go; "many thanks, for you have quite encouraged me. You'll keep my secret, won't you?"

"Oh, yes, you may depend on me. Good-bye and good luck."

* I must explain that a magistrate and collector in charge of a district draws upwards of two thousand rupees a month; a joint, or joint-magistrate, the grade below, from seven hundred to a thousand.

Captain Kummakl needn't have made a point about his secret, as he called it, being kept. He was an honorary member of the 159th mess, and always dined there when in cantonments. After he left that night there was a good deal of betting whether Kummakl, Isteefa, or which of the half-a-dozen others who were well known to be running for Julia's hand would be successful. Kummakl was the favourite. After some further discussion, a gold mohur lottery was proposed and forthwith started. Captain Spot, who drew Kummakl, sold him for five gold mohurs the minute after to Blackburn, who had drawn Isteefa, and Blackburn got ten gold mohurs for the two the next day.

In India society lives pretty much in a glass house, and as making love forms a part of most men's lives, they enjoy the unenviable privilege of making love in glass houses. Alexis fancies that his *penchant* for Lucinda is a secret—when there are fifty pairs of eyes watching his talking to her at the first ball, and when he rides up to her carriage at the band, Lucinda's less favoured admirers make way for him, and leave them together as a matter of course. Two doves that sit together cooing on the branch of a tree in the open face of heaven, in no deeper seclusion than that afforded by the somewhat scanty foliage of the surrounding branches, enjoy as much privacy as you, when you offer the lady of your love in an Indian drawing-room those little attentions which are construed into intended matrimony.

This may be an uncomfortable reflection for those who have a reputation or wish to gain a reputation for being wiser than their fellow men. Some statesman, I think it was Sir Robert Peel, said it was as impossible for a tax to be popular as for a man in love to be wise. I suppose it is a law of nature that the proportion between the two should be maintained everywhere. For if the difficulty of discovering a popular tax in India is tenfold greater than in England, it is certainly ten times as difficult to make love in that country and throw a veil of privacy over an amiable weakness as it is at home.

Next day Kummakl called. Julia was there in the drawing-room looking more lovely than ever. He prolonged the morning call as long as he could with decency, asked permission to accompany the ladies in their morning ride, and took his departure.

Mrs. Mooltawee had a dinner party that evening, but Kummakl had not been invited. I dare say he would have been if he had been in Budgepore when the invitations were sent out, or even if Mrs. Mooltawee had known he was coming in; but then he had come in so suddenly, and not told anyone of his intention. So he dined at mess and was moody and abstracted all the evening, and went home early, when he sat for full two hours in the verandah smoking a great many more cigars than were good for him, and thinking of Julia, how she looked in the carriage at the band when he had exchanged a few words with her, her bonnet, her ribbons, her gloves, her dress, and how she was probably dressed at that very moment while Kummakl was sitting in the verandah with his legs up against the pillar dreaming of her. I say dreaming, for it was nothing else How she looked at the band he had a sort of right to dwell upon, for it was a *bonâ fide* exercise of memory, but as to how she was dressed for the evening was a matter Kummakl had no business at all to reason about, because he had no better data to go upon than most members when they bring a bill into council; that is, he took for granted his facts, grounded on some general ideas about ladies' dress, and drew his conclusions, being perfectly satisfied, because he had only himself to satisfy as to their correctness. And was Julia thinking of Kummakl? I am afraid not. The standing programme, with all the young butterflies who hovered round her, and burnt off their legs and wings, seemed to be ceaseless merriment. They were always saying funny things—at least they were always laughing. How they found so much to laugh about at Budgepore I cannot imagine. I think Julia must have been very tired of all this when night came and she laid her pretty head upon her pillow. But then Julia's intellectual education had not been thought of very much. You see, she was brought up at one of the first schools for young ladies. She was taught every possible accomplishment, from music and painting to getting into a carriage gracefully—and out. A carriage was brought twice a week in the afternoon to the door of Miss Minim's seminary and the young ladies of the head class went through the lesson, a branch of education deemed so important that Miss Minim, who delegated most of the other branches to assistants, superintended this herself. She stood just by the carriage door, which was held open by a footman in gorgeous livery, who preserved, all the time, a countenance as solemn as if he was looking down into the graves of each young lady as she tripped up the carriage steps. One after another, dressed as for a drive, they came out of the hall door, advanced to the carriage steps, put their little feet gracefully upon them, attending all the time to Miss Minim's instructions as to adjustment of dress, position of hands, and every movement, like a soldier going through the old-fashioned manual and platoon. Each young lady had to seat herself in the carriage, and then go through the reverse process of coming down again.

After it was all over Miss Minim used to go for a drive, taking with her one of the governesses, or one of the young ladies who had earned a claim to this distinction by superior gracefulness of deportment.

Julia learnt to write a delicate lady-like hand, and to read; she learnt a little geography and a little arithmetic as far as addition. French, of course, and enough Italian to be able to pronounce properly the words of Italian songs, and to know their meaning—when they had any. She learnt to dance, of course, and took lessons in riding, and when these and other minor contributory accomplishments were mastered, her education was completed. On Sunday, the young ladies went to church once in the morning, where Miss Minim had two long pews in the very centre of the aisle of St. Bonavia's, the fashionable church. The afternoon was spent in walking about the garden in summer in twos and threes, talking generally about their love affairs, real or imaginary. In winter the girls crowded over the fires in their rooms and talked on the same subject. The religious instruction imparted to the minds of her pupils by Miss Minim consisted in a chapter of Mrs. Trimmer's annotations, which she read every evening at prayer time. The curate of the parish, Mr. Mildmay, had made one or two advances in proposing to attend at stated times and give the young ladies religious instruction. But Miss Minim did not see the matter in the same light at all as Mr. Mildmay, and resolutely kept the young priest at arm's length. She did her duty, did Miss Minim. She professed to give her young ladies the best and most accomplished education, and she did so. She did not undertake to give instruction in Latin and Greek or mathematics. If parents wished their daughters to learn such things as these, they must send them to some inferior establishment.

Miss Minim's institution was intended only for young ladies of position; she undertook to bring them up so that they could be ornaments to society, and I only wish every professor in the world succeeded in doing what they undertake to do as well as Miss Minim. That lady used to boast that she knew the world; and I think she did not overrate herself in this respect. "I don't care so much," she used to say, "about a girl's looks. Of course, it is all the better if she is good-looking; but nice, lady-like manners and a graceful bearing in a drawing-room, and good taste in dress, go further in society a great deal than mere beauty of features."

"Go further in society,"—that was the standard Miss Minim worked up to. That was her rule of life, as it were,—the high-water mark of her principles and her designs. That there was any other object in education never for one instant crossed her mind. There is one advantage in not setting one's self a very high standard, namely, that you can the more easily attain to it; and Miss Minim perfected her scholars, whereas, had she set herself to train them for immortality, possibly she might not have succeeded so well.

Beings like Julia Congreve really seem as if they were born exceptions to the conditions under which the human race comes into the world, as if the curse, passed upon Adam and his posterity, did not reach them. As soon as she was born, she had two servants beside her mother to attend to every babyish caprice. When a little older, her two servants were increased to three, to thirty in fact, for every member of her father's somewhat numerous household vied in devotion to the little girl. When she went to England she lived with an aunt, who had no children of her own, and so doted on the little Julia, who was a queen without the cares of state, from her very birth. Having naturally a gentle disposition, never tried or crossed by the exactions of elder brothers or sisters, she never gave occasion for any chastisement harsher than a gentle rebuke. And when she went to school, she fell under Miss Minim's principle of education for young ladies, viz., that refinement, and ease, and grace of manner were incompatible with labour of any kind. Up to the age of eighteen, she never knew a care more weighty than the selection of a ball-dress. A hard or unkind word had never met her ear, or been addressed to her. She did not know her mother, and therefore her death was no cause of real grief to her young mind. Her aunt, with whom she was living when that event occurred, felt a mother's kindness for her, and saw no reason why she should cause her young idol's tears to flow for a loss which could only be brought home to her by the aid of imagination, and forbore to dwell upon the reality of the loss to Julia. Her path of life from the very cradle, was, as if it were strewn with flowers,—with flowers that bear no thorns. Compare the existence of such an one with the lot of the sons and daughters of toil and care, and say whether they do not appear to belong to different races.

Kummakl couldn't sit in his verandah dreaming of Julia all night, so, although the subject to his somewhat narrow mind was by no means exhausted, he gave it up and went to bed, to continue his dream in the land of sleep. But he awoke an hour before daylight, and looked at his watch. He was determined to be early at Mrs. Mooltawee's, for there might be some other fellows there bent on the same errand as himself, and he was resolved to have the pleasure of assisting Julia to mount her horse. He had planned that little plot the night before—indeed he had dwelt upon all the contingencies connected with it for full three-quarters of an hour. Such elastic things our minds are. We can contract them to the smallest dimensions, that the veriest trifle can fill the whole area of the mental vision, or expand them to take in an idea of infinity. And a man's mind does contract a good deal when he is under the influence of any passion, for then the minutest point, no bigger than a pin's head, will swell and swell like Satyavrata's fish, till it fills the whole field of view. Kummakl was up and dressed, and had had his cup of coffee, and yet it wanted half-an-hour of gun-fire, which means a little after day-light. He waited till the gun fired, and then, afraid that after all he should be late, cantered along to Mrs. Mooltawee's. Here he found no sign of anyone stirring, so he gave his horse to the syce and walked about the garden, looking at his watch every two minutes. A quarter of an hour passed before the ladies' horses were brought round, and then he came up a little nearer the house. Then an ayah made her appearance, walking leisurely across from the servants' huts, and disappeared inside a bathing-room door. He wondered whether that was her ayah, and his heart began to warm towards the woman, as if she were a priestess consecrated to the service of his goddess. I venture to say if a genii—a jin, more correctly speaking—had appeared at that moment, and offered to change his identity with that of the ayah's, Kummakl's destiny in the world would have seemed a cheap price to pay for the bargain. He was thinking of this when another ayah appeared, and he didn't know which was Julia's, and he laughed as he thought how the genii might have taken him in. Another half hour passed, when a light step and a rustle of a lady's dress made him look up, and he beheld Mrs. Mooltawee in her riding habit. Julia had a headache, she said, that morning, and was not going out. Ah, poor Kummakl! All the fabric he had been twining through so many hours turned out to be made of gossamer thread after all, and broken up at once!

Mrs. Mooltawee, however, saw his disappointment, and asked him to come to tiffin, as she thought Julia perhaps would like to ride in the evening. So Kummakl's hopes revived with the idea of a *tête-à-tête* ride, and he was cheerful and companionable enough; and when he assisted Mrs. Mooltawee to dismount at the door on their return, she thought he would not be so bad a match for Julia after all.

I have always heard, for I am obliged to speak on these matters from the experience of others, that when a man who has been very much in love gets married, he feels an immense relief, like a ship long tossed on tumultuous seas,—he is in harbour at last. No more toiling and watching, no more waiting for an hour or two for the chance of a look, an opportunity for a word, an occasion for some petty, trifling service, too ludicrously trifling to be described; no more anxious hours and sleepless nights, no more plunges into the depths of despair because a passing shade crosses the features of your lady-love. If your whole happiness and peace of mind for a day, or a week, or a month, is liable to be destroyed by a cross word or a cold look, it is obvious that your happiness stands on very unstable ground. When you are once married, all this fever and anxiety are at an end. A cross word or a cold look does not then signify so much—there is time to heal the wound, or let the cloud pass away. So that

I think our Indian code—I do not mean the Penal Code, but the code of Indian social law—is very merciful, for it shortens materially the period of trial a lover has to undergo. Kummakl had danced twice with Julia, had exchanged a few words in a morning call, and fewer still at the band; he had been one *tête-à-tête* ride with her, had helped her once on her horse, and once to dismount. The next time he saw her was at a large evening party at Mrs. Mooltawee's the day after the ride, when he inveigled her into the verandah, and there by moonlight took her hand, as if he was touching the hand of a being of a superior order from himself, and told her of his love. She withdrew her hand but manifested no displeasure. She neither said "yes" nor "no," but rather sternly, as he thought for her, desired to go inside. He offered his arm in silence, and led her in. Just as they crossed the threshold, they confronted Mrs. Mooltawee, and Kummakl, whose sense of perception was wound up to an inconceivable pitch of acuteness, augured well from a glance which Julia gave her aunt, and which the latter returned with the rapidity of an electric spark.

While the weighty question which Kummakl had put remained unanswered, he felt it was impossible to hold any kind of conversation with Julia, and as the silence was irksome beyond measure, he led her to a seat, and returned to the veranhah alone, for he felt as if the eyes of everyone in the room were upon him; a great mistake, for no one probably was even thinking of him at the time.

As he was standing alone, gazing out on the scene before him, bathed in the splendour of an Indian moonlight, he felt a light touch on his arm. He looked round, and Mrs. Mooltawee stood beside him.

"So you have proposed to my niece?" she said.

"Did she tell you? Yes, I have. Oh, I do so hope you will all consent," said Kummakl incoherently.

"Her father must be written to. I don't suppose he will object. I don't."

"And she?"

"I do not think she will say no."

This was not very decisive, but it raised Kummakl to the seventh heaven. He pressed Mrs. Mooltawee's hand in silent gratitude, and she left him with a smile. His eyes followed her as she went in, and soon sought out Julia. There she was, chattering and laughing with a young fellow of the 159th, as if there was very little weighing on her mind. Kummakl's heart sank for a moment, as the idea crossed him, "Is that the woman to whom I have just made an offer of marriage, and she doesn't seem to consider it worth thinking about? But then she is such an angel."

Kummakl had the good sense to feel that he was not fit company for anyone but himself, and slipped out of the room quietly and went home.

"Well, my dear, you know he has eighteen hundred a month," said Mrs. Dakhil Duftar to Mrs. Mooltawee apologetically, as the two ladies were exchanging a few words on the subject of the offer.

"Yes, but the military pensions are so bad."

"Well, I confess I should have preferred a district for Julia; still, you know, she might have done worse; she might have fallen in love with one of those young officers."

"I don't think Julia will ever fall in love," was Mrs. Mooltawee's reply. "Good night."

"Good night."

THE BUDGEPORE POLITICAL AGENCY.

CHAPTER II.

WE ALL HAVE OUR WEAK POINTS.

So they were married. Some philosophers will tell you that hopes fulfilled are never equal to the anticipation. In Kummakl's case it certainly was not, as I don't suppose any man could have been happier than he was. His brightest dreams had all come to pass. There was Julia, the goddess, enthroned in the very shrine he had built for her. There was he, the worshipper, with the being he worshipped for his own, and, as it seemed, no cloud in the sky to darken the sunlight of his bliss. As for Julia, the destiny to which she seemed born continued to attend her, the pathway of her life was strewn with flowers as it had ever been. She had a beautiful house in a beautiful spot; she had a *boudoir* exquisitely furnished with every artificial luxury that an upholsterer's skill could supply. She had her music and her painting and her embroidery. Her husband was her devoted slave, too loving to bore her with attentions, but ever ready to gratify her slightest whim, to read to her, to ride with her, to walk in the garden with her, and gather flowers for her, to row her on the lake. She had the newest novels, they were the only sort of literature for which her education had given her a taste, and as much society as she wanted, as her Budgepore friends were always glad to come out to spend a day whenever she asked them, and the Nawab's carriages and horses were always at her disposal to bring them out and send them back. She was still a queen as she always had been all her life; every creature that came near her seemed but too glad to do her the slightest service, and she accepted it all with a kindness and grace of manner that captivated every heart.

And here I find myself face to face with a matter which no

chronicler of Indian social history can shirk. He may avoid it or pass it by for a time, but sooner or later it is sure to force itself upon him. Here were two human beings, Lionel and Julia, who knew no more of each other's character than you do of the man who brushes by you in the Strand on your way to the city, yet they had sworn before the altar to live together as man and wife till death should part them. Now, it is no use to pretend to ignore the fact, it is undeniable, and forces itself on our attention every day we read the papers or listen to what goes on around us, that in spite of marriage vows, something a long way short of death does very often interfere to sever the union of Indian married life. And the majority of those who consider the subject account for it by the tropical rapidity with which courtship ripens into matrimony. In former days, it was the common thing for a man, if he heard there was a nice girl at a neighbouring station, to get leave between musters, that is, leave for thirty days, go over, see her, speak to her, dance with her, make an offer and marry her. Sometimes he would complete it all in the one month. At others, he would put it off, and get another thirty days' leave a month or two later, and then go and get married. Nowadays, "leave between musters" is out of fashion, but in nine cases out of ten your Indian marriages are consummated between people who venture their life's happiness upon the most superficial acquaintance of the one whom they make their life's partner. Of course I shall be called cynical, and the opinion will be put down to the withering of the heart's affections under the blighting influence of the disappointed hopes that have left me an old bachelor. But, like Diogenes, I can study from my tub the manners and customs of other men who do not live in tubs. And I believe that our Indian social laws have been blamed for that for which they are not answerable. Marriage is a lottery, and out of a thousand men and women who do marry, not ten know each other's character before they speak the vows that bind them indissolubly together.

If the marriage is one of convenience, as many in the highest circles of society at home are, there is, of course, little or no attempt to read character. Among the middle classes in England and society generally in India, such marriages are less common, for they are contracts between parties who put wealth against rank, and in India there is little or none of either. On the other hand, our marriages are generally made between persons of mature age, whose characters are formed. But love is proverbially blind, and no wonder, for lovers, when together, wear a mask. And neither will discover the true features underneath the mask, no matter whether the courtship lasts for one month or for twenty. No, the unhappy fatality that attends so many Indian marriages is not to be attributed to the brevity of courtship. It is attributable to the habit, in so many cases a necessity that necessity is always taken for granted, of frequent temporary separations between man and wife, and the tone and habits of society in our modern Capuas. No more fatal lesson can be learnt by a wedded pair than that the society of one is not necessary to the happiness of the other. When Alexis and Lucinda have once discovered that they can do without one another, the chain that binds them together is reduced to one link, the social or moral obligation to observe the marriage vows, and the extent to which that obligation is recognised varies not only in different people, but at different times in the same person.

The natives about the agency admired Julia with a sort of distant veneration. They were never tired of extolling her beauty, and the Nawab of Budgepore heard so much about her that he fell desperately in love on hearsay, as the princes in the Arabian Nights and the Bagh-o-Bahar always do with princesses they have never seen. Though he would willingly have given up half his revenues for a Begum like her, he felt it was out of the question his ever possessing one, but he knew that a fresh element had been introduced into the machinery of the agency, and like a wise man he began to turn over the matter in his mind, and ponder upon the method by which it might be used to his advantage.

No European can form the smallest idea of the extent to which the whole life of the Asiatic is made up of intrigue. From the bottom to the top of the social ladder it is the same. Your servants spend all their spare time in intriguing to get a larger share of your favour and outdo their fellows. They will plot, and plan, and scheme for a whole year to get some member of your large household dismissed and another installed in his place, a relative, a friend, perhaps a creditor.

What appears to you a mere trifle not worth a minute's thought, a native will willingly spend days and weeks upon, and think the time well spent if he succeed. And if you like to see how the principle holds good in the highest walks in Asiatic life, read Indian history, and there you will find how the whole of it is nothing but a record of intrigues, commencing with diplomatic scheming and ending in war. To displace a favourite, to dethrone a reigning prince, to subvert a dynasty, were the ends and aims of statesmen and warriors in former days. Dethroning princes and subverting dynasties are matters now generally beyond the compass of either diplomacy or war. But the very same love of intrigue, though confined to limits where the results are necessarily less apparent than they were before British power became predominant, still finds a vent, and is as actively indulged in now that the prize is comparatively small, as it was in the days of Akbar and Aurungzebe.

The prime minister, or dewan, as he was called at Budgepore in the days I am writing about, was a Hindoo, by name Dowlut Rao. He had been installed as dewan before Kummakl's time by his predecessor, the man who was dewan before him, a Mahomedan noble named Mustaffa Khan, having been displaced to make room for a successful rival. For Mustaffa Khan had got into disgrace with the former political agent, who procured his dismissal and the installation of Dowlut Rao.

But an Asiatic takes all such instances of the ups and downs of life very stoically. He knew he had been outwitted. He had made a series of bad moves, and was checked for the time, but not checkmated. There was only one power that could checkmate him, and that was the angel of death, and there had been no summons from that quarter, so that it was clear that fate intended he should one day reverse the order of things and check, perhaps checkmate, his rival in his turn.

The Nawab, who hated Dowlut Rao, and against whose will Mustaffa Khan had been turned out, was quite ready to intrigue to get the latter back again, and, indeed, Kummakl's chief duties lay in thwarting the efforts which the Nawab was incessantly making to get his favourite re-instated.

All sorts of accusations were sent to the Political Agent against Dowlut Rao, and backed up by the Nawab. But Kummakl was duly instructed from the Foreign Office how to deal with these attempts, and to thwart every effort of the Nawab and Mustaffa Khan's party. Mustaffa Khan had tried to poison Dowlut Rao, and Dowlut Rao had tried to poison Mustaffa Khan. The most crafty and deep-laid plots were set on foot to embroil Dowlut Rao with the British Agent, and the most crafty and deep-laid schemes were set on foot to bring Mustaffa Khan somehow or other within reach of the criminal law. But beyond an incessant bubbling at the surface, these attempts produced no real fermentation in the social element at Budgepore. So matters had been going on since Kummakl had taken up the reins of office. He, of course, could no more vie with the authors of all these intrigues in sublety and cunning, than he could have ventured in competing with a pearl-diver for the treasures of the deep. Both parties in turn tried to make him their tool, and both failed, simply because a certain amount of common sense and English straightforwardness, or, as an Asiatic would call it, English obtuseness and want of sublety, kept him from being made a tool of either. Had he laid himself open to be bribed by money by either party, he might have made a fortune long ago. But he had not been long enough there for the natives to have sounded his character to the bottom. They were a little uncertain about him. The very deficiencies in his character puzzled them, and they had none of them dared to venture on the dangerous experiment of a bribe, and as he, of course, never suggested anything of the kind, he had never been subjected to the temptation.

Now, however, a new element altogether was introduced into the complex machinery. Kummakl was the slave of his wife, she was a woman, and if she was to be won, the party that won her would be sure of victory. But how to win so unapproachable a creature? That was the theme that many wise heads and subtle minds spent whole days in pondering upon, after Julia had been a month at the Budgepore Political Agency.

Meantime the subordinates attached to the Agency had a fine time of it. The head clerk, whose name was Cynthea Jones, was subsidized by both parties. He received a hundred rupees a month from Dowlut Rao to secure his influence in his interest, and another from Mustaffa Khan to bind him to his, besides *dalies*, or presents, from each of the noblemen on every Hindoo holiday from the one, and on every Mahomedan holiday from the other. These *dalies*, as they are called, consisted chiefly of vegetables and sweatmeats, cakes, &c., but there was always a gold mohur, or two, neatly wrapped up either in a bunch of plantains or tomatos. Besides this the Nawab, who was not above securing his services, made him handsome presents about twice in the year, taking good care, of course, not to let his minister know of the subsidy. But Cynthea Jones was not the only man who profited considerably by the state of politics at Budgepore. There was not a servant attached to Kummakl's household, as long as he was a bachelor, who did not receive a gratuity equivalent to his pay from each of the rival factions, for each servant individually represented to the servants, respectively of Dowlut Rao and Mustaffa Khan, that he was in high favour with his master, and could influence him by a word dropped into his ear now and again.

When Julia came and it was seen what influence she possessed, you may easily imagine how anxious the contending parties were to hit upon some scheme either to get access to her or to secure her interest, if it were possible. Mustaffa Khan in this matter exhibited the greatest ability or capacity for intrigue, which in an Asiatic passes for ability. He, in thinking over the matter, came to the conclusion that if it was too high a flight of ambition to aim at the mistress, the next best thing was to secure the maid. And so as Julia had two ayahs, an upper and a lower lady's maid, and as the upper one was, as is usually the case, a Mahomedan woman, he soon set the Nawab on the scent, and the result was overtures of friendship from the women servants in the Nawab's household. If among the Asiatics the male sex look upon intrigue as one of the main objects of life, the female live but to intrigue. Their capacity for it is something marvellous. The tenacity of purpose, the skill and cunning with which they weave the fine web of their plot and schemes, even about the merest trifle, is an interesting study in the book of human nature. Perhaps this characteristic is not confined to the Asiatic woman only. I have met with English women almost as fond of the pursuit, but compared with their Aryan sisters they are but clumsy operators. The ayah was not long in understanding how the land lay, and you may be sure she was not slow in turning it to good account. It soon became a common thing for her to spend some portion of every day in the Nawab's seraglio.

Every man has a weak point somewhere in his character, for every human being is open to flattery. There are many kinds of flattery. I do not mean by flattery, necessarily, the application of coarse butter by a clumsy hand, a dull Bœtian sounding of a man's praises in his presence or his ear. But there are other sorts of flattery, consisting of the discovery of the weak points of the character, and a skilful playing with them when found. Many of the greatest minds are subject to some petty vanity, such as you might, indeed, be prepared to find in a girl just fresh from school, but which you are surprised to meet with in a philosopher, a poet, or a statesman.

And as the weak point may be manipulated by flattery, so it may be made to secure a purpose by the opposite treatment. If the skilful flatterer can discover the small aperture between the joints of the harness where he may reach the skin, you may be sure a subtle enemy will be able pretty nearly always to find a similar place where he may wound. Kummakl was like other men. He was certainly not above the average in intellect, and I do not know but in this respect he was very much below it. He had a weak point like the rest of us, and a weak point very curiously situated. Frederick Schlegel, it is said, was so vain of his features that he had a little mirror inside the lid of his snuff-box wherein he was fond of contemplating the reflection of his face even while lecturing. Kummakl's weak point—you may smile as you read it, but can you lay your hand on your heart, my friend, and say you have no similar little vanity—was his feet. He was excessively, inordinately, ludicrously vain about his feet. I can't tell you how many pairs of boots and shoes he had not collected in his dressing-room. If you do not believe me, ask his bootmaker how much his yearly account for boots and shoes amounted to. When a man has a weak point like this, of course, all those who live with him and about him become aware of it. Do you think your native servants do not know your pet particular weakness? Why, it is the subject of constant discussion with them, and many a joke is made at your expense on the basis of it, in the kitchen.

Of course Julia soon found out her husband's little foible, but it was a very harmless one indeed, and it amused her to watch its occasional development. One morning, about three months after their marriage, she was walking with him in the garden; arm in arm they were sauntering down the path, pausing every now and then to gather flowers, and chatting pleasantly, when something caused Julia to stop a few seconds. Ere they continued their walk, she burst out laughing.

"What are you laughing about, Julia?" asked her husband.

"A very absurd idea crossed my mind just at the moment, some nonsense my ayah told me this morning, as she was doing my hair. I encourage the girl in tittle tattle, it amuses me, and your attitude just this moment, Li," (she always called him "Li") "reminded me of something the silly girl said to me this morning—it is too absurd to repeat, really."

"Never mind if it made you laugh—in connection with me too, and has evidently created an impression of some sort in your mind; you may as well tell me, it will make me laugh too, perhaps."

"Well, she said,—you know she gets together with the women servants in the Nawab's palace, and Dowlut Rao's women go there too, and they all talk scandal and nonsense, as women will, and she retails a great deal of it to me. They say that Dowlut Rao makes a joke about your being vain about your feet, Li,—what do you think of that? You know I think it *is* a little *wee bit* true—now confess, isn't it?"

"Pish, what stuff, Julia, you do listen to," said Kummakl, pretending to treat the trifle with the scorn it deserved. They neither of them alluded to the subject again, but Julia had to put a little extra force into her winning ways, ere she could chase away the cloud that that laugh of hers, and the remarks it called forth, had conjured up.

When a man has some of the petty little vanities or conceits I have spoken of, or the weak point the flatterer or the enemy may aim at, nothing galls him so much as to have it exposed and ridiculed. If Kummakl had had any work to do that absorbed his attention, or really occupied his mind, it is certain the disagreeable feeling occasioned by this trifling incident would have been speedily obliterated. As it was, he had nothing the least engrossing to take up his attention. His mornings were generally spent in reading aloud some novel to Julia, and if he had any work, it was nothing more than casting his eyes over the copy of some letter, comparing it with the draft, and signing it. Perhaps once or twice a week he had an hour's work in his office, but not more. This morning Julia happened to be engaged in something else, and did not want to be read to, and Kummakl spent the time in walking up and down the verandah, thinking, brooding rather, over the slight put upon him by Dowlut Rao, in making him the common talk of menials in his own or other households. When you take a trifling annoyance or a petty wrong to your bosom, and cherish it with the warmth of your concentrated attention, it is astonishing how it grows and grows till it assumes the most disproportionate dimensions. Any man in this way may make himself as miserable as he likes, and many men do make themselves very miserable. Kammakl did so, and not only that, but he made himself very angry too. And the poisoned shaft went on rankling in the wound, creating a festering sore that grew worse and worse every minute. A man of stronger character would have taken out the arrow and laid it aside, and not have allowed his mind to dwell upon the matter, seeing how much it discomposed him. But Kummakl had not a very strong character, and his vanity was piqued.

He began from that moment to look on Dowlut Rao with an unfavourable eye. Everything he did or said, if susceptible of two interpretations, appeared to Kummakl's view in the light the least favourable to the minister. It is astonishing, when once you take a prejudice against a man, and what trifles will give rise to a prejudice we all know, how different an aspect everything that man has to do, in connection with you, begins to wear. Before you conceive the prejudice, every little fault or mistake he committed you would explain away or excuse. Now, however, under the influence of another feeling, you have no allowance to make for him. You judge him by another standard altogether. You hold him guilty before you try him, whereas before you held him innocent till you were convinced unmistakably of his guilt.

The most important events of our lives, may we not say even the most important events in history, frequently arise seemingly from the smallest and most insignificant cause. In the life of nations, as in the life of individuals, events are so linked together, that you may often trace the chain all the way back to the occurrence out of which the change of a nation's destiny, or of an individual's whole character and fortunes arose. Most men, if they narrowly scan the past, will find that the great crisis in their lives was generally determined by some accident, as they call it, or some fortuitous circumstance, which they might have controlled had they been previously aware of its approach, or warned to be on their guard. It is a truth which is worth thinking about; that any day, you know not when, you may have to encounter some crisis, petty and insignificant perhaps at the time, which is nevertheless the turning-point of your life's fortunes.

It so happened that just as Kummakl had blown the smouldering fire till it made the kettle boil, and his feelings against Dowlut Rao were anything but charitable, a chuprassee appeared, and announced the very man himself. Now this was an unlucky accident! What brought Dowlut Rao there on that day, of all days in the week or month? He did not often visit Krummakl, not oftener than once perhaps in three weeks, unless Kummakl sent for him. What made him come to-day? I don't know, but I do know that in our every-day life occurrences of this sort do very constantly happen, and this is one instance of what I have just said, that any day we may, any one of us, be called unexpectedly to confront some seeming trifle, which is, nevertheless, destined to colour the whole future course of our destiny.

The reason of Dowlut Rao's visit was this, and Kummakl recollected it as he was going inside to receive his visitor. A short time before, the minister had requested Kummakl to give a berth in the agency office, then vacant, to a relation of his, and Kummakl had replied that, so far as he was concerned, he should be glad to recommend the appointment of Dowlut Rao's relative, but that he, Kummakl, had not the appointment in his gift, the patronage belonging to the head of the department. This was what Dowlut Rao had come about, and Kummakl, as he went inside, resolved in his heart that he would disappoint the man who had insulted him.

The interview began by Dowlut Rao thanking Kummakl for his recommendation of his nephew, which recommendation had been confirmed by Colonel Boozey, the Governor-General's Agent, when Kummakl cut him short by saying curtly, and, indeed, rudely, that he was very sorry that other arrangements had been made. Dowlut Rao at first did not understand him, and Kummakl repeated what he had said rather more curtly than before. The other replied, without exhibiting in his tone the slightest disturbance of temper, that he was very sorry, because he had sent for his nephew all the way from Benares, and he was expected to arrive that very day, that he would not only thus be put to a great expense needlessly, but that, what was worse, he would be held up as a laughing-stock to all his family; the respect in which he was held, his honour and reputation (there is no exact English translation for the word *izzut*), was injured irrecoverably, and he hoped the Political Agent would rescind his decision.

Kummakl sat silent all through this little speech, and then replied as before, with a little asperity of temper. Dowlut Rao then rose to go, intimating, in the politest possible phraseology, that he was sorry for what had occurred, but he hoped Captain Kummakl would have no objection to the matter being referred to higher authority, which, considering that the appointment had to be confirmed by that higher authority, was reasonable enough.

It is not worth while to follow this matter out further. The reference, indeed, ended in Dowlut Rao's nephew being installed in the post in spite of Kummakl's opposition, but from that day forward there was a deadly feud between these two men.

It was about a fortnight after this that Kummakl came into his wife's room one morning, after he had been into his office, and said,

"I'm glad the Mooltawees are coming over here, Julia, to-morrow, because you will not be alone. I have to go out into the district for a day or so, and must start at once."

"Where are you going, Li? can't I come too?"

"No, dear—unless you can ride a camel. There has been a row in a village about twenty miles from here, and I must go and see what it is all about. Several lives have been lost, and a lot of property destroyed."

It was as Kummakl told his wife. There had been an affray or a disturbance in a large village, or a cluster of villages, about twenty miles from the capital, and most conflicting were the reports of it brought in to the agency. So that Kummakl had no choice left him but to repair to the spot himself.

When he got there it was all over. The dead bodies of those slain in the fight had been burnt and buried, and it was impossible even to find out how many lives had been lost. But on enquiring into the *casus belli*, Kummakl was told by all the people who belonged to the party of the aggressors, that the reason they had risen was on account of the oppressions and exactions of the dewan, Dowlut Rao.

Kummakl had not ridden far on his way back before he fell in with a native gentleman, a petty chief and zemindar, who had an estate in that neighbourhood, and was going out hawking. Thinking that he might be able to give some information about the late disturbance, Kummakl joined him and rode a little in his company. In reply to the question as to whether he knew anything about the affair, Inayet Ali, for that was the man's name, said, "Oh, yes, it is noised all over the country; everybody about here knows that Mustaffa Khan, the ex-minister, induced these people to create this disturbance, and then to say they were driven to it by the dewan's exactions, because, as every one has heard of the disagreement between the dewan and your honour, Mustaffa Khan thought it a good opportunity to light a fire."

"So," thought Kummakl, as he rode homewards, "every one in the province, it seems, knows about the little tiff between the dewan and myself; they know, of course, that that old meddler Colonel Boozey decided against me in that case. I wonder if what Inayet Ali says is true, he is a Mahomedan too, and his interests must lie, one would think, the other way."

When Kummakl, as Virgil says, "revolving these things in his breast," reached his office, he was met by the head clerk, Mr. Cynthea Jones, who said he had a man waiting whom he had met with accidentally in the city, and discovered equally accidentally that he had some important information to give about the disturbance.

The fortuitous nature of Mr. Cynthea Jones' connection with the man with valuable information consisted in the fact that he had that morning received in hard cash a hundred gold mohurs, or sixteen hundred rupees, to introduce the "man with valuable information" to the Political Agent.

The valuable information served to complicate the matter still further, and sadly to perplex poor Kummakl's brains. The man who Mr. Cynthea Jones introduced was a very respectable Hindo banker of the city, and he said he would undertake to swear that the disturbance had been got up by the Dewan, who had instructed people to say that it had been got up by Mustaffa Khan to throw discredit upon him. And the man moreover said that he had overheard the Dewan himself giving instructions.

The day of his return Kummakl did not see much of his wife alone, as the Mooltawee's were still there. The next day they left early in the morning, and Julia complained of not feeling well, and did not get up. He took no great notice of her ailment, supposing it to be a temporary indisposition that would soon pass off. She got up in the afternoon, and then he could not help observing traces of illness upon her features which he had not noticed before, and which gave him some alarm. Upon mentioning to her his apprehensions, and hinting about sending for Dr. Golee, she at once quieted his fears, saying there was nothing really the matter with her, and on no account was he to send all that distance for Dr. Golee.

"By the way, Li," she went on to say, "about that affair, you know, that you have been away about. There is a man, my ayah tells me, who is capable of giving you some very valuable information. I know it was a difficult matter to unravel, from what I have heard you say, so I told her I would tell you, but I did'nt know whether you would care to hear what the man has to say."

"Oh, yes, I have no objection to hear what he has to say; tell her to send him to me to-morrow."

"Oh, no, that won't do at all. You see, Li, the man says he is afraid his life will be taken if he is seen giving the important evidence he has to give: you must see him here, or in some private place where there are no witnesses."

"It will be very difficult to find such a place, Julia. If I wanted to get a man into the Agency without it's being known, I don't believe I could do it, however much I tried."

"Well, I'll tell her to bring the man here to-morrow, to my room; he can come as a cloth-seller" (kaprawalas, men who are walking milliners' and linen-drapers shops in India, which thus come to the ladies instead of the ladies going to them), "and you can see him here."

"This little manœuvre, which was successfully carried

out, put three hundred rupees into the ayah's pocket. Kummakl saw the man, who showed him a scrap of paper covered with writing in the Hindee character, and said it was part of some written instructions the Dewan had given to the people in the neighbourhood, who were his own tenants, to say that it was Mustaffa Khan who had originated the disturbance with the view of throwing discredit upon him, the Dewan. All this information, you must know, Kummakl duly recorded.

That evening, after dinner, he had retired to the verandah to smoke a cigar, and his bearer or valet, who had just brought him a light, said he had an "urzee" or petition to make. Kummakl asked him what it was, when he said that he had a brother who lived at the village where the disturbance had taken place, who had had his house burnt and almost all his property destroyed, and he wanted to know to whom he ought to apply for compensation, that was all.

"This man," thought Kummakl, "will be able to give me some useful information. He appears to have been on the spot, and being a poor man and not mixed up with the intrigues of these people, will, no doubt, tell an unbiassed tale." He asked where the man was, and the bearer said that he had just that instant left him to return to his home, but if the "huzoor" would see him, he had no doubt he would be able to overtake him and bring him back. Kummakl told him to go at once and fetch him, and off the bearer went, successful beyond anticipation, and hearing the two hundred rupees, he was to receive for the night's job, chink in his imagination.

Kummakl examined this man very closely as to the whole occurence, which he related in the minutest detail, describing the position of his own house in the village, and giving the names of his neighbours, telling him how the disturbance began, and in fact the whole history from beginning to end.

It was cleverly done, for the narrator, although it was quite true that he was the "bearer's" brother, yet came from Seetapore in Oude, and had never been to Budgepore before in all his life, and had only arrived two days previously. He declared, however, that he witnessed the whole thing, and saw and heard Mustaffa Khan's emissaries first, and then Mustaffa Khan himself lay the plot, instigate the people to rise, and instruct them to say that the disturbance was got up by the Dewan with the view of implicating him, Mustaffa Khan, by inducing his own tenants to swear that he, Mustaffa Khan, did originate it.

Next morning early, as Kummakl was going out for his morning ride alone, for Julia very often did not accompany him now, his sweeper came up and made a low salaam, and begged for leave of absence for a few days, as his father, who lived in the village where the disturbance had been, had been killed during the affray, and there was no one left but a younger brother, whom he wanted to look after, as well as to bring away whatever of the property there might be left about the place. Of course he got the leave granted, and was told to bring his younger brother to Kummakl on his return. Lucky fellow, he pocketed a hundred and twenty-five rupees by that stroke of policy. Two days after, he came with his brother, a lad of about fifteen, who repeated word for word what the bearer's brother had said about Mustaffa Khan.

But my chronicle will swell to the same size as poor Kummakl's record if I put down all the stories that were told him.

Of course the matter was sent up to Government, and Kummakl was ordered to make a full investigation (which he did, taking the evidence of a hundred and twenty witnesses) and write a report. No doubt the case was a difficult one rather to unravel; still there was not so much difficulty about it, but what Kummakl would have been able to arrive at a clear and just conclusion, had he set about it with an unprejudiced mind. But Mustaffa Khan, who in reality had originated the whole thing from the very commencement, was far too astute to introduce the *finale* of his piece before the introductory part had been played out. He knew perfectly well that if the affray and the inquiry into it took place while Dowlut Rao was on good terms with Kummakl, it would inevitably end in the whole thing being found out and the decision going against him He waited, therefore, till either he could hit upon a scheme for getting up a bad feeling between the two, or until something should occur which would enable him to sow distrust in the name of the Political Agent against the Dewan. The only difficult part of the game to play was the first step; all beyond that was plain sailing.

We have seen how he succeeded in that. The visit of Dowlut Rao to Kummakl on the very day that his feelings were first aroused against him was an accident—one of those accidents that constantly occur to favour the designs of a bold man playing for a high stake. The fatal error Kummakl made was in allowing his mere private feelings to influence his conduct. But it is an error into which many men of his position would have fallen, and one into which any man of his mental calibre would be sure to have fallen. He went into the case with a strong bias against Dowlut Rao, and reported against him. The Government, of course, had nothing to guide them but this report, and the result was that Dowlut Rao was turned out of the Dewanship and Mustaffa Khan installed in his place. This move, however, only had the effect of changing the position of the pieces on the board. Dowlut Rao naturally commenced plotting and intriguing to recover the advantage he had lost. Kummakl, between two such men as Dowlut Rao and Mustaffa Khan, may be compared to a London hack cab-horse trying to overtake two thoroughbreds. By reason of race and position, Kummakl was their superior, but in intellect they were very far his superiors. It was not a very high order of intellect, you may say, seeing that subtlety and cunning formed so large an element in it. But I do not know that Kummakl's was much higher. No doubt, in a display of physical courage, they would have had no chance with the British officer, but then the three parties were not in a position where the display of physical courage or muscular development was likely to be called forth.

THE BUDGEPORE POLITICAL AGENCY.

CHAPTER III.

AN UNWELCOME VISITOR.

KUMMAKL's anxiety about Julia's health was not allayed by her repeated assurance that there was nothing particular the matter. She so resolutely declined to have Dr. Golee sent for, that her husband, who always yielded to her wishes in everything, did so in this case also. She had given up her out-of-door exercise, her rides, her walks in the garden. Day by day she appeared to Kummakl, who watched her with the anxious eye of love, to be growing weaker and weaker. And when the autumn came, and it was refreshing after the heat of the day to sit in the verandah in the evening and watch the sun setting over the hills, she was so weak that she could not walk that distance without the support of her husband's arm. Still, to all his anxious inquiries, and to all his entreaties to let him send for medical advice, she only returned the answer that she was merely suffering from temporary lassitude brought on by the heat of the weather.

This delusion, however, could not last for ever, and one evening, as Kummakl seated himself beside her, after arranging her easy chair and placing her on it, so that she faced the setting sun, and the rosy tints on the western horizon seemed to be reflected from her mass of golden hair, she said, taking Lionel's hand in her own,—

"Do you know, dear Li, I think I have done wrong in persisting in not having the doctor sent for. I don't think he will do me any good, but you may send for him to-morrow. I don't feel worse, exactly, this evening, but I do feel as if there was something the matter, and I have been thinking to-day about mamma's early death, and trying to recall the little I ever heard about it."

"Wait one instant," said her husband, "I'll be back directly."

He left her to go and send an express off to Dr. Golee, and then returned and re-seated himself at her side. He did not encourage her to speak of her ailments, but feeling an inexpressible relief from her having allowed him to send for Dr. Golee, he led her thoughts and conversation away as much as possible from the present. They talked over the past; they did not talk of the future. Minds are differently constituted, and some like dwelling on the past, and others on the future. When people are very happy in the present they do not care to dwell upon the future; they would rather think and talk of the past, and trace the steps by which they have mounted to the culminating point of their bliss. They do not care to look forward, because, as there is a condition in life when any change must be for the better, as we commonly express it, though what we mean is that the chances are very much in favour of any change being for the better, so there is a condition in life when you can hardly conceive any change but what must be for the worse. You are happy with the fulfilment of your highest hopes, and then—if fate would but let things remain, your happiness might be permanent. So Lionel and Julia talked over the past, how they had first met, and what was the impression they each derived of the other, and Julia acknowledged that it was only after they had married that Lionel had really won her love. Before that she had not known what love was. She had consented to marry him because her friends thought it a good match and every one spoke of him as a man likely to make a woman happy. They talked together calmly and peacefully, yet there was a tone of sadness in their words as there was a weight and presentiment of coming trouble on the heart of both. As evening drew on, Julia said she did not feel equal to sitting up at dinner and would go to bed. So she went, and Kummakl repaired to his solitary dinner-table. He did not expect Dr. Golee out before the following evening; but he felt as if there was no further cause for anxiety, for he fancied that all his wife wanted was some tonic medicine. In fact both of them had been foolishly speculating on their own little knowledge, you may say ignorance, of physics, and had adopted altogether erroneous conclusions as to the cause of Julia's declining health. But when Dr. Golee the following evening came out of her room after his examination of the patient, he had a very grave face indeed.

"Your wife, Kummakl," he said, "is very ill indeed, much worse than I had any idea of."

"She would not let me send for you before. I have entreated and begged her to let me send for you, but she said no, it was no consequence, it would all pass off, and so on."

"Don't reproach yourself the least about that. If I am right in what I conjecture, for I cannot make up my mind at once very certainly, I may be misled by appearances—but if I am right, it would have made no difference at all whether you sent for me before now, or later. Do you know what it was her mother died of?"

"No; I never heard, and she does not know either. She was in England at the time, and it seems her friends never talked to her much about her mother."

"Well, I will write a prescription for some simple medicine, which can be made up in your native dispensary here, and then I will be off. But I will come back in a couple of days. I do not think it is a case where medical attendance can be of much avail. All you have to do is to follow the directions on the bottle, and keep up her strength and spirits as much as possible. I shall be able to judge when I see her the second time better as to whether my first conclusions are sound or not."

The first person Dr. Golee visited when he returned to Budgepore, was Mrs. Mooltawee, and the first question he asked her, and rather abruptly as she thought, was,

"What did Mrs. Congreve die of?"

"Rapid consumption."

"Very rapid?"

"Yes. So rapid, that six months before her death, no one dreamed there was anything the matter with her. Why do you ask?"

"Because Mrs. Kummakl is very ill. I was sent for to see her for the first time the night before last, and went over yesterday. My worst fears of her case are confirmed by what you have now said. It is a similar case to her mother's."

"Poor Lionel!" said Mrs. Mooltawee, "he is so devoted to her!"

Poor Lionel indeed! Never for one instant had the thought crossed his mind that his idol, his darling, his cherished Julia, the only being in the whole universe he cared for, the only being he worshipped, should be taken from him. He knew, of course, that death is the lot of all mankind, but he never realised in the slightest degree, never contemplated for a single moment, that the stern reaper would have the heart to cut down his beautiful flower. If you had asked him the question, whether he thought Julia was immortal, and whether his present happiness was to last for ever, he would have answered of course in the negative, with some of the commonplace platitudes people keep for the subject of mortality and a future state, as old-fashioned ladies bring out their best china tea-cups to do honour to some respected guests, whose visits are few and far between, and always occasions of considerable ceremony. But for death—hideous death, to come into his house and scatter with one blow all that made life dear to him, was something as new as it was terrible. He stood rooted to the spot where Dr. Golee had left him, for some five minutes, and never stirred a muscle, Then, with a very deep sigh, such as would have made anyone sad to hear, he sunk into a chair and covered his face with his hands. The squall had come upon him suddenly, when he least expected it. There was no ballast, and he was shipwrecked.

He remained in that posture till summoned to assist Julia into the open air. He forgot he had not been to see her since Dr. Golee's visit. Was she, too, aware of the nature of her illness? He must be careful, and not show by any sign or expression the serious view the doctor took of the case.

"Did Dr. Golee tell you what he thought of me?" was the direct question she put her husband, scanning his countenance closely as she spoke, as if conscious there was something to conceal, and determined it should not escape her.

"Yes, dearest; he said that you were worse than he expected."

"Was that all, Li? Now, don't try to conceal anything," she said, half in earnest and half in sport. "I will know what he said, and you have never disobeyed me yet—tell me."

"Well," said Kummakl, hesitatingly, "let me see, he did not certainly say what he thought about your case, because he said he had not definitely made up his mind, but he did say you were worse than he expected."

"You told me that before, you foolish old creature. Do you think I can't see that there is something you are trying to keep back from me? Come Li, I must know. You once swore you would never refuse to do anything I told you; and I tell you to let me know what Dr. Golee said about me."

"I declare I have told you everything, Julia, that he said. He did say one thing more, certainly; he asked me if I knew what your mamma died of."

"Ah!" said Julia to herself, "that was it then."

After a long pause, during which she remained buried in thought, her large grey eyes fixed on the sky, she turned her head towards her husband, and said.

"Li, dear, you will be very, very lonely without me."

Man as he was, he burst into tears. She alone of the two remained unmoved, to all outward appearance. Ashamed of the betrayal by his emotion of all his worst fears and the doctor's impressions, he rapidly recovered himself. She was the first to speak. There was a little of reproach in her tone.

"Are those tears for yourself, or for me, Li?"

"Forgive me, Julia, for being so weak and foolish. I cannot bear to think of your being so ill, and—"

"And what?" she said, seeing him hesitate, "and no hope, is that it, Li?"

Kummakl had determined not to let her see or know how anxious he was, and what the doctor thought of her case, but fate was too strong for him. Every word he said, he seemed to make the matter worse.

"No, not that Julia—and I not able to do a thing to relieve you."

Again there was a pause—which was broken by Julia, as if she was giving expression to some conclusion she had arrived at after a long train of thought, saying half out loud and half to herself,

"What a mistake!—what a mistake!"

"Yes," said Lionel, "I wish you had let me send for Dr. Golee before."

"It was not that I was thinking of, and don't let that prey on your mind, for it was my fault, Li, and if Dr. Golee had come ever so long before he could have done no good. It was not that I was thinking of, but what a mistake my life has been!"

Kummakl looked at her anxiously. He thought that, perhaps, she was regretting their marriage.

She went on, half speaking to herself,

"Yes, what does it all come to? What is it all worth? I was never taught to think. I never had anything put before me more serious to think about than the preparations for a picnic or the trimming of a dress. I was taught to dance, to play, to paint flowers, to dress well, to make an impression in a drawing-room full of well dressed idlers, and what is it all worth now? What will it be worth to me ten days hence perhaps—when I am face to face with——Oh, Li," she added, turning her face towards him, "why didn't *you* tell me of these things?"

"Indeed, Julia, I wish you would not talk about these things. It makes me so wretched to hear you. You are not yourself now—you are so ill and weak, these gloomy thoughts crowd on your mind, and you cannot throw them off. Let us go on with the novel I was reading when Dr. Golee came."

"No, Li, I won't finish that novel. The page is turned down where you left off reading to me, you can finish it yourself when——Oh, Li! what would I give, what thousands of worlds if I had them, had I been taught to read fewer novels, and to think and read more about this."

"Julia, you are an angel. No angel in heaven is purer or lovelier than you."

"Hush, Li, don't talk like that now. An angel of earth I might have been, for don't you see I was taught to be one, to dress and to dance, and to make myself agreeable, but the angels in heaven must be very different sort of beings. The fact is, I have had this journey all my life before me, I never made any preparation for it, and now I am all unprepared. Go and get a Bible, Li, and read me something out of it."

Kummakl did as he was bid, but he felt some doubt as to whether there was such a thing as a Bible in the house at all. At last he recollected seeing one under a heap of old papers in his office; thither he went, and there he found the book he was in quest of, very dusty.

"What part shall I read, Julia?" he said, seating himself by the side of her couch, for she had meantime been wheeled into her room, and turning over the leaves listlessly like a man who has a new book and does not know where to begin.

Julia gave him no answer, but intimated that she left that to him. I think perhaps she would have found it difficult to have referred him to any part in particular.

So Kummakl, left to his own devices, and by a vigorous effort recalling some reminiscences of his childhood connected with the book before him, turned to the early part of Genesis, where he recollected he used as a child to find the story of Noah and the flood. And having found the place, he began, and read to his wife the whole of that wonderful history of the destruction of the human race, with the exception of the few saved in the ark. And Julia, though she had been told the story when she was young, and though she had heard the portions of the same narrative read occasionally as the first lesson in church when her mind was running on the latest fashion in dress or her last flirtation, or the bonnet of the lady in front of her, she now seemed to hear it for the first time.

"Ah, Li," she said, when he had finished, "I dare say people used to go to balls and picnics in those days, one round of gaiety from morning to night, till all of a sudden the flood came, and then it was too late; there was a chance for them before that, though—eh, Li, what do you think?"

Kummakl had never had such a proposition put before him, and was totally unable to deal with it.

"I don't know," he said, and they both relapsed into silence.

Thus these two young and loving hearts, like two children suddenly benighted when out at play together are scared when they are brought face to face with some real and terrible danger, went groping along, as it were, in the dark, trying to find for themselves a way out of the woe that encompassed them. Each loved the other so dearly that either would willingly have sacrificed life for that other's sake. Lionel would, if he could, have given up his own life for the sake of accompanying his darling on that gloomy journey that lay before her. But all his love and devotion could avail nothing in the present crisis.

Of a future state, of death, of immortality, in the view religion places these things before men's minds, they had between them not so much knowledge as any one of the mass of the heathen by whom they were surrounded. They, at any rate the Hindoos and the Mahomedans, had so far realised those great truths that they had attended to the outward forms of religious worship all through their lives. As for their morality and their obedience to the divine law written in their hearts, if the heathen had broken that, Lionel and Julia might have done the same, had they ever been tested. His knowledge of Christianity actually was confined to uncertain reminiscences of the story of the fall, of the flood, just now recalled in all its fulness to his memory, of the passage of the Israelites over the Red Sea, and Pharaoh with his army being drowned, and of David killing a giant with a stone. Even his knowledge, or rather recollection, of these incidents was vague. Vaguer still and more misty was his idea of the fundamental truths of the Christian religion. That a Redeemer had died to save mankind he had often been told, but he never knew what it meant, in fact never thought about it, or tried to find out what it did mean.

Julia's ideas were still more cloudy. She had a beautifully bound church-service, with crimson velvet covers, gold rim and clasp, and a gold cross on the outside, which her godmother gave her for a present when she left school to come to India. She had been in the habit of going to church at Budgepore once on Sunday in the morning, before she was married, when she heard Green Baize, the chaplain, gabble over the service, and then read very badly what sounded very like a part of the preface of some old book on divinity. As for listening, or directing her attention or thought to either the service or the discourse, she didn't know any body was expected to. She had been confirmed when she was sixteen, and then had had to learn by rote the church catechism and to read with a number of other girls all through Secker, which was done as mere drudgery; when it was over she had a ticket given her, and went along with the others all dressed in white muslin up to the altar rails, where the ceremony was performed and the bishop's hands were laid on her head. She had never taken the sacrament, and if she had been asked what it was, could have given no answer. She had been carefully educated in all the refinements of civilised life, but no one ever dreamed of teaching her to think. Her aunt, with whom she lived for a few years in her childhood, had taught her to say her prayers every morning and evening, but when she went to school the other girls laughed at her for going it, and she left it off, and speedily forgot even the words she used to repeat by rote. All through her life every effort had been made by those about her to strew her path with flowers, and to keep carefully away every idea that could cloud with a passing gloom the sunshine of her pleasures. She had been accustomed from her infancy to be flattered, and caressed and admired, and yet the excellence of her natural disposition was such that all this flattery and admiration had never made her vain or exacting, or even thoughtless of the happiness of others. Brought up amid all the refinements and elegances of life, no coarse ideas dimmed the natural purity of her mind. With her exquisite beauty, her loveliness and winning ways, and her gentle and amiable temper, she seemed to want but the training for heaven to make her indeed an angel. But now she was face to face with death, and she was called to go forth into the unknown region alone, and for the first time in her life she was forced to think of what her lot would be there.

After the conversation, a portion of which I have related, and which continued for some little time in the same strain, the two loving hearts so soon to be parted, groping as it were after Truth, Kummakl rose and left her upon some household business. He had not been away half an hour when he was startled by the ayah's scream. He hurried back to her room, and there he found the ayah standing wringing her hands over the prostrate form of Julia, who was on her knees with her head upon the couch and her hands clasped over her head.

She was apparently lifeless. Lionel had never before seen her in the posture of prayer, for such it was, though she had fainted. With the ayah's assistance he raised her and laid her on her bed and took off her dress, when he was inexpressibly relieved to observe signs of returning animation. He left her for a moment and hurried out to send an express for Dr. Golee, and then returned to the bedside, where he found her sufficiently recovered to recognise him. They put her into bed, and she fell asleep, clasping her husband's hand. He was afraid to move it lest he should disturb her, and he sat there hour after hour till his whole body ached from remaining so long in one posture that the pain was almost unendurable; still he did not stir till two o'clock, when Dr. Golee arrived. His entry into the room, though silently made, awoke her. He heard what had happened, ordered some fresh stimulants, gave a few directions to Kummakl, and then hurried back, for he had to be at Budgepore in the morning to attend a committee upon a bottle of port wine supplied by the Commissariat to the hospital, which had been reported unsound.

The next day Mrs. Mooltawee came over, but Kummakl refused to give up his place at Julia's bedside. Her aunt was inexpressibly shocked at the ravages disease had already made on the form of her lovely niece. Her good feeling prevented her from intruding much upon the grief and sympathy of the young husband and wife, but her mere presence in the house was an immense relief to Lionel. During the day Julia bade him read to her again, and told him to select some part of the New Testament, and he by chance opened it at the latter part of the Gospel of St. John, which he read through to the end. It was strange how the old neglected Bible which had lain so long covered with dust under a heap of papers in the office, rose in value. It was their only mainstay in the sudden calamity which had overwhelmed them both.

But I have lingered too long over the scene. Day by day Julia got weaker. Kummakl never left her day or night except for a few minutes at a time. Once or twice the thought had crossed his mind that he would destroy himself so as to die at the same moment with his beloved idol, and accompany her to the unknown region whither she was travelling so fast, for strange as it may seem, he believed in the immortality of the soul, and felt that there was an existence after and apart from life which he would fain have shared with her. But some instinct bade him chase the idea from his mind. It was not love of life, for life he did not care for without her; it was not fear, for he fancied he should be with her, and whatever there might be of a fearful nature to be apprehended, he would willingly have encountered for the sake of supporting her under it. But it was some instinct that warned him off the path, and he endeavoured to dismiss the notion from his thoughts, though it would rise again and again, till it was too late to carry it out, for Julia was gone, and he did not feel certain that he should overtake or find her in the land whither she had fled.

THE BUDGEPORE POLITICAL AGENCY.

CHAPTER IV.

THE CAB-HORSE BETWEEN TWO THORRUGHBREDS.

UTTERLY worn out by long watching and grief, Kummakl had hardly physical strength or consciousness left to realise the truth when they tried to force it upon him. He was alone in the world, and how inexpressibly lonely he felt! But there was work for him to do, for all the time of Julia's illness he had neglected everything, and now had to bring up arrears.

Dowlut Rao had retired to his estate upon his dismissal from the dewanship, and then set himself to work to discover some means of unravelling the plot by which his rival had supplanted him. Among his own tenants who were all more or less cognizant of the transactions which had preceded the outbreak in the village, he had famous opportunities for discovering the truth. But it was one thing to discover it so as to satisfy himself, and another to make matters so clear as to satisfy the authorities who were prejudiced against him.

Mustaffa Khan, meantime, enjoyed to the full the emoluments and powers of his office, and none the less because he dwelt in fancied security. The agent he had employed in the duty of inciting the people to the affray was the brother of his favourite wife, a man named Jaffer Ally Khan. There was, indeed, one circumstance that occasionally caused him a little uneasiness, and that was the fact that Jaffer Ally, who was far too prudent a person to undertake the work entrusted to him without some written instructions from the then ex-dewan, had received and was in possession of a document signed and sealed under Mustaffa Khan's own hand conveying those instructions. The latter had no suspicion of his brother-in-law's fidelity, but in this whirligig world there was no foreseeing what might not turn up, and it might so happen that Jaffer Ally one day or other should conceive the desire of doing him, Mustaffa Khan, an injury, and in such a contingency there was no concealing the ugly truth that he had the means ready to hand. Dowlut Rao had also become aware of the existence of this document, and would have given a very large sum of money to get hold of it. Many an offer he did make to Jaffer Ally in a roundabout way, all of which offers were duly reported, of course, to Mustuffa Khan, who was forced to reward fidelity, and to secure it, too, by large presents. And Jaffer Ally made a good thing of it, for while he held possession of the papers the dewan was in reality his slave. So matters went on, and so I daresay they would have continued to go on some time longer, had not Mustaffa Khan's passions intervened. So long as Jaffer Ally's sister held her sway in the harem and her husband's affections were undisputedly hers, she had no cause to mix herself up in the intrigues; but in an evil moment for them both she got a very pretty maid into the harem to wait upon her, against whose charms Mustaffa Khan's philosophy and self-interest were alike powerless. His wife discovered one day the intrigue (indeed it had passed far beyond the preliminary stages of intrigue) between her husband and the slave girl, and a domestic fracas ensued. High words passed, mutual reproaches that between husband and wife can never be forgotten, and seldom are forgiven. Mustaffa Khan made a deadly enemy of the woman who through her influence with her brother had his fate in her hands. She communicated what had occurred to Jaffer Ally, who bade her to beware of poison, and came and resided himself near the dewan's residence on purpose to watch over his sister's welfare.

The warning which sprang from a thorough acquaintance with Mustuffa Khan's unscrupulous character was not misplaced. One night, Jaffer Ally received from the hand of a trusty messenger a packet containing some sweetmeats which his sister sent him, with a message, saying she had reason to believe they were poisoned, for her husband had, after a hasty and suspicious reconciliation, sent them to her as a peace-offering. Jaffer Ally experimented with them upon a dog, and the rapid death of the animal, in horrible convulsions, left no doubt on his mind of his sister's danger and her husband's intentions. Next day he called on Mustaffa Khan and demanded, as the price of safety, an immense sum of money, or a large grant of land in lieu of it, and an instant divorce or separation from his sister, whose life was no longer safe under his roof. Mustaffa Khan refused, denied the charge, and desired him to do his worst. Jaffer Ally then left. It was about six o'clock in the evening, and after enclosing the document in a cover sealed with his own seal addressed to Kummakl, he left it at the Agency, mounted his horse, and rode straight off towards Dowlut Rao's estate. He never lived to reach it. Just as evening drew on, as he was crossing a lonely moor, he was fired at from behind a bush. The shot missed. He reined in his horse and faced about, drawing his pistol at the same time. At that moment two men rushed upon him, one seized his horse's bridle, and the other thrust a spear through his body, but not before he had fired with an unerring aim. He fell with his assailant, the latter dying instantly, for he was shot through the heart; the other lingering in agony, in which condition the man who had seized his horse, after letting the animal go, came and searched all over his person carefully, as if looking for some article concealed about him. Next morning it was reported to Kummakl that Dowlut Rao had assassinated a servant of Mustaffa Khan's, and his brother-in-law Jaffer Ally.

This tragedy took place about three months after Julia's death, during which Kummakl had been dragging out a wretched existence, finding life almost insupportable, and longing to get away from a scene so full of sad reminiscences, and the gloomy shadow of happiness that had flown for ever. That evening he was sitting alone in his room, meditating over his past life and longing for the means of retiring from the service and the country, when Mustaffa Khan was announced. Kummakl had, of course, received the packet left by Jaffer Ally, and through his private moonshee (for he could not read the language himself) had mastered its contents. His genius, however, never very acute, and blunted, perhaps, by the domestic sorrow he had recently undergone, failed to trace any connection between the tragedy of the preceding evening and the document itself. Mustaffa Khan knew, of course, by this time where the paper was. Had he known it in time to stay the execution of his plans, Jaffer Ally might have been alive, for it was no part of his business to incur useless risks, and the murder of his brother-in-law had turned out to be a most useless one. No sooner had Kummakl's private and confidential moonshee left the room after reading the paper to his master, then he sent a short note over to the dewan, telling him he had something of importance to communicate. The dewan came over to the Agency and in the moonshee's private room saw the paper which had been to him the cause of so much uneasiness. The moonshee, of course, was ready to assist with any advice or device he could suggest, but the ordinary resources in such cases were of no avail here. If the alteration of a date or a name, or the insertion of a few words here and there, such as can easily be managed with most vernacular documents so as entirely to alter their whole purport and meaning, could have been effected in this case, all difficulties might have been removed at once. But the nature of the contents of the document was such that no tampering with the words or sentences or dates could have the slightest effect upon its general tenor. Some of my readers may like to see a translation of it. The document was as follows:—

"To the honoured brother of the harem of his faithful servant Jaffer Ally Khan greeting (salam).

"Be it known that for certain reasons, it is necessary that the fire of discord should be lighted in the mouzas (villages) of Mobaruckpore, &c. (here follow the names of several villages which need not be transcribed). This is to show that I have authorised Jaffer Ally Khan to act for me in this matter, and will confirm all that he deems necessary to do in the prosecution of this design.

"At the Sheesmehal of Budgepore, 15th Rubbee-ool-awwul, A. H. 1278."

"What a cursed thing it is," said Mustaffa Khan, after conning it over two or three times, twisting it about between his finger and thumb as he spoke. "There is no doing any thing with it at all! We might as well try to alter the texts of the holy book itself?"

"Yes," said the moonshee, "your Highness should have sent for me to draw it up and not attempted it yourself. It was the work of a scribe, not a minister, to write out a paper of this kind—scribes know how to do it properly. My father, who was a wise man——"

"Yes, I know, he was—I wish he was here now to tell me what I had better do—well, but what of him?"

"He used to say to me—he was, your Highness knows, one of the record keepers of the Civil Court at—he used to say to me, and he taught me how to do it, never to write a document in such a way that it could not easily be corrected."

"Corrected, yes, that is right, documents should always be capable of being corrected—I wish I could correct this," said Mustaffa Khan, with a dry satirical humour, foreign to the Asiatic character. "Cannot we correct this—we have the words 'fasad-i-atish' (fire of discord)—if that phrase was altered,—but let me see, what shall it be?"

But the dewan was puzzled—he looked and looked again at the paper, and shook his head and muttered, as if saying words over to himself, "alif dal," and so on, mentioning the letters by their alphabetical names.

The moonshee watched him with an amused expression of countenance. Perhaps he enjoyed the other's dilemma—as he relished an intrigue—or he foresaw golden opportunities before him. At any rate, it was not to his profit to help the dewan out of his difficulties at this stage.

"It's no use," he said at last. "Even if we could think of anything to alter this 'fasid-i-atish' into, it would be of no use, the sahib particularly noticed the expression, made me repeat it three times over, and then repeated it to himself. He has written it in his memory."

With an oath, which I do not care to repeat, invoking some very unpleasant consequences upon Kummakl's head, whom he designated as that accursed Kaffir, Mustaffa Khan tossed the paper on the table, and got up to leave the room.

He went straight from the moonshee's apartment to Kummakl's. By the time he had reached the latter, his feelings bore no trace of the anger or vexation they had worn a minute previously.

The dewan's object in visiting Kummakl, was mainly to discover if he could learn what that officer thought about the revelation recently made. He calculated that he would probably lead the conversation to it himself, nor was he mistaken, for after a few remarks had passed between them on the usual topics of mere formality, Kummakl said,

"I am very sorry to see, dewan sahib, that it was you, after all, who stirred up the ill-feeling at Mobaruckpore."

Mustaffa Khan laughed a pleasant little laugh.

"The sahib has seen it, then! Is it not cleverly done? Even my seal and signature so well imitated, that it would be difficult to discover the forgery."

"Forged you say it is!" said Kummakl, looking him steadily in the face. "It had every appearance of being genuine."

"Nevertheless, I shall show your honour that it is a clever forgery."

"Well," said Kummakl, "I shall do nothing further in the business till I have reported the matter, and then, If I am ordered to investigate the case, I will call on you to substantiate what you have said. If you can do so, I shall be very glad."

Before Mustaffa Khan went home, he had an interview with the moonshee for two minutes in his private room, and exacted a promise that he would call at his house that night and bring the paper with him.

When the moonshee got there, Mustaffa Khan was waiting for him, and, as soon as the attendant had withdrawn, he produced another document, the counterpart of the genuine one in the moonshee's possession, and desired the latter to compare the two. He did so very carefully, but confessed himself unable to detect the slightest difference. Mustaffa Khan watched him with an amused expression of countenance, and, when he had completed his examination of the papers, he said,

"Now, let us exchange papers, you see there can be no harm in your taking this one and letting me have the other, for they are so exactly alike, that you can detect no difference whatever between them." At the same time, he put into his hand an order on a native banking firm in the town for five thousand rupees. The argument was conclusive. The exchange was made, and the moonshee next morning placed the document received the night before from Mustaffa Khan, with the other papers in the case, wondering much what the astute minister could possibly mean by giving him a really genuine document, signed by himself, and sealed with his own seal, in lieu of one which was indeed the exact counterpart of the other, but had come from the custody of one who might have been his enemy.

Kummakl, of course, reported the affair, and solicited orders how to act; meantime, events occurred which served still further to complicate matters.

One or two evenings after his interview with Kummakl, Mustaffa Khan, on returning from the Nawab's palace, where he had been detained nearly the whole day on business, was distressed by the announcement that the girl to whom he was so much attached, and his passion for whom had been at the bottom of his recent misfortune, was dangerously ill. It was so indeed. He found her stretched on the floor in convulsive agonies most painful to witness. A physician had been sent for as soon as the symptoms appeared, by some of the household, and was in attendance when Mustaffa Khan reached home, but his services were of no avail. The shrieks of the poor girl and her sufferings were terrible to watch, but as with many oriental houses belonging to the better classes, the building was so constructed that the sounds could not penetrate to the outer air, and it is perhaps just as well they cannot.

The day passed uncomfortably enough for the dewan, who was distracted between his love for the girl, and distress at witnessing her sufferings, which terminated towards evening in death, and his anger at the perpetrator of the deed, for no one in the household doubted that the girl had been poisoned by Jaffer Ally Khan's sister, Zeenut Mahal, in revenge for her brother's death. He vowed himself revenge too, but would take it by-and-by at his own time.

In the evening, Kummakl was waited on by Dowlut Rao, who had come in haste on a summons, secretly conveyed to him from Zeenut Mahal, imploring him to save her and avenge her brother's death. He lost no time in obeying the summons, but found difficulty in acting now he had arrived. He could not gain access to Mustaffa Khan's harem of course without violence, and he knew it would be useless to attempt to influence the Nawab; so, after turning the matter over in his mind, he went to Kummakl, and told him the whole story. Jaffer Ally had been waylaid and murdered by Mustaffa Khan's own men, and in order to secure possession of the document which was now in the Sahib's possession (Kummakl wondered how Dowlut Rao came to know this). His sister was an inmate of Mustaffa Khan's household, and in danger of her life. Would not the sahib be convinced at last that he, Dowlut Rao, has been a victim of a conspiracy, and unjustly ejected from the dewanship?

Kummakl replied, of course, that he, Dowlut Rao, was suspected of having instigated the murder, the more so because the possession of the document would be of more use to him than to any one else. In vain the ex-dewan protested his innocence, and urged all the arguments he could in support of it. Kummakl shook his head, and said that of course he could give no decision in the case, but should await the orders of Government. So Dowlut Rao left and returned to the house where he was accustomed to put up when he visited the city, whence he despatched a messenger to communicate privately with Zeenut Mahal, whose co-operation he saw would now be absolutely necessary.

It would lengthen out my story into an "Arabian Night" were I to relate in detail all the plotting and counterplotting that went on between the foes and their retainers. It will be sufficient to say that eventually Zeenut Mahal managed to escape from her husband's house, and to the intense horror and scandal of all pious Mussulmans and virtuous Hindoos in the city of Budgepore, took refuge under the protection of no less a person than Dowlut Rao himself. There was, of course, great excitement in the city, though no violence was attempted. Zeenut Mahal was a valuable witness on Dowlut Rao's side, for she was cognizant with the part her brother had taken in the affair, and with all that had transpired since. But Mustaffa Khan upset all the inferences deducible from her testimony, and declared that the word of such a perfidious woman, who could abandon her husband's house and seek the protection of a stranger and an unbeliever, was not worthy of any credit. Poor Kummakl was fairly bewildered, and when at last an order came for him to send up a report of the whole occurrence, he found his literary powers scarcely able to bear the strain put upon them.

According to promise he sent for Mustaffa Khan, and told him that he was about to report on the affair, and that if he had anything to urge in substantiation of his averment that the document which afforded so important a link in the chain was a forgery, he was ready to hear it. Mustaffa Khan, who had come prepared for the inquiry, began by drawing Kummakl's attention to the paper.

"You see, sahib," he said, "it has every appearance of being genuine."

"It has, indeed."

"Very well, and now the signature is easily imitated."

"But the seal—is not that your seal?"

It must here be explained that the kind of seal referred to in use among orientals in Mustaffa Khan's position, is not an impression upon wax as the word would ordinarily denote, but a device stamped on the foot of a document by the seal impressed in ink.

"Has the sahib a magnifying-glass?"

Kummakl unscrewed the magnifying lens from a pair of binoculars and handed it to the dewan.

"Now," said he, "there are in this office hundreds of official documents bearing my seal; will the sahib send for a bundle of them?"

A pile of abont a hundred and fifty vernacular documents, all impressed with the dewan's seal, were brought by the moonshee, who made the errand a pretext for remaining in the room, as he was really anxious to learn what line of argument the dewan was about to adopt. He took the official documents one by one, laid each one separately on the table before Kummakl, and placed his seal over the mark impressed on them, showing that the edge of the seal exactly fitted the circumference of the impression. It took some time, but he went patiently through them all, and there was not one that was the difference of a hair's breadth between the impression and the seal.

"Now," he said, "we will try the same test with this," and placing the document which he averred to be a forgery upon the table and smoothing it out with his hand, he applied the seal to the impression, and showed that there was about an eighth of an inch between the outer circumference of the impression and the edge of the seal itself. It was apparent when carefully compared, but any one might have looked at it a thousand times without the actual test, and not observed the least difference.

The dewan then put the lens in Kummakl's hand and desired him to examine carefully the lines of the letters on the impressed stamp with those of the seal itself and of the mark on the other documents. Kummakl did so, and found that although to the naked eye there was not the slightest difference observable, yet when examined with the magnifying glass the letters did not at all correspond. Kummakl was then desired to examine equally closely the signature, and that too, on inspection under the glass, exhibited many slight differences which would readily escape the naked eye of even an accurate reader.

There is no need to lengthen out my tale. The document was pronounced a clever forgery, and Mustaffa Khan was acquitted of all complicity in the transaction imputed to him. The Nawab confiscated Dowlut Rao's jagheers (estates) and he left the territory and took service as a native officer in the — regiment of Irregular Cavalry. But the moonshee was in possession of too dangerous a secret for the dewan to allow him to remain at Budgepore, and an accusation was very easily brought against him which procured his dismissal. Mustaffa Khan then sued him in the Nawab's civil court for the five thousand rupees, which he said was a loan, and of course got a decree, which he executed ruthlessly against the moonshee, who had accumulated a good deal of property. It was, however, all seized in execution of the decree and for the expenses of the suit, and he left Budgepore a beggar. He afterwards met Dowlut Rao, and told him the story of the exchanged documents, which Dowlut Rao told his commanding officer, and so the story came round to me. The commanding officer interested himself much in the case, and referred it to Government, who, however, "declined to interfere," and administered a severe reproof to the officer for exceeding the limit of his official duties in meddling with the case at all.